DEVELOPMENT OF INDIAN TRIBES

DEVELOPMENT OF INDIAN TRIBES

Edited by
Dr. Prakash Chandra Mehta

DPH

DISCOVERY PUBLISHING HOUSE
NEW DELHI-110002

First Published-2006

ISBN 81-8356-112-8

Published by

DISCOVERY PUBLISHING HOUSE

4831/24, Ansari Road, Prahlad Street.
Darya Ganj, New Delhi-110002 (India)
Phone: 23279245 • Fax: 91-11-23253475
E-mail:dphtemp@indiatimes.com

Printed at:

R.S. Offset Printers & Binders

New Seelampur
Delhi–110 053

Preface

The tribals are primitive and prefer living in isolation i.e. in dense forests or remote areas which are generally cut-off from civilized area. Hence, tribals have limited contacts with other societies. The habit of isolation helps them to preserve their social customs, traditions and beliefs to a large extent. The territorial distribution of tribes overlaps the political boundaries of the state and territory.

The tribals constitute a share of about eight per cent of the country's population and spread over about 1/5 part of the country's land with more than 500 different tribal groups having special cultural traits and identity.

The term development has been used in a wilder sense, it is a slow process of civilization. The purpose of development is to provide increasing opportunities to all the people for a better life. It is essential to bring about more equitable distribution of income and wealth for promoting social justice and efficiency of production, to provide a greater variety of facilities viz. education, health services, nutrition, housing, etc.

Development is an elusive concept and involves mobilization of natural resources, augmentation of trained manpower, and utilisation of natural resources etc. It is a multi-dimensional process.

Keeping in view the importance of the subject I have tried to discuss the different aspects of development modes of tribals. I have given prime importance to commission and committees constitute from time-to-time for review the government policies and give recommendation of programmes/schemes for the betterment and welfare.

In first chapter I have discussed thoroughly the concept and policy of development including special provisions provided in constitution. In second chapter the role of commissions and committees have been discussed while in third chapter Tribal women and Educational programmes have been discussed. In fourth chapter development of Tribals in Madhya Pradesh is discussed while in fifth chapter Aies of Tribal Development have been discussed. Similarly anthropological analysis, gender disability, development of primitive tribes and Naikas is also discussed in detail.

I hope this volume would be milestone for the planners and scholars. I am grateful to all the learned scholars who have contributed me in this onerous work. I am indebted to Shri Tilak Wasan of M/s Discovery Publishing House, New Delhi for efficient publication. I am also thankful to members of my family for their inspiration and association.

Dr. Prakash Chandra Mehta

45, Ravindranagar

Udaipur–313 003

(Rajasthan)

Tel:. 2490417(0294)

Contributors

1. **Dr. (Mrs.) Bindu Ramachandran**, Lecturer, Dept. of Anthropology, Kannur University, Kerala Thalassery Campus, P.O. Palayad, Thy, Kannur (District) – 670 061
2. **Prof. (Dr.) I. Satya Sundaram**, 12/354-I, Rustumbada, Machilipatnam (Kerala) – 521 001, Tel.: 086672-226242
3. **Dr. Md. Azeez Mohidden**, Research Associate (Cultural), Anthropological Survey of India, Manav Bhavan, SRC, 93/12 & 94/12, Boyad, Mysore (Karnataka) – 570 026
4. **Dr. Naba Kumar Duary**, Research Associate (Cultural), Anthropological Survey of India, Indian Museum Campus, 27, Jawaharlal Nehru Campus, Kolkata (W.B.) – 700 026
5. **Dr. Prakash Chandra Mehta**, 45, Ravindranagar, Udaipur (Rajasthan) – 313 001, Tel.: (Res.) 2490417 (0294)
6. **Dr. Pratibha Kumari**, Research Officer, Q. No. 249, Type-III, Sector-I, R.K. Puram, New Delhi–110 066
7. **Dr. V.K. Srivastava**, Advisor (Ecds), Bhopal (M.P.), Mohini Villa, 187, Kalpana Nagar, Piplani, Raisen Road, Bhopal (M.P.) – 21, Tel.: (Res.) 3091864 (0755), Fax: 91-755-573822

Contents

1

Development of Indian Tribes

Dr. Prakash Chandra Mehta

The tribal scene in India presents a very complex picture. Different regions have had different administrative history and, therefore, they are having different administrative structures. Since personnel policies are complementary to the administrative structure they present an equally varied picture. Pre-independence tribals living in forests, hills and even on the plains were isolated from the mainstream. The status of tribals were unsatisfactory during princely and colonial regime. It was a policy of neglect and saga of exploitation. Due to this, their land and forest were slowly and gradually grabbed by the rich people like landlords and money lenders. They were turned into bonded labourers, leading a life of extreme poverty and misery. The excessive encroachment on their rights in land and forest let to be expression of anger in the form of risings. Thus independent India inherited from the British colonial system 'a complex tribal problem', in view of our commitment to the objectives of justice, social, economic and political equality of status and opportunity as enshrined in the preamble to the constitution. The result was that makers of the constitution had to pay special attention towards the 'complex tribal problem' and came out with solutions in order to eradicate it for ever. The dire need of day was to engulf the gap between tribals and non-tribals.

The concern of the constituent members of the constitution for protection and promotion of the interests of the deprived sections is amply reflected in the preamble of the constitution, which is amended in 1976, succinctly proclaims the aims and objects of the constitution, i.e. to constitute India into a Sovereign, Socialist, Secular, Democratic Republic and to secure to all its citizens.

The scheduled areas and scheduled tribes commission (1961, Chairman Shri U.N. Dhebar) in the context of tribal welfare and development observed that "the constitution arranged for the provisions of resources and provided institutional apparatus. We feel that so far as the basic framework of the constitution is concerned it cannot be considered inadequate. Some of the safeguards for the tribals in the constitution were originally only for ten years. In fixing this period, the constitution had envisaged an effective follow-up programmes which would have obviated the need for their continuance. This hope has not materialised and the period has been extended, but we are of the opinion that this has not been due to any deficiency in the constitution itself. It is the result of deficiency in performance."

The rights of the scheduled tribes are sought to be preserved first, through the fundamental right. These rights apply generally to all citizens as well as the scheduled tribes. A number of specific provisions have made in the constitution to protect the rights of the tribals. In constitution both protective and development aspects have been considered. The protective aspects relate to the protection of the rights of the tribals in land and forests alongwith the safeguards against usurious or exploitive elements. The 'developmental' aspects related to the welfare measures.

The constitution deliberately, laid emphasis on both aspects protective as well as development. The constitution members of the constitution were keen that the tribals join the mainstream of the national life, while retaining their traits and cultural heritage. Keeping in view the tribal status in constitution, therefore, made special provisions for their social and economic development. The provisions are contained in Articles 46,244, 330,332, 334,335, 338,339, 342 and schedules V and VI to the constitution of India. The constitution also permits for change in laws, according to the tribal situation of concerned area.

Who are Tribals

The so called "Tribals" of India are the indigenous people of the land, in the sense that they have been long settled in different parts of the country before the Aryan speaking people penetrated India to settle down first in Kabul and Indus valleys and then within a millennium and a half, to spread out over large parts of the country along the plains and river valleys. At a much later stage of history they here came to this land as civilized foreigners in small numbers like the Achaemenians, the Hellenistic, Greeks, the Parthans and the Romans, nomadic-pastoral tribes in very large numbers and a wave after wave from the steppes of central Asia and this over a period of more than a millennium and a half, beginning with the sakas and closing with the trunks and Mongols and finally, again in several waves, rural and semi-agricultural. Tibeto-Burmano from across the north and north-eastern borders of the country. In between the later there were small influxes from time to time of the Arabs, Iranians and Abysinians from East Africa and Tibeto-Burmans from Burma and Arkan region.

There is linguistic and archaeological evidence to suggest that pro-Aryan indigenous 'Janas' were settled originally on the plains and rivers and valleys of the land. But they were not all in the same stage of development. Many of there are still in the food gathering economy, not knowing, the use of metal; and perhaps on the thresh-hold of a real food producing economy. They seem to have lived in isolated settlements, in shelters and various levels of constructional activities, some are even in natural or dug-out shelters. They spoke a variety of languages. Their religion consisted in the belief in and practices called 'Primitive religion' and they seem to have lived in closed, well-knit social units presided over a headman or chief and controlled by a group of elders. In a word, these indigenous so called "tribes" were just slowly but certainly obliged to move bit by bit, to farther and farther areas until they came to find their refuge in relatively more inaccessible regions of forests and hills, large mountain slopes. The process went on centuries and millennia, in a very slow and steady, but in a very relentless manner very slow and steady, but very relentless manner, until very recent times since when state legislation has been trying to put a break to it because of a rising consciousness among the people themselves.[1]

The term "tribe" refers to cultural and historical concept. It is used in terms of the folk urban continuum along which different groups are classified, given a certain order of material culture and a stage of technological growth and classified as tribes.

The definition of "tribe" as it has emerged that "a social group usually with a definite area, dialect, cultural homogeneity and unifying social organisation having several subgroups, such as clams or sibs."

The term 'tribe' have been defined by various writers in their own specific views. Anthropologists, sociologists, economists and administrators have different approach to the problem of defining the term.

According to Oxford Dictionary "tribe is a group of people in primitive or barbarous stage of development acknowledging the authority of a chief and usually regarding themselves as having a common ancestor."

The tribe is "a social group of simple kind, the members of which speak a common dialect, have a single government, act together for common purposes, and have a common name, a contiguous territory, a relatively uniform or way of life and a tradition of common descent.[2]

A.B. Bardhan defines the tribe as a "course of socio-cultural entity at a definite historical stage of development. It is a single, endogamous community, with a cultural and psychological make up going back into a distinct historical past."[3]

D.N. Majumdar defines the tribe as "a collection of families or common groups bearing a common name, the members of which occupy the same territory, speak the same language and observe certain taboos, regarding marriage, profession, or occupation and have developed a well assured system or reciprocity and mutuality of obligations.[4]

Kamaladevi Chattopadhyaya[5] explained the term tribe as "a tribe ordinarily has an ancestor or a patron deity. The families or groups composing the larger units are linked through religious, social and socio-economic functions.

Verrier Elwin[6] further explained this term as "but let me turn to the history of the term and concept 'tribe'. Derived from a Latin root, the middle English term "tribuz" meaning the three divisions into which the early Romans were grouped, came to evolve into the modern English 'tribe'. With the Romans, the 'tribe' was a political division which Greeks seem to have equated it some what with their 'fraternities' at times, with the geographical divisions at others. In Irish history, however, the term meant families or communities of persons having the same surname. In certain other areas of western world and certain period of history, it stood for a division of territory allotted to a family or community.

Similarly various authors have described the tribes by different nomenclature. Dr. Ghurye named them Backward Hindus', Dr. Das and Das rename them as 'Submerged humanity', few named them Aboriginals, Primitive tribe, Adivasi, Vanyajati, Vanabasi, Adimjati, Pahari etc. In the ancient literature of India the veds, the Puranas, the Ramayana, the Mahabharta the tribals appeared as Nishad, Sabarars, Kiratas and Dasyns. They are believed to be the earlier among the present inhabitants of the country.

In constitution the term 'Tribe' have not been defined clearly any where. Only the term 'scheduled tribe' explained as "the tribe or the tribal communities or parts of or groups within tribes or tribal communities" which the president may specify by public notification (article, 342). As these groups are presumed to form the oldest ethnological sector of the people.

The term 'Adivasi' (Adi=original and 'vasi'= inhabitant) has become current among certain people. The International Labour Organisation has classified such people as "indigenous". According to I.L.O. Convention 107 (1957) the aboriginals or tribals have been defined as the tribals or semi-tribals groups of the Independent countries deprived socially or economically and having their own customs, traditions and traits or they have their own special customary laws/conventions."

Hence in this way the term "tribe" have been clearly defined by various social scientists and eminent Anthropologists and identified as a separate group of the persons having their own identity and cultural traits. The tribals have their own mode of management to control their group or society. The customary laws of tribals are still unwritten, but they obey them strictly.

The difficulty in setting out formal criteria for defining the tribe arises from the fact that tribes in India are and have been for some decades in transition. All of them live in various stages of cultural and economic conditions. Because of this transitory process of evolution no scientific and standard definition has so far been evolved.

The concept of 'scheduled tribe' has not become an objective one. The term 'scheduled tribe' as conceived by administrators is different from that of anthropologists and sociologists. Today they recognise a tribe by the list of scheduled tribes declared by the Govt. For the non-tribes a tribe does not exist as a single cultural entity.

The idea behind defining the term tribe is to evolve ways and means of gradual adjustment of the tribal population with the changing conditions and slow integration in the national mainstream. They have suffered from social injustice and economical constraints too long.

Tribal Development

The term development has been used in a wider sense, it is a slow process of civilization. The purpose of development is to provide increasing opportunities to all the people for a better life. It is essential to bring about more equitable distribution of income and wealth for promoting social justice and efficiency of production, to provide a greater variety of facilities like education, health services, nutrition, housing etc.

The aims of development were spelled out in 1970's in the Preamble of the International Development Strategy for the second United Nations Development Decade.

According to I.L.O. development involves 'humans' as distinct form material product. It is defined as a process which involves improvement in the quality of life of the weaker sections and a greater participation and involvement of the masses in the process of decision making in the economic, social, political and cultural life of a society. In his book Cruel choice, Denis Goulet[7] has said,

"Development is not a cluster of benefits given to the people in need; it is rather a process by which a populace acquires a greater mastery over its own destiny" Schumpeter[8] defined development as only such changes in economic life as are not forced upon it from without, but arise by its own initiative from within".

According to Dedley seers[9] "development means creating conditions for the realisation of human potential."

Development is an elusive concept and involves mobilization of natural resources, augmentation of trained manpower, capital and technical know-how and their utilisation for attainment of constantly multiplying national goals, higher living standards and the changes over from a traditional to a modern society. The essence of development is generally perceived as industrialisation and modernisation. Development is a multi-dimensional and multilinear process."

"Development is usually conceived as an aspect of change that is desirable, broadly predicted or planned and administered or at least influenced by governmental action. Thus the concept of development consists of (a) an aspect of change (b) a plan or prediction, and (c) involvement of the government for the achievements of that planned or predicted goal. The term development is also used for the process of allowing and encouraging people to meet their own aspirations."[10]

Development and modernisation are not interchangeable terms as development results in a community where as moderanisation is a particular case of development.[11]

The main aim of development is to increase national as well as per capita income and to raise the standard of living of the people and secure justice, freedom, equality and security for them in society. The focus of development is now increasingly on (a) equitable distribution of wealth and income; (b) full utilization of manpower; (c) better utilization of natural resources; and (d) protection of human environment, etc.[12]

Hence, development means change plus growth, i.e. it includes growth, modernisation, increase in social facilities, etc.

Nehru's Concept

Nehru's international outlook is well known. During pre-independence days, he kept peering beyond the Indian frontiers and was influenced by events, aborad. After independence, he influenced the international scene considerably by being the chief architect of the non-aligned movement. Of particular interest in his reference in his Autobiography to the oppressed people's meet in 1927 at Brussels. The conference was held against the background of the feeling that, in the struggle for freedom against imperialism and colonialism, common joint deliberation as well as possible joint action were desirable. He was attracted towards socialist movements and lauds the policy Lenin and his successors adopted in the Soviet Union encouraging the languages and helping growth of linguistic minorities. He held the view that in this country, not only should tribal languages be allowed to continue but they should be encouraged to flourish. Linguism became one of the prominent currents in the national socio-political mainstream even during Nehru's time and has become stronger subsequently. Contrary to the assumption that a linguistic force is destructive only, Nehru believed that the contributions of the linguistic groups can deepen and widen, thereby strengthen the national mainstream. He was convinced that tribal contributions would enrich India's cultural mosaic. There has been some progress in development of tribal languages and their linkages with the educational curricula. The Central Institute of Indian Languages, Mysore is reported to be engaged in work on 57 tribal languages. The Tribal Research Institute have been doing their bit. With clear policy and directions the progress can be accelerated. The content and pattern of educational relevant for different scheduled tribe communities have to be carefully evolved with particular reference to their socio-cultural milieu. But whether it is the question of tribal education in general or tribal languages in particular, there is need to keep the tribal in focus and proceed keeping his views in the picture.

The recurrent theme in Nehru's thought is that of integration and consolidation of India after Independence. He observed:

After the achievement of Independence, the basic problem of India taken as a whole, is one of integration and consolidation. Political integration is now complete but that is not enough ... so the greatest problem of India today is psychological integration and consolidation, to build up unity which will do away with provincialism, communalism, and various other 'isms' which disrupt and separate.

In expressing this view, Nehru was touching on the most crucial problem, as we can now visualise from the vantage point of history. His emphasis was fully justified; in our own times it needs even heavier emphasis. The question is relevant in the total national perspective. But in the present context, the north-eastern ethnic aspirations have been fulfilled through a variety of measures like constitutional provisions, creation of states of Meghalaya, Nagaland, Mizoram, Arunachal Pradesh, etc. Ethnic strings sometimes assume violent shape. The question of Jharkhand has long been with us and now the new demand of Bodo land is being voiced; both these are conceived within the federal framework. Not all ethnic aspirations are unwholesome; fulfilment of the legitimate once releases creativity. The entire issue has to be considered and appreciated in the overall context of nation-building, national integration and consolidation. More thought and action have to be directed towards the cementing forces of nation-building, that Nehru was able to comprehend so much about tribal, their life and culture, with so little contact with the spread over so long in his busy life of multifarious activities during the freedom struggle and subsequently as Prime Minister of a newly independent emerging India. Part of the reason may have been his ardent spirit and part his keen mind. He was a committed humanist as well as rationalist radical. He touched the tribal psyche when he called for their advancement along with preservation of their identity.

The Panchsheel were visualised as five pillars for tribal development. It is mentioned by some that they represent a basic survival system. They are more than that. With Gandhian ideas in the background, the Panchsheel and other policy parameters evolved into a growth-oriented charter. The conditions have been changing and becoming more complex over the years.

The Nehru's Panchsheel (five points) are:

1. *Non-imposition:* The tribals should be allowed to progress according to their own pace and understanding of the situation.

2. *Respect of tribal customs:* This respect applies particularly to their customs about land ownership, allocations for use of forest resources within their jurisdiction.
3. *Development tribal youth:* The leadership for tribal development and social change should be encouraged from amongst tribal youth.
4. *Simplicity of administration:* Proliferation of bureaucracy should be avoided. The voluntary agencies or suitable local organs should be involved to carry out the developmental tasks.
5. *Emphasis on human growth:* The quality of human living is more important than compliance with physical targets of programming.

There is greater differentiation among the tribal communities, some having raced ahead of others. Various forces have been transforming them. New challenges are emerging. The new situations call for fresh evaluation. But the validity of the second Panchsheel demanding respect for tribal rights in land and forest is greater today than in his own day. The call for light administration and tribal development through tribal social and cultural institutions, contained in the third and fourth Panchsheels, have a special significance, as our experience of planned development during the past five decades shows; without direct tribal participation, the advance is slow and uncertain.

Today, it is necessary to examine whether under the broad canopy of the Panchsheel, the existing policy formulations and instruments are adequate. For example, the legislation in regard to alienation of tribal land needs a fresh look. The policy in regard to establishment of big projects consuming tribal land and causing tribal displacement needs to be appraised afresh. Induction of big administrative machinery in tribal areas should be subjected to close examination to prevent its oppressiveness.

Their use of national resources did not outstrip resource regenerative capacity. Almost every scheduled tribe community devised its own eithnoeco-technology, in fact a whole ethnosystem. Left to themselves, they might have been able to develop them further. But they have now to contend with inexorable march of moderanisation. The forces of technology and economics have been closing in on tribal areas, relentlessly transforming the character of tribal communities. The techno-eco-culturation tends to transmute them into the personality of their non-tribal neighbours. Some tribal elite groups favour modern education and technology for extricating the mass from backwardness and illiteracy. With accelerating tempo of modernization, the distinctive tribal character, of which Nehru was enamoured, is likely to be obliterated, making the tribals and not-tribals of a piece. But there is a contrary. Social tribal groups have sprung up in support of preservation of tribal identity and culture. Tribal resurgence is world-wide. In our country it has taken a marked turn. Thus, we are back to the old controversy of feasibility of tribal advancement without sacrifice of their culture and identity.

Although the Presidential responsibilities for the administration of scheduled areas is managed by Home Ministry as was the case during British times, the process of planned development brings together inputs from various national-building departments to be focused in tribal areas. The allocation for tribal welfare have a demarkable like from 50 crores in the First Five Year Plan to Rs. 1,571 crores in Seventh Plan. In the subsequent plans; the trend is to make plan outlays for tribal development proportional to the tribal population.

Concepts of Economic Development

Economic development is the process of securing a higher level of productivity in all the sectors as the economy which primarily depends upon the technological advances the community is able to make.

Economic growth with social justice is one of the most important goal of developing economy like ours. Harmonious growth of inter-sectoral income, trade and income distribution are some of the pre-requisite of accelerated economic development. In the process of growth, agriculture and industry depend on each other for raw materials and market, besides, it is often argued that declining output ratio of agriculture and industry increases the net domestic product and affects the income distribution pattern in the economy. Several writers have commended the importance of an "agricultural surplus" for the economic growth or economic development. The tribals have poor-agricultural surplus, in this way they suffer economically.

Conceptually "development is the faithful limitation of the developed" holds John Kenneth Galbraith (and others) recognises three types of economic development.

1. Symbolic modernisation;
2. Maximized economic growth; and
3. Selective growth.

1. Symbolic Modernisation

Symbolic modernisation is a deceptive expression of economic development because the well being of the people is not much advanced by symbolic modernisation and it may be retarded for those who must pay the bill. In the past, moreover, much symbolic modernisation has been a strategy for making the people into believe that some thing was being done. A poor country like India where more than three fourth of the population lives below the poverty line Symbolic modernisation by constructing Asia's best "Ashoka Hotel" as public undertaking is certainly meaningless to a commoner in the street.

2. Maximized Economic Growth

Test of increased income and product (i.e. through obtaining maximised economic growth) obviously has much to commend it and stands up to objective test of performance.

3. Selective Growth

At back of much development planning has been the belief that benefits must accrue as a matter of priority to the more needy sector of population. Resources so painfully conscripted from the people, must return benefit to the same people. This politically salutary principle of Selective Growth has, however, led to diverse and even contradictory conclusions as its application. Planned proportionate development of the economy is an objective economic law of socialism.

The common factor in all these three types of economic development is a change from a given situation to attain a better situation. There are a number of norms to measure these changes. Also there are a number of perspectives to look at these changes, for example, the social change, the economic change, the political change, the technological change etc. Thus, the change factor is a basic component of development, improvement in one situation is normative of desirable change.

The democratic approach to economic planning and implementation leads to equitable distribution of economic resources. One of the directive principles of economic planning in India has its in Socialistic economic mode, which perhaps is more meaningful to achieving the political goal of making it impossible. This is possible by Striving to attain the ideal of democratic socialism. The chances of attaining the orderly process of development are closely related to the effectiveness of measures to distribute the gains of development equitably or at least reasonably equitably among the income groups, regions and sectors.

George Dalton has vividly analysed the different dimensions of the problem of development. What economists call development, political scientists call "Modernisation", Sociologists, role differentiation; and anthropologists "Cultural change". These accompanying political and social changes make economic development processes even more complicated. In tribal regions, mostly comprising non-market economy, it is difficult to apply the tools of measurement of economic development as most of them are not relevant.

Characteristics of Tribals Economy

The socio-economic structure in tribal communities is markedly different from that of the non-tribals or advanced groups of people. They have a very simple technology which fits well with their ecological surroundings and conservative outlook. Moreover, their economy can be said to be subsistence type, they practice different types of occupations to sustain themselves and live on "Marginal economy". We find the tribals of India belonging to different economic stages, from food gathering to industrial labour, which present their overlapping economic stages in the border framework of the stage economy. And the last important point to be emphasised is that a tribe is usually considered an economically independent group of people having their own specific economy and thus having a living pattern of labour, division of labour and specialisation, gift and ceremonial exchange, trade and barter, credit and value, wealth, consumption norms, capital formation, land tenure and good tangible and intangible economic status, all these have their own specially which identified the tribal economy in the border set-up of Indian economy.

The first and foremost characteristics of the tribal economy is the close relationship between their economic life and the natural environment or habitat, which is, in general, the forest. Exception to this are the tribals inhabiting their own islands. The Bhils of western India depend on Forest for Mahua and biri (Tendu) leaves (Tandu Patta) to a great extent.

Tribal—A Concept of Forest Ecosystem

The linkage between the tribal and forests is traditional. Tribals are economically and ecologically inseparable from forests. Be it food, fodder or fuel needs, the tribal inescapably and assuredly depended on his surrounding forests for sustenance even during troubled times of droughts.

Their dependence on forests is such, that they constitute the integral components of forest ecosystem. Forests have been the pivot on which tribal habitat and life revolves and has evolved so far; their religion-cultural artifacts, beliefs and practices, technologies and tools have been nurtured and cultivated under perennial plant associations and benign environment.

The tribals are usually surrounded by thick forests or they live in hilly regions away from the modern world. The forests are an integral part of the tribal economy. The objects is to focus attention on the integration of forest policy with that of economic development of tribals. The forest and the tribals are inseparable; very rightly, the tribals consider the forest as their nourishing mother. The use of forests and their produce is traditional to tribal economy as food-gatherers and agriculturists. In drought situations the forests are the only source of subsistence for the tribals.

Goals of Tribal Development

The goals of Tribal Development in India were best summarised in Nehru's foreword to Varrier Elwin's book on NEFA as follows:

1. People should develop along the lines of their own genius and we should avoid imposing anything on term. We should try to encourage in every way their own traditional arts and culture.
2. Tribal rights in land and forest should be respected.
3. We should try to train and build up a team of their own people to do the work of administration and development. Some technical people from outside will no doubt be needed, especially in the beginning, but we should avoid introducing too many outsiders into tribal territory.
4. We should not over administer these areas or overwhelm them with multiplicity of schemes. We should rather work through and not in rivalry to their own social and cultural institutions; and
5. We should guide results not by statistics or the amount of money spent, but by the quality of human character that is involved.

This five point formula enunciated by Nehru (optimises) as the corner stone the government policy. This was further elaborated by Elwin, who emphasised the need for the tribal people to come to terms with their own past, avoiding danger of pauperism and without creating a sense of inferiority. Elwin stressed on recognising the contribution of the tribal people in helping the Indian society as a whole so that they may feel as part and parcel of India as any other citizen.

Dr. B.S. Guha explained the tribal welfare goals in such a manner that "schemes for tribal welfare must fulfil two essential conditions namely, conformity to the social values and patterns of the people for whom they are intended and the psychological receptivity and ability of the tribal population to absorb them. Theoretical perfection of a scheme or its suitability to people in general must not be regarded as the criterion for tribal people. Ignorance of these basic facts and inability to appreciate them are responsible for the failure of many development which by themselves are unexceptionable.

Dr. Guha further commented about the tribal development that isolation and absence of intercourse with other communities are injurious to a people. The views put forward here are motivated by these consideration only and not framed with the purpose, conscious or unconscious, of attaining to keep the tribal people as "Museum specimens" as is so often wrongly attributed to the anthropologists. To allow a tribe to retain its traditional value and mode of life in its natural setting and give it the chance to develop along its own genius is the very reverse of the museum specimen idea."

In the context of tribal development, it aims at increasing the incomes and strengthening the material aspects of tribal culture through better utilisation of the environmental resources i.e. forests, minerals, flora and fauna, agriculture, horticulture, animal husbandry, industrial potential as was as skill of the tribal people.

The goals of tribal development can be summarised into:

(i) long term objectives; and

(ii) short term objectives

The long term objectives are (a) To narrow the gap of development between tribals and non-tribals (b) To improve the quality of life without disturbing their ethnicity. The short term objectives are (a) elimination of exploitation by all means, by rapid Socio economic development; (b) improving organisational capabilities; and (c) building up inner strength of the tribal people.

Tribal development is often taken as synonymous with rural development. The tribal situation in the country presents a varied picture. Some areas have high tribal concentration, while some have no tribals. There are about 250 tribal communities speaking about 105 languages and 225 subsidiary languages. The developmental parameters of each tribe is different and it depends on the inhabitants and their setting conditions. The tribal development scene was categorised in two parts. (i) areas of tribal concentration, and (ii) dispersed tribals. The review of first tribal plan 1974-79 was also discussed in the Report of the Working Group on Tribal Development. During sixth plan 1980-85 under the Chairmanship of B.G. Deshmukh. In respect of tribal concentrated areas "it was decided to accept in area development approach with focus on tribals and for dispersed tribals, family oriented programmes were decided for being taken up".

Approaches for Tribal Development

There are mainly five approaches which have been employed so far in the welfare of tribals in India. These are:

1. Political approach;
2. Administration approach;
3. Religious approach—with special reference to missionary approach;
4. Voluntary agencies approach; and
5. Anthropological approach.

1. Political Approach

The Political Approach for the tribal welfare may be understood in the context of the pre and post independence period. The colonial rule created "excluded" and "Partly excluded" areas and gave separate political representation to the tribes. Nationalists opposed these measures as part of a diabolic conspiracy to a new separatism.

After independence the constitution has given the tribes a number of safeguards considering them to be the weaker section of the population. In the first instance a period of ten years was given to achieve the goal, but as the problem was too complicated to be solved in a single decade, it has persisted through decades. We are to continue to guard the tribal interests. A number of articles of the Indian constitution provide proper safeguards for the tribal people.

2. Administrative Approach

The Administrative Approach is closely followed by the political approach. The Government of India has constituted a vast administrative machinery for tribal welfare.

At state level, the Governor has been made responsible and on his behalf the Chief Minister and Welfare Minister are incharge of the special schemes to be implemented in the tribal areas. In some major concentrated tribal areas, the state has an independent Tribal Welfare Ministry. The Welfare Ministry is advised by two bodies. The Tribes Advisory Council and the Tribal Research Institute in framing the policies and programmes for tribal welfare.

3. Religious Approach

The Religious Approach has been attempted by different religious agencies like Christian missionaries, the Ramakrishna mission, the Arya Samaj and other local religious institutions which are engaged in the welfare work for the tribals. At the same time conversion of tribes to a new faith, viz. Christianity, has also taken place. This conversion activity has formed groups among the tribals.

The Christian Missionaries have been active in tribal India. Though they have been primarily interested in evangelization, the welfare works educational, economic, hygienic and social called "work of mercy", have invariably followed it. For both types of work spiritual and material, the missionaries did realise the importance of understanding the tribal culture and language. These they considered essential for communicating with them effectively. Missionary welfare activities have been viewed by different persons in different ways. But if it detribalises and disintegrates these communities without offering the many alternative satisfaction, the approach can be said to be a problem for the tribals.

4. Voluntary Agencies Approach

Under the Voluntary Agencies Approach, social works, social welfare agencies, social movement agencies, social reformers, etc. are working to uplift the weaker section of our society in their own ways.

Voluntary social service organisations have done considerable humanitarian work in the tribal areas; but their idealism and spirit of service have not been matched by their understanding of tribal organisation, values and problems.

5. Anthropological Approach

The fact of the matter is that there is not an anthropological approach; there are anthropological approaches, which instead of offering an omnibus solution to tribal problems, have led to thinking of specific solutions to specific problems.

Anthropological knowledge in the changed situation of the country as a Welfare State is again of great importance. By and large anthropologists believe in the ultimate integration of the tribes into the mainstream of Indian life. After Independence, some anthropologists came out with several papers and addresses, dealing with the importance of applied anthropology in tribal welfare programmes. They made a re-valuation of anthropological position and came out with the theory of "planned acculturation". A vast organisation of anthropological researches is available with us to help and guide the welfare work. The various tribal research institutes are engaged in conducting researches on scheduled castes and scheduled tribes. Besides, many university department in the country undertake research on them.

If the welfare projects are implemented with understanding and caution the first effective step against primitiveness will have been taken.

To identify the various approaches which have been in operation in respect of tribal development. The tribal development will have to be examined in the overall context of development planning in India.

The tribal policy of the British rule was at best of indifference and at worst of oppression. They left the field of tribal welfare wide open for the Christian missions to launch their humanitarian activities. The main thrust of the missionary activity among the tribals was on evangelical services. After independence the government of India paid some attention to tribal problems. The Govt. initiated three important measures; provision of special constitutional concessions, programmes of tribal development and the protectionist policy. The focus of constitutional concessions has been on reservations for tribal in educational institutions, jobs and parliament and state assembly seats. This radical approach to tribal development manifested itself in the form of tribal development.

In the 8th Five Year Plan Tribal Sub Plan area, M.A.D.A. (Modified Area Development Approach) and Scattered development plans and primitive tribe development plans for the tribal development approach have been stressed. In this plan family oriented schemes have been also stressed to uplift the tribal families. The community development programmes are given importance on second priority.

Planning in Tribal Areas

Micro-plans generally adopt area approach as the technique of planning which makes the following specific presumptions:

(i) The growth stimuli have an even geographical spread efforts.

(ii) The benefits of development percolate evenly to the lower strata of society.

(iii) The socio-economic topography of the region is even, which, by implication, means that are "Spread-effect" and "percolation effect" will automatically set in and it is only a matter of time for the benefits to spread out both socially and geographically, and

(iv) Manpower is like any other fact or production demand for different skills can be satisfied over a larger region with no implications for the local community.

The situation in the developing countries is extremely complex inhibiting both the "spread effect" and the "percolation effect". The additional stipulation of "full employment" will provide the necessary corrective. In this context, manpower cannot be treated as any other factor of production. "Micro Planning for full employment" appears as a distinct methodology of planning. The micro-world of each area will present its own matrix of natural resources, socio-economic structure, institutional frame of manpower.

Planning for tribal development in our country is based on the actual experience in these areas for the last five decades. The National Committee on the Development of Backward Areas under the Chairmanship of Shri Sivaraman (Sivaraman Committee) has recommended the "sub-plan approach" with suitable adaptation for other backward areas. For the better planning and development of tribals some committees were formed by Govt. of India under the Chairmanship of prominent politicians/Govt. officials. These committees are detailed in the working group report of VI plan 1980-85. The scheduled Areas and Scheduled Tribes commission set-up under the chairmanship of Shri U.N. Dhebar in 1961 referred to this policy approvingly and observed that "the problem of problems is not to disturb the harmony of tribal life and simultaneously work for its advance; not to impose anything upon the tribals and simultaneously work for their integration as member and part of the Indian Family". A study team appointed by the Planning Commission headed by P. Shilu AO opined that" the aim of tribal-welfare policy should be defined as the progressive advancement, social and economic, of the tribals with a view to their integration with the rest of the community on a footing of equality within a reasonable distance of time. The period has necessarily to vary from tribe to tribe and it may be five or ten years in the case of certain tribes".

Another important committee was Renuka Ray (1959), he emphasised that while each aspect of development is important in its own place, while Dhebar Commission (1961) stressed integrated approach, "According to them, problem of economic development for the bulk of the tribals cannot be solved unless that resources of land, forests, cattle wealth, cottage and village industries are all mobilised in an integrated basis". In 1972 under the Chairmanship of S.C. Dube an Expert Committee was set up for advising on formulation of a new strategy during the fifth five year plan defined the task of tribal development.

Selection Criteria of Tribal Areas for Tribal Development

The selection criteria of the tribal development area are discussed in the Report of the working Group on Tribal Development during Sixth Plan 1980-85 in detail. According to the report. "The Tribal sub-plan was initially expected to include all the Scheduled Areas and Tehsils/Block with more than 50 per cent tribal population. As per this approach tribal majority states namely Arunachal Pradesh, Meghalaya, Mizoram, Nagaland, Lakshadweep and Dadra and Nagar Havali were not included since development plans of these states/U.T's. were primarily meant for the scheduled tribes themselves. However, according to the formulation, substantial tribal population was covered by the tribal sub-plans in Madhya Pradesh, Orissa, Bihar, Rajasthan, Gujarat, Manipur, Himachal Pradesh, A & N Island and Goa, Daman and Diu. In other States where the tribal population was of lower concentration these forms were relaxed with a view to cover a reasonable proportion of the states tribal population, a minimum scheduled tribe population threshold of about 20 thousand was adapted in delineating the tribal sub-plan areas in Maharashtra, Andhra Pradesh and Assam. In the case of Tamil Nadu and Kerala, the norms were further reduced to a S.T. population of about 10 thousand. In Tripura and West Bengal, groups of villages with more than 50 per cent tribal concentration were included. In Karnataka and Uttar Pradesh, where the tribal population is small and dispersed, family based approach was adopted. The tribal sub-plan area was further divided into 180 Integrated Tribal Development projects for operational purposes."

In constituting the tribal sub-plan areas in the Fifth Plan period, the development Blocks were taken as the smallest unit, when the Blocks were carved out. Originally, the norm for a Community Development Block was 60 thousand population and for a Tribal Development Block 25,000 thousand population. However, in actual practice, the average would be about 40 thousand and one lakh respectively. Those Blocks which had more than two third tribal tribal population were converted into T.D. Blocks, mostly in the Third Plan Period. Many Blocks having S.T. population between 50 per cent and 66 per cent continued as C.D. Blocks. When the tribal sub-plans areas; C.D. Blocks which had more than 50 per cent of the tribal population were included, by the end of sixth plan 181 ITDP's, 248 MADA pockets and 72 primitive tribal projects were in operation in the country and covered 75 per cent of the tribal population.

Regional Classification

The tribals are an intrinsic part of our national life and through their rich cultural heritage they have been contributing a lot to the complex amalgam. The tribals settled down in India in pre-historic times, inhabiting mostly the sparsely populated parts of hills and forests of sub-Himalayan and North-eastern regions in the mountain belt of Central India between, Narmada and Godavari rivers, and in the southern parts of the western Ghats extending from Wynad to Kanyakumari.

The territorial distribution of many tribes overlaps the political boundaries of the state and territory. For a better understanding of the demographic situation of the tribals, the states and territories have been classified into seven regions as mentioned below.[13]

1. *North-eastern Region:* This region comprises the states of Arunachal Pradesh, Assam, Manipur, Meghalaya, Mizoram, Nagaland and Tripura.
2. *Eastern Region:* This region includes the states of Bihar, Orissa, Sikkim and West Bengal.
3. *Northern Region:* This region belongs to states of Himachal Pradesh and Uttar Pradesh.
4. *Central Region:* This region consists of only one i.e. Madhya Pradesh.
5. *Western Region:* This region is the part of the states of Rajasthan, Maharashtra, Gujarat, Dadar and Nagar Haveli, Goa, Daman and Diu.
6. *Southern Region:* This region comprises the stress of Andhra Pradesh, Karnataka, Tamil Nadu and Kerala.
7. *Island Region:* This region constitutes Andaman and Nicobar island, and Lakshadweep.

Financial Allocations for Tribal Development

The tribal majority areas in the country are broadly divided in the three categories, viz (i) predominantly tribal states/union territories; (ii) scheduled area; and (iii) Non-scheduled areas in the states. All the tribal-majority states and union territories are placed in a special category for allocation of funds. The development and administration of tribal areas is accepted as a special responsibility of the central government even though they are integral parts of the concerned states. The question of making financial provisions for their development were considered in detail by the constituent Assembly itself.

The schemes have been divided into two categories, viz. (i) Central Sector programmes which are fully financed by the Central Govt. (ii) the Centrally sponsored programmes which are partly financed by the Central Govt., and rest of the expenditure is met out by the concerned state govt.

Dr. B.D. Sharma explained the elements for state programmes[14] as "the financial resources for developmental programmes in a state may comprise the following elements.

(i) Investment in the central and centrally sponsored schemes;

(ii) State revenues;

(iii) Share from central revenues;

(iv) Plan assistance from the central government under the Gadgil formula; and

(v) Grants under Article 275(1) on the basis of the recommendations of the Finance Commission.

The utilisation of State funds is broadly classified under two categories. Plan and Non-plan. The plan technically covers all those items which are included in the state or the Central plan. The non-plan includes expenditure on general administration as also on the maintenance of development schemes".

The special central assistance for tribal sub-plans is allocated between different states on the basis of three criteria as under:

(i) the tribal population of sub-plan area;

(ii) the geographical area of the sub-plan; and

(iii) the per capita gross output of the state.

The weightage for these three elements has been fixed in a certain proportion. While the first two criteria are simple, the quantum of assistance on the basis of the third criterion is determined with reference to the difference between the inverse of the States per capita gross product and the inverse of the per capita gross national product. Thus, the sub-plan, besides having a share from the state plan, also gets benefit of Special Central Assistance, the assistance under 'Gadgil Formula' as also the devaluation on the basis of recommendations of the Finance Commission are the block grants of states. These can be used by team according to their needs, subject to the guidelines of the Finance Commission and Planning Commission.

Broadly the financing agencies rendering their services in the tribal areas are Central Government, State Governments, Institutions viz. Commercial Banks, Co-operative Banks, NABARD and voluntary organisation.

Tribal Situation in India

According to 1991 census 67.76 million persons were belonging to Scheduled Tribes in different States and Union Territories, excluding Assam and Jammu & Kashmir, constituting 8.08 per cent of the total population. The percentage of S.T. population has marginally increased from 7.83 per cent in 1981 to 7.95 per cent in 1991. The S.T. population has increased by 25.67 per cent during the decade 1981-1991. The growth is high in comparison to the total population of the country (23.79 per cent). In some of the states and Union Territories, the population was predominantly S.T. viz. Mizoram 94.75 per cent, Laksha Dweep (93.15 per cent), Nagaland (87.10 per cent), Meghalaya (85.83 per cent), Dadra and Nagar Haveli (79.98 per cent) and Arunachal Pradesh (63.66 per cent). Among the 15 major States, Madhya Pradesh had the largest proportion of S.T. population (23.27 per cent) followed by Orissa (22.21 per cent).

Out of the total S.T. population of 67.76 million, about 49 per cent of the S.T. population live in three States viz. Madhya Pradesh (27.73 per cent), Maharashtra (10.80 per cent) and Orissa (10.38 per cent), while Haryana, Punjab, Chandigarh, Delhi and Pondicherry have not a single S.T.

Only 7.39 per cent of the S.T. population of India reside in urban areas as compared to 25.73 per cent of the general population and 18.72 per cent of S.C. population. Thus, about 93 per cent of the S.T. population are rural based. Out of the major 15 States, only 3 states viz Karnataka, Maharashtra and Tamil Nadu had more than 10 per cent of S.T. population residing in the Urban areas, the respective percentages being 14.94, 12.47 and 12.01. The percentage of S.T. population residing in Urban areas in other States are Andhra Pradesh (7.6 per cent), Assam (3.4 per cent), Bihar (7.0 per cent),

Gujarat (8.1 per cent), Kerala (3.5 per cent), Madhya Pradesh (4.8 per cent), Orissa (5.1 per cent), Rajasthan (4.6 per cent), Uttar Pradesh (5.9 per cent) and West Bengal (5.2 per cent). The State-wise details of S.T. population are discussed in Appendix-I to III.

The Children in the age group 0-6 constitute 20.18 per cent of the S.T. population in India as against 17.94 per cent for total population and 19.63 per cent for S.C. Population. Thus, the S.T. population has a relatively higher Children population as compared to general and S.C. population. The sex ratio for S.T. population was 972 (per 1000 males). This is favourable to women as compared to general (927) and S.C. (922).

Literacy

According to 1991 census 29.6 per cent of the S.T. population in the age group 7 years and above were literate, the literacy rate being 40.65 per cent for males and 18.19 per cent for females. There figures are much lower than the corresponding figures for the total population of India. If we were to take out the population of North-Eastern States like Nagaland, Mizoram, Meghalaya, Manipur which have a predominantly higher literacy rate among the S.T. population, while the literacy rate among other states are extremely low viz. Andhra Pradesh (17.16 per cent), Rajasthan (19.44 per cent). In case of females, the literacy is extremely low viz Rajasthan (4.4 per cent), Andhra Pradesh (8.7 per cent), Orissa (10.2 per cent), Madhya Pradesh (10.7 per cent), Bihar (14.8 per cent) and Uttar Pradesh (15.0 per cent).

Workers

The work participation rate of S.T. population is 49.30 per cent which is much more higher than that for the general population (33.46 per cent) and for the S.C. population (39.25 per cent). This is primly due to very high participation rates among the S.T. women. In case of males, the work participation rate of S.T. population is 54.74 per cent which is somewhat higher than total population (51.55 per cent) and S.C. population (51.48 per cent). But the female work participation rate among the S.T. is 43.71 per cent as against 25.98 per cent for S.C. and 22.25 per cent for total population of the country. The female work participation rate is generally quite high in most of the States and Union Territories. The highest female work participation rate among the S.T. was found in Andhra Pradesh (50.63 per cent) and lowest in West Bengal (23.43 per cent).

96.03 per cent of the main workers among the S.T.'s are in the primary sector, 3.85 per cent in the secondary sector and 6.12 per cent in the tertiary sector with in the agriculture sector, 54.51 per cent of the S.T. main workers are cultivators, while 32.69 per cent are agricultural labourers. This is a sharp contrast to S.C. as well as the total population of the country. The State-wise percentage of workers are given in Appendix-IV.

Review of First Tribal Sub Plan 1974-79

The tribal development scene was critically reviewed on eve of the Fifth Plan. The problem of tribal development was broadly classified into two categories (i) areas of tribal concentration, and (ii) dispersed tribals. In respect of the former, it was decided to accept in area development approach with focus on tribals. For dispersed tribals, family oriented programmes were decided for being taken up. Thus, the strategy of Tribal Sub Plan Area was evolved in the Fifth Plan introduced Bihar, Gujarat, Himachal Pradesh, Karnataka, Kerala, Madhya Pradesh, Maharashtra, Manipur, Orissa, Rajasthan, Tamil Nadu, Tripura, Uttar Pradesh, West Bengal, Andman and Nicobar Island and Goa, Daman & Diu.

The tribal sub-plan was initially expected to include all the Schedule Areas and Tehsils/Blocks with more than 50 per cent tribal population. However, according to the formulation, substantial tribal was covered by the Tribal Sub-plan in Madhya Pradesh (74.83 per cent), Orissa (68.41 per cent), Bihar (76.75 per cent), Rajasthan (43.67 per cent), Gujarat (72.42 per cent), Manipur (93.71 per cent), Himachal Pradesh (59.15 per cent), and A & D islands (99.45 per cent), and Goa, Daman & Diu cent (per cent). In other States where the tribal population was of lower concentration, the norms were relaxed with a view to cover a reasonable proportion of State's tribal population; a minimum S.T. population threshold of about 20,000 was adopted in delineating the T.S.P. areas in Maharashtra, Andhra Pradesh and Assam. In the case of Tamil Nadu and Kerala, the norm was further relaxed to a S.T. population of about 10,000. So in the T.S.P. area was divided to 180 I.T.D.P.'s for operational purpose.

The Investment in the Tribal Areas from the First Plan to the Fifth Plan are:

(Rs. in Crores)

Plan	*Total Plan Outlay*	*Tribal Development Programmes*	*Percentage*
First Plan	1,960	19.93	1.0
Second Plan	7,672	42.92	0.9
Third Plan	8,577	50.53	0.6
Annual Plans (1966-67)	6,756	32.32	0.6
Fourth Plan*	15,902	75.00	0.5
Firth Plan (1974-79)*	39,322	1,182,00	3.01

* Outlay.

The tribal sub-plan 1974-79 basically represented disaggregation of sectoral programmes and the total outlay was derived figure from the sector-wise qualification. This process cannot be expected to present a viable area plan. Hence the first ttibal sub-plan 1974-79 accorded the highest priority to elimination of exploitation. Exploitation in the tribal areas mainly occurs in the fields of liquor, vending, land alienation, money lending, forestry trade including collection and disposal of minor forest produce and labour including forest labour in brief, the fifth plan be treated as initiation of tribal development measures.

The developmental measures geared in the sixth, seventh and eighth plan of the States as govt. are trying their best to uplift the poor tribals. It is expected that in the 21st century they will be in a better position in comparison to 20th century.

Tribal Development in Rajasthan

Rajasthan is one of the major States in the country where concentration of tribal population is high. The dominating tribals of the State are Mina, Bhil, Garasia, Sahariya and Damor. The tribals can be seen throughout the State, the solution part has high concentration of the tribals in comparison to western parts of the State.

According to 1991 census the tribal population of India constitute 67,758,380 persons (62,751,026 rural and 50,007,354 urban) i.e. 8.08 per cent of the tribal population, while Rajasthan the tribal population constitute 5,474,881 persons, 15,220,549 rural and 254,332 urban) i.e. the percentage is just double (12.44 per cent) of the total State population. While in 2001 census it was 12.56 per cent. The details of district-wise population according to 2001 census is given in Appendix V.

The scheduled Tribes Amendment order 1976 included the following 12 groups of tribes as under:

1. Bhil, Bhil Garasia, Dholi Bhil, Dungri Bhil, Dungri Garasia, Mewasi Bhil, Rawal Bhil, Tadvi Bhil, Bhagalia, Bhilala, Panara, Vasava, Vasave;
2. Bhil-Mina;
3. Damor, Damarai;
4. Danka, Tadvi, Tetaria, Valvi;
5. Garasia (excluding Rajput-Garasia);
6. Kathodi, Katkari, Dhor Kathodi, Dhor, Katkari, Son Kathodi, Sonkatkari;
7. Kokna, Kokni, Kukna;
8. Koli Dhor, Tokre Koi, Kolcha, Kolgha;
9. Mina;
10. Nalkda, Nayaka, Cholivala-Nayaka, Kapadia, Nayaka, Mota, Nayaka, Nana Nayaka;
11. Patelia; and
12. Seharia, Sehria, Sahariya.

The total population of the state according to 1981 census was 34,261,862 (17,845,154 males and 16,407,708 females). The total tribal population according to 1981 census was 4,183,124 (2,150,767 males and 2,032,357 females) which constitute 12.21 per cent of the states total population.

According to 1971 census 774,036 tribals have increased in comparison to 1961 census. This increase was about 32.92 per cent to the 1961 S.T. Population and 1,057,618 were added to the previous population of S.T. At the time of 1981 census, the increase was 33.84 per cent to the 1971 S.T. Population. The increase was just double to the 1961 S.T. population. According to 1971 census the S.T. population was 12.21 per cent. Hence, the increase was very low i.e. 0.08 per cent only. Thus we can say that the growth rate of the general population was much higher in comparison to the S.T. population.

The Minas constitute the highest percentage i.e. 49.88 per cent, second stand Bhil i.e. 44.11 per cent, Garasia stands third i.e. 2.84 per cent, Sahariya stands fourth i.e. 0.988 per cent and Damor stands fifth 0.75 per cent, while the list of Kokna, Kokni, occupy the lowest position in the rank. They have negligible percentage i.e. 0.004 per cent only. Bhil, Mina, Naikda and Nayaka are found throughout the state. The concentration of tribal population in the District Banswara and it covers 72.63 per cent, Dungarpur stands second i.e. 64.44 per cent, Udaipur stands third i.e. 34.33 per cent, Sirohi stands fourth i.e. 23.11 per cent, Sawai-Madhopur stands fifth i.e. 22.67 per cent of the total population. The lowest concentrated area are Bikaner and Nagaur having only 0.18 per cent tribals of their total population.

In Rajasthan the tribal development block strategy was followed. One special multipurpose tribal development block was started in Kushalgarh (Banswara) in the year 1956. This approach continued in the Third and Fourth five year plans. Besides the programmes for provision of infrastructure like transport and communication, others such as irrigation, medical and public health and some protective legislation were also placed. Rajasthan Tenancy Act, 1955, Rajasthan Abolition of Sagri Act, 1961, Rajasthan Money Lender's Act, 1963 and Rajasthan Relief of Indebtedness Act, 1957, were some of the important legislative measures initiated for the protection of the tribals.

The programme of T.D. Block was reviewed in the Third Five Year Plan and it was brought out that the programme approach followed thus far did not have the desired impact.

Area Specific and Family Oriented Approach

During the Fourth Five Year Plan some area specific and family oriented schemes were started in this series Small Farmers

Development Agencies (SFDA) and Marginal Farmers and Agricultural Labour Development Agencies (MFALDA) were the first two programmes. After the political change in 1977, the Government of Rajasthan launched "Antyodaya" scheme to make a direct attack on poverty. It aimed at identifying the poorest of the poor in rural areas and then making provision for a package of facilities for these tribals on priority basis. The "Antyodaya" programme was a micro level effort. The special feature of the scheme was that the poorest of the poor in each village were selected in every Gram Sabha.

Many appraisal studies have been made of the area specific and family oriented programme launched with the specific objective of strengthening the economic position of the rural poor. All these programmes have failed because they did not take any cognisance of the existing exploitative institutional framework. As long as this exploitative possibility for making a dent in the poverty whether by expanding employment or by upgrading the productive capabilities of the poor.

Tribal Sub-plan Approach

In view of the drawbacks of the earlier area based programmes viz. Tribal Development Block and Tribal Development Agencies, a new strategy was evolved in the Fifth Plan to formulate separate sub-plan for the tribal concentration areas. This was intended to achieve an intensity on the tribal areas and devise measures to suit their ethos.

Article 46 of constitution of India has entrusted the government with the responsibility of promoting the economic and education interests of the scheduled castes and scheduled tribes. Efforts were made to fulfil this constitutional obligation in five year plans, but a new strategy for development of tribal area was evolved during Fifth Five Year Plan which has continued upto date. In Rajasthan in the year 1974, 18 tehsils were included in Tribal Sub-Plan Area (T.S.P. Area) belong to five districts. The details of T.S.P. Area is given in the Table 1.1 and 1.2.

Table—1.1 Tribal Sub-plan Area

S. No.	District	Tehsil		Panchayat Samiti		Area in sq. km.	No. of Villages	Inhabitated Villages
		Fully	Partly	Fully	Partly			
1	2	3	4	5	6	7	8	9
1.	Udaipur	Kotra	–	Kotra	–	1,133.82	304	301
		Jhadol	–	Jhadol	–	1,469.74	256	255
		Sarada	–	Sarada	–	1,082.73	157	157
		Dhariyawad	–	Dhariawad	–	1,202.81	244	242
		Salumber	–	Salumber	–	934.43	222	220
		Kherwara	–	Kherwara	–	1,088.57	234	233
		–	Girwa	Girwa	Girwa	976.76	81	81
	Total	**6**	**1**	**6**	**1**	**7,888.84**	**1,498**	**1,498**
2.	Banswara	Ghatol	–	Ghatol	–	1,268.19	316	310
		Garhi	–	Pipalkhunt	–	710.55	167	166
		Banswara	–	Banswara	–	1,182.90	325	320
		Bagidora	–	Bagidora	–	859.74	259	259
		Kushalgarh	Kushalgarh Sajjangarh	–	–	1,046.30	396	390
	Total	**5**	–	**8**	–	**5,067.68**	**1,463**	**1,445**

(Table Contd...)

1	2	3	4	5	6	7	8	9
3.	Dungarpur	Dungarpur	–	Dungarpur	–	1,673.23	429	429
		Bichiwara						
		Simalwara						
		Aspur	–	Aspur	–	683.25	144	142
		Sagwara	Sagwara	–	–	1,454.27	264	261
	Total	**4**	–	**5**	–	**3,810.75**	**837**	**832**
4.	Chittorgarh	Pratapgarh	–	Pratapgarh	–	1,458.16	353	317
		Arnod	–	Arnod	–	696.55	177	173
	Total	2	–	2	–	2,154.71	530	490
5.	Sirohi	–	Aburoad	Aburoad	–	848.17	81	80
	Total	–	**1**	**1**	–	**848.17**	**81**	**80**
Grand Total	**5**	**17**	**2**	**22**	**1**	**19,770.15**	**4,409**	**4,336**

Table—1.2 Tribal Sub-plan Area of Rajasthan (Census 2001)

S. No.	District of Scheduled Area	Total Rural Urban	Total population			S.T. Population			% of S.T. to total population	Sex Ratio	
			Persons	Males	Females	Persons	Males	Females		S.T.	Total
1	2	3	4	5	6	7	8	9	10	11	12
1.	Udaipur	T	1433565	719289	714276	1013728	508272	505456	70.71	994	993
		R	1381320	692219	689101	1008183	505350	502833	72.99	995	995
		U	52245	27070	25175	5545	2922	2623	10.61	898	930
2.	Banswara	T	1501589	760686	740903	1085272	547277	537995	72.27	983	974
		R	1394226	705110	689116	1073930	541412	532518	77.03	984	977
		U	107363	55576	51787	11342	5865	5477	10.56	934	932
3.	Dungarpur	T	1107643	547791	559852	721487	355748	365739	65.14	1028	1022
		R	1026787	505664	521123	703877	346558	357319	68.55	1031	1031
		U	80856	42127	38729	17610	9190	8420	21.78	916	919
4.	Chittaurgarh	T	356488	182091	174397	196213	99754	96459	55.04	967	958
		R	321066	163614	157452	193772	98399	95373	60.35	969	962
		U	35422	18477	16945	2441	1355	1086	6.89	801	917

(Table Contd...)

1	2	3	4	5	6	7	8	9	10	11	12
5.	Sirohi	T	114818	59326	55492	76526	38864	37662	66.65	969	935
		R	114818	59326	55492	76526	38864	37662	66.65	969	935
		U	–	–	–	–	–	–	–	–	–
	Total	T	4514103	2269183	2244920	3093226	1549915	1543311	68.52	996	989
		R	4238217	2125933	2112284	3056288	1530583	1525705	72.11	994	994
		U	275886	143250	132636	36938	19332	17606	13.39	911	926
6.	Rajasthan	T	56507188	29420011	27087177	7097706	3650982	3446724	12.56	944	621
		R	43292813	22426640	20866173	6717830	3445719	3272111	15.52	950	930
		U	13214375	6993371	6221004	379876	205263	174613	2.87	851	890

The Table—1.1 reveals that T.S.P. area has been composed of 18 tehsils i.e. 23 Panchyat Samities (Blocks) or 5 district having the major tribes Bhil, Mina, Garasia and Damor. According to 1981 census the population of tribal sub plan area was 18.30 lakh, while the total population was 27.57 lakh (13.78 lakh males and 13.79 lakh females). The Scheduled Tribal population of Sub Plan Area constitutes 66.39 per cent (66.15 per cent female and 66.63 per cent female) of the total population of the area. The tribal population of the state according to 1981 was 41.83 lakh which constitutes only 12.21 per cent of the total population of the state. In this manner 43.75 per cent of the tribal population of the total tribals of the state reside in the sub plan area.

Keeping in view of the situation prevailing in the tribal areas, priority in the sub-plan was given to the elimination of the exploitation of the tribals. For operational purposes the tribal sub-plan areas have been organised into I.T.D.P. (Integrated Tribal Development Projects). The programmes under the T.P.S. Area supported by the sectoral outlays in the state, central programmes and the institutional finance.

In Tribal Sub-plan Area the development strategy follows and area development approach with focuses on the development of tribal communities. Infrastructure development programmes i.e. community and individual beneficiary programmes were taken up for the tribal concentrated areas. After the evolution of the programmes it was realised that in T.S.P. area and in scattered groups or parts of the state. To cater the needs of the non-covered tribals, special programmes were started in the state of Rajasthan in 1977-78 for the development of Sahariya (Primitive tribal) residing in Kishanganj and Shahabad Panchayat Samities of Baran District formerly (situated) in Kota District. The details of Sahariya area are given in the Table 1.3.

Table—1.3 Sahariya Development Project

S. No.	District	Name of Panchayat Samiti	Area in sq. km.	Percentage of Sahariya population to total population	No. of Villages	Inhabited Villages
1.	Baran	Sahabad	1,469	30.50	236	147
		Kishanganj	1,429	34.64	199	171
	Total	2	**2,898**	**32.84**	**435**	**318**

According to 1981 census 0.34 lakh Sahariya have been covered under Sahariya Development Project.

In 1978-79 the modified Area Development Approach (MADA) was evolved. The strategy of MADA was adopted for contiguous villages having a population of at least 10.000 tribals forming 50 per cent of the total population. The pockets of tribal concentration are dispersed over 3,589 villages of 44 MADA blocks covering 67 Panchayat Samities of 17 districts. The MADA programme had covered 10.33 lakh tribal population the details of MADA are given in the Table 1.4.

For those tribals who were not covered under the MADA programmes, one new strategy in MADA programme was evolved known as "Cluster Area". The criteria for the cluster was that the villages having a population of at least 5,000 persons with 50 per cent or more tribals in it would constitute it. Hence under this scheme 11 clusters were formed from 159 villages of 8 districts covering a tribal population of 0.37 lakh. The details of cluster area is given in the Table 1.5.

Table—1.4 Details of MADA Blocks of Rajasthan

S. No.	*District*	*Name of MADA Block*	*Number of Villages*	*Population as per 1991 Census*		
				Total	*S.T.*	*%*
1	2	3	4	5	6	7
1.	Alwar	1. Rajgarh-Alwar	131	110007	57784	52.52
		2. Thanagazi	61	26894	14732	54.77
		3. Lachmangarh	29	33047	16805	50.85
		Total	**221**	**169948**	**89321**	**52.56**
2.	Dholpur	4. Baseri-Bari	53	48650	25817	53.07
3.	Bhilwara	5. Jahajpur-Mandalgadh	196	94361	49696	52.66
4.	Bundi	6. Bundi	56	34640	16967	49.98
		7. Bundi-Keshorai Patan	56	34371	17188	50.00
		8. Hindoli-Bundi	40	29073	14412	49.57
		9. Keshoraipatan	3	23069	12286	53.26
		10. Nainwa-Bundi-Hindoli	65	36157	18111	50.09
		Total	**248**	**157310**	**78964**	**50.20**

(Table Contd...)

1	2	3	4	5	6	7
5.	Chittorgarh	11. Bari Sadri-Chhoti Sadri	151	55511	28598	51.52
		12. Begun	118	30829	18523	60.08
		13. Begun-Chittorgarh-Gangrar	72	12924	6560	50.76
		Total	**341**	**99264**	**53681**	**54.08**
6 & 7.	Jaipur & Dausa	14. Lalsot-Chaksu-Dausa-Baswa	412	246562	136007	55.16
		15. Jamawa Ramgarh-Chaksu-Bassi-Dausa-Sanganer-Amer	298	188706	108673	57.59
		16. Sikrai-Baswa	75	74759	41382	55.35
		Total	**785**	**510037**	**286062**	**56.09**

(Table Contd...)

1	2	3	4	5	6	7
8.	Jhalawar	17. Aklera	127	44396	25715	57.92
		18. Jhalarpatan-Khanpur	117	37343	22888	61.29
9 & 10.	Kota & Baran	19. Atru-Chhipa Barod-Chhabra	36	18742	9216	49.17
		20. Chippa-Barod	50	21397	14336	66.53
		21. Pipalda-Mangrol-Digod	112	58399	29762	50.96
		22. Chhabra	53	18143	10311	56.60
		23. Ramganj mandi-Ladpura	44	17890	8556	47.83
		24. Baran-Mangrol-Sangod	29	16217	8593	52.83
		Total	324	150788	80774	53.57

(Table Contd...)

1	2	3	4	5	6	7
11.	Pali	25. Bali	21	40879	23971	58.63
12 & 13.	Sawai Madhopur & Karoli	26. Bamanwas-Gangpur	40	27568	17391	36.08
		27. Bamanwas	41	32957	19051	57.81
		28. Gangapur-Karauli	26	47107	26002	55.20
		29. Nadoti-Hindaun	30	34332	17061	49.69
		30. Hindaun-Todabhim	40	47158	26278	55.72
		31. Karoli	41	40913	20700	50.60
		32. Karoli-Sapotra-Bonli	77	66293	37920	57.20
		33. Mahuwa	58	45512	26261	57.70
		34. Bonli	70	54088	29054	53.72
		35. Sawai Madhopur-Khandar	80	84630	46466	54.49
		36. Todabhim-Nadoti-Mahuwa	76	84261	47245	56.07
		Total	**579**	**564819**	**313429**	**55.49**

(Table Contd...)

1	2	3	4	5	6	7
14.	Sirohi	37. Pindwara-Sirohi-Reodhar	55	56799	42734	75.23
15.	Tonk	38. Dewali-Todarai singh-Tonk	61	39497	20841	52.77
		39. Niwai	71	32163	17155	53.33
		40. Uniyara	74	31136	17722	56.91
		41. Uniyara-Tonk	40	12739	6846	53.74
		Total	246	115535	62564	54.15
16 & 17.	Udaipur & Rajsamand	42. Girwa-Nathdwara-Mavli	59	45122	23635	52.38
		43. Gogunda-Kumbhalgarh-Nathdwara	117	85173	50327	59.09
		44. Vallabhnagar	103	37710	19653	52.12
Total	**17**	**44**	**279**	**168005**	**93615**	**55.72**
	Grand Total		**3592**	**2258134**	**1249231**	**55.32**

Table—1.5 MADA cluster of Rajasthan

S. No.	District	Name of Cluster	No. of Village	Percentage S.T. Population to Total Population
1.	Bundi	1. Pipalda	30	51.50
2.	Kota	2. Digod	19	49.39
	Baran	3. Atru & Baran	9	51.69
3.	Jhalawar	4. Khanpur	13	51.54
		5. Aklera (E)	22	50.02
		6. Aklera (S)	12	60.12
4.	Ajmer	7. Kekri	11	58.93
5.	Rajsamand	8. Nathdwara-Rajsamand	19	54.93
6.	Bharatpur	9. Weir (S)	4	51.39
		10. Weir (N)	11	55.61
7.	Sawai-Madhopur	11. Khandar	9	58.41
	Total 8	**11**	**159**	**53.56**

For the rest of the tribals who were not covered in any of the schemes mentioned above, one new scheme "Scattered are development scheme" was introduced by the State Government. This remaining tribals, 12.96 lakh came under its developmental programmes of them.

Strategy of Tribal Development During Sixth and Seventh Plan

The new strategy for development of tribal area was evolved during Fifth Five Year Plan which was continued during sixth and seventh plan also. The broad objectives of sixth and seventh plan were:

(i) A progressive reduction in the incidence of poverty and unemployment;

(ii) Improving the quality of life through minimum needs programme;

(iii) A reduction in the inequalities of income and wealth;

(iv) Infrastructure development for fuller exploitation of potential of the tribal region.

Flowing from these broad objectives, the strategy of the seventh plan combined are development approaches with individual beneficiary approach. The individual beneficiary programmes include human resources development activities and provision of economically remunerative and viable-project. Following activities and areas were identified for concerted efforts of development to achieve the objectives:

1. Emphasis on increase in agriculture production in small holdings through Horticulture, Sericulture, Vegetable farming, Castor and Soyabeen farming.
2. Expansion of irrigation facilities through Mahi Bajaj Sagar Dam, Jakham, Som-Kamla-Amba and Som-Kagdar irrigation project, lift irrigation schemes, anicuts and deepening of wells by blasting.
3. Human resources development through creation of MINI ITI's and other vocational training centres, expansion of education by providing greater incentives and hostel facilities to tribal students.
4. Waste land development through plantation.
5. Fisheries development.
6. Priorities to afforestation.
7. Eradication of guineaworm through community education, installation of handpumps and conversion of stepwells into draw-wells.
8. Programmes for isolated tribal communities.
9. Improvement of sheep quality through the introduction of half and quarter breed rams.
10. Awareness raising among tribals through social animators and voluntary agencies.
11. Saving tribals from exploitation by money lenders and Sahakurs through formation of LAMPS.

Strategies Adopted During Seventh Plan

1. First objectives was to take-up beneficiary programmes to Horticulture, Sericulture, Vegetable growing and

marketing, Poultry, Dairy, Fisheries, Community Diesel Pumpsets, Community lift irrigation, Blasting of wells, etc. were taken up.

2. Regarding exploitation of tribals, various laws and bylaws have been enforced by the State and Central Government to protect the tribals as under:

   (a) The Rajasthan Tenancy Act, 1955 as amended from time-to-time. It provides protection to tribals against alienation of their land.

   (b) The Rajasthan land Revenue (Allotment of land for agricultural purposes) Rules, 1970. S.T. are given priority in allotment of land.

   (c) The Rajasthan Relief of Agriculturist's indebtedness Act 1957. It provides relief to tribals in their indebtedness.

   (d) Abolition of Bonded Labour.

   (e) Regulation of Money Lending.

   (f) Excise Policy.

   (g) Payment of Minimum wages.

   (h) Personnel Policy.

      (i) Reservation in Government Services (12 per cent).

      (ii) Maintenance of Roster Registers.

      (iii) Vacancies are carried forward.

      (iv) Relaxation upper age limit (upto 33 years in State Services).

      (v) Relaxation in prescribed qualifications.

      (vi) Levying of lower application fee.

   (i) Reservation in allotment in House of Rajasthan Housing Board (14 per cent for S.C./S.T).

   (j) Forest concessions.

      (i) Concession to take timber for the use of agriculture implements and for house building.

(ii) Tribals are allowed to take away two cart loads per family of thorns and bushwood for fencing the agricultural fields.

(iii) Fuel wood and gas-free head loads for own consumption and for sales also.

(iv) Royalty rate 1/8 from tribals.

(v) Free grazing in forests areas.

(vi) Right to collect minor forest produce to tribals and sell it to LAMPS which function as an agent of RTADCF.

3. For the development of human resources and improvement of skill of tribals; various types of educational incentives in the form of uniform, books, stationery articles, Hostel facilities etc. are being given. For improvement of skills and gainful employment, the following training programmes are being undertaken:

   S.T.C. B.Ed., Stockmen training, G.N.M. Training, Ayurved Compounders Training, Pre-service Coaching i.e. R.A.S. Banks, Railways etc. I.T.I.'s Mini I.T.I's, and vocational Crafts training, Fisheries training, Sheep and wool training and Handloom training.

   Near about 5,000 tribal candidates are being trained under these programmes every year so as to provide themselves employment.

4. As a result of special investment made in the T.S.P. area. area, there is generally a better infrastructure available now. The tribal areas have better network of schools, medical institutions and roads, on the basis of both population, size and area.

5. Proper care and attention has been given to rehabilitate displaced tribal families in T.S.P. area. For the development of tribal women, programmes like sericulture, applied Nutrition and I.C.D.C./I.C.D.S. Weaving and Knitting centres, organisation of Chetna Camps, Khadi and Village Industries etc. are being undertaken.

6. To upgrade the environment in T.S.P. area the following programmes have been introduced.
   (i) Creation of nurseries of minor forest produce through Tribal Area Development Co-operative Federation (TADCF) and Ayurved College.
   (ii) Plantation of waste lands of tribals.
   (iii) Roonky Bhaila project.
7. Poverty Alleviation Programmes: Under the poverty alleviation programme, it has been targeted to economically assist 3.06 lakh tribal families during seventh plan. The year-wise achievement has been as follows:

Year	*No. of family benefitted under poverty alleviation programmes*
1985-86	73,044
1986-87	86,616
1987-88	94,075
1988-89	75,713
1989-90	69,201

Sector-wise Allocation and Expenditure During Seventh Plan

An expenditure of Rs. 43,126.40 lakhs was incurred in T.S.P. area on the implementation of various development schemes of tribals during seventh plan against a provision of Rs. 45,697.46 lakh. The sector-wise allocation and expenditure made during seventh plan are given in Table 1.6.

During 1985-86 an expenditure of Rs. 8,000.46 lakh (92.25 per cent) was incurred against an allocation of Rs. 8,672.66 lakhs in 1986-87 against a provision of Rs. 10,478.88 lakh, there was an expenditure of Rs. 10,328.38 lakhs (98.56 per cent). An amount of Rs. 7,435.27 lakhs were allotted during 1987-88 against which Rs. 7,381.31 lakhs (99.27 per cent) was spent against an allocation of Rs. 10,702.24 lakh. During 1990-91 Rs. 12.246.99 lakh (92.56 per cent) was spent against an allocation of Rs. 13,230.42 lakhs and Rs. 17,718.11 lakh was spent during 1991-92.

Table—1.6 Sector-wise Allocation and Expenditure During Seventh Plan

(Rs. in lakhs)

S. No.	*Sector*	*Allocation*					*Expenditure*				
		S.P.	*S.C.A.*	*I.F.*	*C.S.S.*	*Total*	*S.P.*	*S.C.A.*	*I.F.*	*C.S.S.*	*Total*
1.	Agricultural & Allied Service	2,165.56	760.03	180.36	948.27	4,053.22	1,759.03	794.14	142.17	844.29	3,530.63
2.	Rural Development	2,460.83	72.62	1,361.93	3,172.41	7,067.79	2,215.96	66.36	1,167.27	3,019.89	6,469.48
3.	Irrigation	13,007.06	369.09	–	–	13,376.15	13,086.10	526.80	–	–	13,612.90
4.	Power	8,075.30	7.32	–	87.03	8,169.65	7,391.45	5.30	–	51.03	7,447.78
5.	Industries & Minerals	1,310.81	12.60	393.00	32.14	1,748.55	1,121.85	7.71	242.24	28.49	1,400.29
6.	Transport & Communication	1,156.41	–	384.21	137.25	1,677.87	1,133.27	–	658.06	105.38	1,896.71
7.	Scientific services & research	27.53	–	–	–	27.53	13.22	–	–	–	13.22
8.	Social & Community service	5,214.97	1,762.53	237.12	1,545.35	8,759.97	4,985.52	1,534.55	175.63	1,413.50	8,109.20
9.	Economic Service	34.94	–	–	0.21	35.15	28.17	–	–	0.29	28.46
10.	General Service	246.17	533.15	–	2.26	781.58	218.79	397.69	–	1.25	617.73
	Total	**33,698.58**	**3,517.34**	**2,556.62**	**5,424.92**	**45,697.46**	**31,989.36**	**3,287.55**	**2,385.37**	**5,464.12**	**43,126.40**

Sector-wise Target and Achievement during Seventh Plan

Sector-wise target and achievement during seventh plan has been in Table 1.7.

Table—1.7 Sector-wise Physical Progress During Seventh Plan

S. No.	*Schemes*	*Unit*	*Seventh plan*	
			Target	*Achievement*
1.	Area under H.Y.U. Programme	Hect.	1,255.185	107,361
2.	Distribution of Fertilizers	M.T.	68,912	71,668
3.	Seed Distribution	All	46,237	27,114
4.	Plant Protection Majors	Lakh	1,597	1,267
5.	Sericulture	No.	3,090	2,714
6.	Horticulture	No.	8,429	7,812
7.	Lift Irrigation	No.	64	33
8.	Diesel Pumpset	No.	919	936
9.	Deeping of wells by blasting	No.	7,123	7,803
10.	Construction of anicuts	No.	46	74
11.	Poultry	No.	4,654	4,504
12.	Dairy Co-operative Societies	No.	305	173
13.	I.R.D.P.	No.	61,210	72,368
14.	Village to be Electrified	No.	4,100	4,799
15.	Wells to be Emergised	No.	764	862
16.	Construction of Roads	No.	303	304
17.	Primary Schools to be Opened	No.	770	296
18.	Running of Ashram Schools	No.	58	58
19.	Scholarship to Pre Metric S.T. Students	No.	11,482	11,482
20.	Water Supply (villages covered)	No.	694	1,021
21.	Distribution Nets and Boats	No.	600	592

The source so funding to Tribal Sub-plan Area are as follows:

1. Flow from State Plan
2. Flow from Centrally Sponsored Schemes.
3. Special Central Assistance
4. Institutional Finance.

Financial Assistance

During the last few years with a huge financial allocations considerable work has been done under the tribal sub-plan. Heavy investment has been made by the government, along with other resources. Since the Second Plan, an amount of Rs. 1,008.39 crores has been spent in T.S.P. area on various tribal development schemes are given in Table 1.8.

Table—1.8 Plan-wise Expenditure in Tribal Sub-plan Areas

S. No.	*Plan*	*Expenditure (Rs. in crore)*
1.	Second Plan (1956-61)	5.84
2.	Third Plan (1961-66)	9.33
3.	Fourth Plan (1971-74)	10.64
4.	Fifth Plan (1974-78)	71.73
5.	1978-79	33.29
6.	1979-80	36.46
7.	Sixth Plan (1980-81 to 1984-85)	287.37
8.	Seventh Plan (1985-86 to 1989-90)	431.26
9.	1990-91	122.47
	Total	**1,008.39**

The sector-wise expenditure has been detailed in the Table 1.9.

Table—1.9 Sector-wise Expenditure in Tribal Sub Plan Area

S. No.	*Major Sectors*	*Expenditure (Rs. in crore)*	*Percentage of Total Investment*
1.	Agriculture and Allied Services	227.02	22.51
2.	Irrigation and Power	508.77	50.45
3.	Co-operation	18.05	1.79
4.	Industries and Minerals	38.41	3.81
5.	Transport and Communication	45.89	4.55
6.	Social and Community Services	158.17	15.69
7.	Economic and General Services	12.08	1.20
	Total	**1,008.39**	**100.00**

The Table 1.9 reveals that maximum amount i.e. 50.45 per cent has been spent of development of irrigation and power. Agriculture, Forest, Animal Husbandry, etc. accounted for 22.51 per cent, while social and community services received 15.69 per cent of the total investment. The expenditure during Annual Plan 1991-92 was 188.68 crores, out of which 124.94 crore in Institutional Finance and rest 38.92 crore have been spent under centrally sponsored scheme. Hence from 1956 to 1991 a huge amount of Rs. 1,197.07 crores has been spent on tribal development for various developmental programmes. Rs. 188.68 crores have been proposed to be spent during 1992-93 under various heads for tribal development programmes.

The Objectives and Strategy in the Eighth Plan

The focus in the Seventh Plan was on raising the economic status and fuller realisation of the development potential of the tribals and the tribal areas with the objective of giving them social and economic justice. The strategy also specifically aimed at improving the living environment of the tribals by giving them better social and civic amenities and facilities. The Working Group has recommended that the objectives of Seventh Plan would continue for the Eight Plan period. The objectives for the Eight Plan are detailed below:

(a) A progressive reduction in poverty and unemployment there by reduction in income inequalities.

(b) Improve the quality of life through a minimum need programme.

(c) Development and strengthening of infrastructure basis for further economic exploitation of the tribal sub-plan area.

(d) Development of confidence of tribals along the desired lines through intensive educational efforts.

Despite the efforts to diversity economic activities in non-formal sector, the efforts to diversify economic activities in non-formal sector, the predominant sources of livelihood in T.S.P. area continues to be agriculture. The main thrust would be on the development of fisheries, sericulture, horticulture, plantation on waste land and growing vegetables during the Eight Plan these areas would provide supplemental income and new avenues of employment to the tribals, human resources development th 'ough education and vocational/craftsman training would be taken up to improve the skills of the tribals. Expansion of irrigation facilities and electrification of tribals. Expansion of irrigation wells construction of culverts to linkup farflung villages' improvement of cattle breed through BAIF, Mining activities, have also been given due emphasis in the Eight Plan.

Special Central Assistance and Proposed Programmes

All the schemes of 1991-92 will continue during Eighth Plan, except construction of fish nursery at Bhimpur and Development of Mahi Command Area. With a view to providing employment to tribals, 5 mini co-operative societies will be formed in T.S.P. area and mining lease will be granted to these societies for extraction of mineral deposits. 10 new Ashram Chhatrawas has been proposed to be opened. One S.T.C. training school will be opened at Dungarpur, 15, centres of BAIF (Bharat Agro Industries Foundation) have been proposed to be order to popularise the fruit plantation the Horticulture Development programme will be taken up on large scale and 8,600 new orchards will be established on cluster basis in T.S.P. area. Similarly afforestation of bamboos and other minor forest produce will be done on waste lands in 5,000 hectares 2 loom training centres will be converted into a training cum production centre.

National Strategy of Ninth Plan

The Ninth Five Year Plan (1997-2002) has the strategy to achieve a seven per cent growth rate (.G.D.P.) for the economy. The seven per cent GDP would be through a 9.3 per cent annual growth in industrial production, 4.5 per cent in agriculture, while the fiscal deficit is to be brought down to 4 per cent GDP. The approach document has sought an increase in grass domestic savings rate from the Eighth Plan average of 27.37 per cent to 26.2 per cent to 26.2 per cent in the Ninth Plan. The main objectives of the Ninth Plan are:

(i) Generation of adequate productive employment and eradication of poverty.

(ii) Acceleration in the growth rate of the economy with stable price.

(iii) Provision for basic minimum services of safe drinking water, primary health care facilities, universal primary education and connectivity to all villages in a time bound manner.

(iv) Ensuring food and nutritional security for all, particularly the vulnerable sections of society.

(v) Containing the growth rate of population.

(vi) Ensuring environmental sustainability of the development process through mobilization and participation of people; and

(vii) Empowerment of women and socially disadvantaged groups.

Hence, it aims to ensure food and nutritional security for all, particularly the vulnerable sections of society.

The Ninth Plan, therefore, contemplates to where in a newer of people oriented planning in which the government and the people particularly the poor, can fully participate. Though this particularly planning process, it is expected to ensure equity and accede the growth rate. The Ninth Plan is in process and it would be able to fulfil the ambitions of tribals in the initiation of 21st century and may able to bring them more nearer to national main stream.

Review of the Strategy and Development Model

The overall review of the tribal development measures adopted during the 20th century do not fulfil the ambitions and requirements of the tribals, even than the govt. fails to provide them basic minimum needs for their survival. The half part i.e. 50 years of the century were administered by the British Govt., they do not bother about their needs and welfare. Whenever they create or any sort of agitation in some area, the Britishers and rulers try to compel them to withdraw the agitation or may be crushed by hook or crook. The British govt. introduce few reform measures for their better mens in trouble some tribal areas of the country viz. Chhota Nagpur, Kherwara, etc. The foundation of Mewar Bhil Core is also one of them. During this period the Missionary Christian work in the remote areas were creditable. The British Govt. have also demarcated some tribal areas for their development according to their administrative convenience. Hence, the tribals during the first half of century were exploited by the then rulers. After independence the Central Govt. as well as State Govt. paid attention towards the deprived tribal areas, but within 25 years the steps taken towards regarding their development were negligible. Actually the tribal development measures taken by the Central as well as State govt.'s from the Fifth Five Year Plan, in other words we can say the initiation year of tribal development measures was the year 1974.

After independence, the Govt. of India making special provisions in the Constitution of India right from its implementation, but the misery is they were not seriously implemented after passing a long period. Actually the tribal development voyage is of 25 years duration i.e. from 1974 to date. The tribal development measures adopted by the govt. is not enough, they are failed to improve the economic condition of the tribals. After introduction of several betterment schemes, the poor tribals are still today facing severe economic constraints.

Their economy is forest based. They are not perfect in agriculture, having small uneconomic holdings, lack of irrigation facilities, indebtedness and so many socio-economic problems they are facing today. Till they can not be solved by the Govt. Hence the tribal development measures adopted by the Central and State Govt's reflects lacunas and to some extent they get success. There is an urgent need to review the overall strategy of tribal development measures. Keeping in view their present socio-economic status, the plans should be prepared at grass root level and their basic minimum needs for subsistence must be included. Till now the tribal development plans are prepared by the bureaucrats and politicians, in the A.C. rooms. They are not aware about the tribal needs, even they do not know their where abouts. The misery is, such plans are implemented throughout the country without any perception, while they were formed aimlessly or for a certain purpose. The misery with such plans, fails in initiation or do not see a longer period. Such sort of planning may create unnecessary economic burden on the govt. in other words we can say this is only a wastage of resources. There is an urgent need to stop such sort of practice. In my opinion there is an urgency of review of present tribal area development planning, so the poor tribal may survive in the better developing conditions and may live in the tense free environment and may get all the minimum needs as the other class of society enjoys. The planning should be in such a manner, that they may touch the minimum survival level to which is essential.

It is recommended that following measures i.e. development model should be adopted for the development of tribals residing in the country:

1. Re-scheduling the tribes i.e. there is an urgent need to review the S.T. list as per constitutional provisions presently in force.
2. Re-demarcation of tribal sub-plan and MADA areas. The norms for the demarcation of tribal areas also need a review.
3. In the tribal sub plan area, local persons should be given top priority in the employment, if necessary the employment may be given to the persons belonging within the state, but outside persons should be strictly restricted.
4. State should implement or prepare legislation as empowered in the Article-244 of the Constitution i.e. Vth and VIth schedule for the Administration of Scheduled and Tribal Areas. The employment restrictions may be imposed by this schedule. Other essential measures according to area need, the Governor may be given powers under the Schedule Vth and VIth protect the Tribal Rights and empowered to issue ordinance according to area need.
5. Changes in I.P.C. is essential i.e. in certain I.P.C. Codes few crimes are cognizable offence, but in tribal society they are permissible. Keeping in view the tribal traits, essential amendments should be made. So the tribals may get relief from the courts and police administration. Regarding this matter the "Tribal Social Panchayats" may be recognised.

6. Pre-planning socio-economic survey at village level should be conducted, so the basic minimum needs of the area may be demarcated. Such survey should be conducted after every 10 years, like census. By this way we may be able to review the overall progress of the measures adopted and be able to review the situation and requirements of the area.

7. Village profile of every tribal village may prepared and reviewed after every five years.

8. The planners should use the surveyed data and plan out the programmes according to the local needs. The District Planning Forum should be constituted. In the Districts Planning Forum local tribal participation should be given prime importance i.e. fifty per cent of the members must be tribals. The tribal members may be the resource persons of the area like *Gameties, Mukhis, Patels* of each tribal group. They will be more helpful in local planning and able to reflect the local needs and problems they are facing today. Secondly, 25 per cent members must be eminent social workers, Sociologists and Economists. At last rest 25 per cent members may be Govt. officials and politicians of the area. By this way District Planning Forum may be framed. Similar procedure may be adopted at State level also.

9. The Schemes/programmes recommended by the District Forum may be reviewed at State Forum and may finalise them according to the area need. The programmes/schemes by such way prepared and implemented would be more effective then the present system.

10. The Tribal Right's provide by constitution must be safeguard. Their land and forest rights should be given top priority.

11. Voluntary participation should be encouraged i.e. voluntary organisations tasking pains in the development of tribal areas, should be adopted the area or village for overall development or for certain special services. The partly funds may be provided by the govt.

but strict financial and review of the programmes must be carried out quarterly. The officials of NGO's or V.O'.S may be given proper training about the programmes schemes and area where they serve.

12. The Local Self Govt. must be given more powers for the implementation of the programmes/schemes and the local persons may have the powers to review the situation according to the area need.
13. Cottage and local employment generation schemes in the tribal area must be given top priority. The efforts may be, the person should get the employment at nearby their native place, for this purpose forest based programmes/schemes must be given top priority.
14. The V.O.'s may be forced to install/generate local industries in the tribal areas. The co-operative sector may be able to meet out such requirements of the area. So to meet out the local needs, co-operative movement must be strengthen.

Hence, it is very necessary to review the tribal development strategy according to the above suggestion, the tribals may be geared up for thc upliftment upto the mark and able to see better future in 21st century. Keeping in view the changing planning measures the tribal identity and age old social and cultural traits must be preserved, unless their identity will be vanished.

REFERENCES

1. Niharranjan Ray: "*Introductory Address*" in S.C. Dube (Ed.) Tribal Situation in India, (1972), p. 8.
2. P.G. Krishnan: "*Constitution and Tribal Welfare*": Cochin University Law Review, Vol. IX No. 1 and 2, March & June, 1985, pp. 45-66.
3. A.B. Bardhan: *The Tribal Problem in India*, Communist Party of India Publications, New Delhi, 1973, pp. 16-17.
4. D.N. Majumdar: *Races and Cultures of India*, Asia Publishing House, Bombay, 1961, p. 367.
5. Kamaladevi Chattopadhyaya: *Tribalism in India*, (1978), p. 1.
6. Verrier Elwin: *A New Deal for Tribal India (1963)*, p. 17.
7. Mishra, R.P., (Ed. 1983): *Local Level Planning and Development*, Sterling Publishers Pvt. Ltd., New Delhi-16.

8. Sharma, Soumitra (1983): *Development Strategy and the Developing Countries*, South Asian Publishers Pvt. Ltd., New Delhi-2.

9. Seers, Dudley: "*What are We Trying to Measure*", Journal of Development Studies, April 1972, p. 21.

10. Basu, (Dr.) Ashok Ranjan: *The Tribal Development Programmes and Administration in India*, National Book Organisation, New Delhi, 1985, p. 27.

11. Alfred Diamant: "*European Models of Bureaucracy and Development*", International Review of Administrative Sciences, Vol. 8, No. 3. 1967, p. 310.

12. The United Nations, Development Administration: Current Approaches and Trends in Public Administration for National Development (New York, No. E7IIH-I), p. 8.

13. Mehta, Prakash Chandra, *Demographic Profile of Tribals*, Tribe Vol. XXI-XXIII, January 1989 to December 1991, Tribal Research Institute, Rajasthan Udaipur, pp. 54-55.

14. Sharma, (Dr.) B.D.: *Planning for Tribal Developments*, Prachi Prakashan, New Delhi, 1984, p. 85.

APPENDIX—I

State-wise Distribution of Tribals in India (According to 1981 census)

S. No.	State/Union Territories	1981 census				
			Scheduled Tribes Population			% of S.T. Population to total population
		Population	Male	Female	Persons	
1	2	3	4	5	6	7
	India	665,287,849	26,038,535	25,590,103	51,628,638	7.76
1.	Andhra Pradesh	53,549,673	1,618,689	1,557,312	3,176,001	5.93
2.	Arunachal Pradesh	631,839	220,046	221,121	441,167	69.82
3.	Assam	Census was not conducted				
4.	Bihar	69,914,734	2,915,492	2,895,375	5,810,867	8.31
5.	Goa	Upto 1981 the state was with Daman and Diu				
6.	Gujarat	34,085,799	2,453,566	2,395,020	4,848,585	14.22
7.	Haryana	12,922,618	–	–	–	–
8.	Himachal Pradesh	4,280,818	99,727	97,536	197,263	4.61
9.	Jammu & Kashmir	5,987,389	–	–	–	–
10.	Karnataka	37,135,714	926,235	895,968	1,825,203	4.91
11.	Kerala	25,453,680	131,243	130,232	261,475	1.03

(*Contd...*)

1	2	3	4	5	6	7
12.	Madhya Pradesh	52,178,844	6,003,304	5,983,727	11,987,031	22.97
13.	Maharashtra	62,784,171	2,923,955	2,848,083	5,772,038	9.19
14.	Manipur	1,420,953	196,455	191,522	387,977	27.30
15.	Meghalaya	1,335,819	537,635	538,710	1,076,345	80.58
16.	Mizoram	493,757	231,261	230,646	461,907	93.55
17.	Nagaland	774,930	332,943	317.942	650,885	83.99
18.	Orissa	26,370,271	2,939,863	2,975,204	5,915,067	22.43
19.	Punjab	16,788,985	–	–	–	–
20.	Rajasthan	34,261,862	2,150,767	2,032,357	4,183,124	12.21
21.	Sikkim	316,385	38,211	35,412	73,623	23.27
22.	Tamil Nadu	48,408,077	264,288	255,938	520,226	1.07
23.	Tripura	2,053,058	297,612	286,308	583,920	28.44
24.	Uttar Pradesh	110,862,013	121,506	111,199	232,705	00.21
25.	West Bengal	154,580,647	1,559,288	1,511,368	3,070,672	5.63

(Contd...)

1	2	3	4	5	6	7
	Union-Territories					
1.	Andaman & Nicobar Island	188,741	11,586	10,775	22,361	11.85
2.	Chandigarh	4,516,105	–	–	–	–
3.	Dadra and Nagar Haveli	103,676	40,486	41,228	81,714	78.82
4.	Goa, Daman and Diu	1,086,730	5,512	5,209	10,711	0.99
5.	Delhi	6,220,406				
6.	Lakshadweep	40,249	18,865	18,895	37,760	93.8
7.	Pondicherry	604,471	–	–	–	–

State-wise Distribution of Tribals in India (According to 1991 Census)

Sr. No.	*State/ Union Territories*	*1991 census*				
		Scheduled Tribes Population				*% of ST Population to total population*
		Population	*Male*	*Female*	*Persons*	
1	2	*8*	9	*10*	*11*	12
	India	846,302,688	34,363,271	33,315,109	67,758,380	8.08
1.	Andhra Pradesh	66,508,008	2,142,817	2,056,664	4,199,481	6.31
2.	Arunachal Pradesh	864,558	275,397	274,954	550,351	63.66
3.	Assam		1,461,560	1,412,881	2,874,441	12.82
4.	Bihar	86,374,465	3,357,563	3,259,351	6,616,914	7.66
5.	Goa		199	177	376	0.03
6.	Gujarat	41,309,582	3,131,947	3,029,828	6,161,775	14.92
7.	Haryana	16,463,648	–	–	–	–
8.	Himachal Pradesh	5,170,877	1,102,40	108,109	218,349	4.22
9.	Jammu & Kashmir	7,718,700			Census not held	
10.	Karnataka	44,977,201	976,744	938,947	1,915,691	4.26
11.	Kerala	29,098,518	160,812	160,155	320,961	1.10
12.	Madhya Pradesh	66,181,170	7,758,174	7,640,860	15,399,034	23.27

(Contd...)

1	2	8	9	10	11	12
13.	Maharashtra	78,937,187	3,71,7783	3,600,498	7,318,281	9.27
14.	Manipur	1,837,149	322,720	309,453	632,173	34.41
15.	Meghalaya	1,774,778	760,234	757,693	1,517,927	85.53
16.	Mizoram	689,756	329,817	323,746	653,565	23.15
17.	Nagaland	1,209,546	545,156	515,666	1,060,822	87.70
18.	Orissa	31,659,736	3,512,891	3,519,323	7,032,214	22.21
19.	Punjab	20,281,969	–	–	–	–
20.	Rajasthan	44,005,990	2,837,014	2,637,867	5,474,881	12.44
21.	Sikkim	406,457	47,504	43,397	90,901	22.36
22.	Tamil Nadu	55,858,946	293,012	281,182	574,194	1.03
23.	Tripura	2,757,205	434,225	419,120	853,345	30.95
24.	Uttar Pradesh	139,112,287	150,420	137,481	287,901	0.21
25.	West Bengal	68,077,965	1,938,955	1,869,805	3,808,760	5.59

(Contd...)

1	2	8	9	10	11	12
	Union-Territories					
1.	Andaman & Nicobar Island	280,661	13,750	13,020	26,770	9.54
2.	Chandigarh	642,015	–	–	–	–
3.	Dadra and Nagar Haveli	138,477	54,102	55,278	109,380	78.99
4.	Daman and Diu	1,271,394*	6,073	5,651	11,724	11.54
5.	Delhi	9,420,644	–	–	–	–
6.	Lakshadweep	51,707	24,160	24,003	48,163	11.54
7.	Pondicherry	807,785	–	–	–	–

* Including Goa.

Source:

1. Census of India 1981, Series-1, Part-II-B(iii). Primary Census Abstract (Scheduled Tribes), pp. XIX-XXI and 4-15.
2. Census of India 1981, Series-1, Part-II-B(i), Primary Census Abstract (General Population Tables), pp. XXX-XXXIII and 4-23.
3. Census of India, 1991, Series-1, Paper-1 of 1993, Union Primary Census Abstract for S.C. and S.T., pp. 11, 44-67.
4. Census of India 1991, Series-1, Paper-1 of 1992, Vol-II, pp. 15-19.
5. Mehta, Prakash Chandra: Bharat-Ke-Adivasi, Shiva Publishers Distributors, Udaipur, 1993.

APPENDIX—II

Ranking of States and Union Territories by Size of Scheduled Tribes Population (1991 Census)

S. No.	*State/Union Territory*	*Total S.T. Population*
1.	Madhya Pradesh	15,399,034
2.	Maharashtra	7,318,281
3.	Orissa	7,032,214
4.	Bihar	6,616,914
5.	Gujarat	6,161,775
6.	Rajasthan	5,474,881
7.	Andhra Pradesh	4,199,481
8.	West Bengal	3,808,760
9.	Assam	2,874,441
10.	Karnataka	1,915,927
11.	Meghalaya	1,517,927
12.	Nagaland	1,060,822
13.	Tripura	855,345
14.	Mizoram	653,565
15.	Manipur	632,173
16.	Tamil Nadu	574,194
17.	Arunachal Pradesh	550,351
18.	Kerala	320,967
19.	Uttar Pradesh	287,901
20.	Himachal Pradesh	218,349
21.	Sikkim	90,901
22.	Goa	376
	Union Territories	
1.	Dadra and Nagar Haveli	109,380
2.	Lakshadweep	48,163
3.	Andaman & Nicobar Island	26,770
4.	Daman & Diu	11,724

Source: Census of India 1991, Series-1, Paper-1 of 1993, Union Primary Census Abstract for S.C. & S.T.

APPENDIX—III

Ranking of States and Union Territories by Scheduled Tribes Concentration (1991 Census)

Rank	*State/Union Territory*	*Percentage of S.T. Population of Total State Population 1991*
1.	Mizoram	94.75
2.	Nagaland	87.70
3.	Meghalaya	85.53
4.	Arunachal Pradesh	63.66
5.	Manipur	34.41
6.	Tripura	30.95
7.	Madhya Pradesh	23.27
8.	Sikkim	22.36
9.	Orissa	22.21
10.	Gujarat	14.29
11.	Assam	12.82
12.	Rajasthan	12.44
13.	Maharashtra	9.27
14.	Bihar	7.66
15.	Andhra Pradesh	6.31
16.	West Bengal	5.59
17.	Karnataka	4.26
18.	Himachal Pradesh	4.22
19.	Kerala	1.10
20.	Tamil Nadu	1.03
21.	Uttar Pradesh	0.21
22.	Goa	0.03
	Union Territories	
1.	Lakshadweep	93.15
2.	Dadra and Nagar Haveli	78.99
3.	Andaman & Nicobar Island	9.54
4.	Daman & Diu	11.54

Source: Census of India 1991, Series-1, Paper-1 of 1993, Union Primary Census Abstract for S.C. & S.T.

APPENDIX—IV

Percentage of Main Workers in Primary, Secondary and Tertiary Sectors Among Total Population and Scheduled Tribe Population (1991 Census)

S. No.	State/Union Territory	Percentage of Workers					
		Primary		Secondary		Tertiary	
		Total Population	S.T. Population	Total Population	S.T. Population	Total Population	S.T. Population
1	2	3	4	5	6	7	8
	India	67.53	90.03	11.97	3.85	20.50	6.12
	States						
1.	Andhra Pradesh	71.25	90.40	10.48	4.79	18.27	4.81
2.	Arunachal Pradesh	67.44	87.16	8.66	2.98	23.90	9.86
3.	Assam	73.99	89.38	5.56	1.68	20.90	8.54
4.	Bihar	82.36	90.47	4.64	3.29	13.00	6.24
5.	Goa	32.29	21.98	21.98	37.59	45.73	40.43
6.	Gujarat	59.76	86.63	17.86	6.56	22.38	6.81
7.	Haryana	58.84	–	13.18	–	27.98	–
8.	Himachal Pradesh	69.28	79.22	9.99	6.46	20.73	14.32
9.	Karnataka	67.37	85.29	13.17	6.44	19.46	8.27
10.	Kerala	48.02	87.93	18.17	3.91	33.81	8.16

(Contd...)

1	2	3	4	5	6	7	8
11.	Madhya Pradesh	77.54	94.36	8.37	2.35	14.09	3.29
12.	Maharashtra	61.51	87.47	15.80	5.40	22.69	7.13
13.	Manipur	70.00	86.94	9.66	1.77	20.34	11.29
14.	Meghalaya	74.81	82.15	3.73	2.48	21.46	15.37
15.	Mizoram	65.99	71.13	5.07	3.44	28.94	25.43
16.	Nagaland	75.26	83.20	3.48	2.17	21.26	14.63
17.	Orissa	75.83	91.48	7.51	3.83	16.66	4.69
18.	Punjab	56.08	–	14.84	–	29.08	–
19.	Rajasthan	71.63	92.39	9.87	2.53	18.50	5.08
20.	Sikkim	68.40	70.60	11.12	8.42	20.48	20.98
21.	Tamil Nadu	61.81	87.10	16.18	4.96	22.01	7.94
22.	Tripura	64.08	89.28	6.41	1.29	29.51	9.43
23.	Uttar Pradesh	73.01	84.36	9.98	6.41	18.01	9.23
24.	West Bengal	56.46	90.85	17.82	4.80	25.69	4.35

(Contd…)

1	2	3	4	5	6	7	8
	Union Territories						
1.	Andaman & Nikobar Islands	34.50	21.07	25.14	58.43	40.36	20.50
2.	Chandigarh	4.46	–	27.82	–	67.72	–
3.	Dadra & Nagar Haveli	71.81	85.88	16.13	7.75	12.06	6.37
4.	Daman & Diu	37.32	46.16	25.40	31.01	37.28	22.83
5.	Delhi	2.85	–	32.43	–	64.72	–
6.	Lakshadweep	25.02	29.30	25.27	24.26	49.71	46.44
7.	Pondicherry	39.24	–	19.99	–	40.77	–

* Excludes figures of Jammu & Kashmir where 1991 census was not taken.

Source: Census of India 1991, Series-1 of 1993, Union Primary Census Abstract for S.C. & S.T.

APPENDIX—V

District-wise Tribal Population of Rajasthan (2001 Census)

S. No.	District	Total Population			Scheduled Tribe Population			% of S.T. to Total Population
		Person	Male	Female	Person	Male	Female	
1	2	3	4	5	6	7	8	9
1.	Ajmer	2181670	1129920	1051750	52634	27346	25288	2.41
2.	Alwar	2992592	1586752	1405840	239905	127707	112198	8.02
3.	Banswara	1501589	760686	740903	1085272	547277	537995	72.27
4.	Baran	1021653	535137	486516	216869	113058	103811	21.23
5.	Barmer	1964835	1038247	926588	118688	62938	55750	6.04
6.	Bharatpur	2101142	1133425	967717	47077	25195	21882	2.24
7.	Bhilwara	2013789	1026650	987139	180556	93089	87467	8.97
8.	Bikaner	1674271	886075	788196	5945	3272	2673	0.36
9.	Bundi	962620	504818	457802	194851	102678	92173	20.24
10.	Chittaurgarh	1803524	918063	885461	388311	197416	190895	21.53
11.	Churu	1923878	987781	936097	10063	5339	4724	0.52
12.	Dausa	1317063	693438	623625	353187	186464	166723	26.82
13.	Dhaulpur	983258	538103	445155	47612	25954	21658	4.84

(Contd...)

1	2	3	4	5	6	7	8	9
14.	Dungarpur	1107643	547791	559852	721487	355748	365739	65.14
15.	Ganganagar	1789423	955378	834045	14744	7948	6796	0.82
16.	Hanumangarh	1518005	801486	716519	10029	5367	4662	0.66
17.	Jaipur	5251071	2768203	2482868	412864	217546	195318	7.86
18.	Jaisalmer	508247	279101	229146	27834	14890	12944	5.48
19.	Jalor	1448940	737880	711060	126799	66610	60189	8.75
20.	Jhalawar	1180323	612804	567519	141861	74014	67847	12.02
21.	Jhunjhunu	1913689	983526	930163	36794	19054	17740	1.92
22.	Jodhpur	2886505	1513890	1372615	79540	41450	38090	2.76
23.	Karauli	1209665	651998	557667	270630	145962	124668	22.37
24.	Kota	1568525	827128	741397	151969	80616	71353	9.69
25.	Nagaur	2775058	1424967	1350091	6497	3503	2994	0.23
26.	Pali	1820251	918856	901395	105814	54928	50886	5.81
27.	Rajsamand	987024	493459	493565	129198	65657	63541	13.09
28.	Sawai Madhopur	1117057	591307	525750	241078	128446	112632	21.58
29.	Sikar	2287788	1172753	1115035	62512	32493	30019	2.73
30.	Sirohi	851107	437949	413158	210763	107905	102858	24.76
31.	Tonk	1211671	626436	585235	145891	76159	69732	12.04
32.	Udaipur	2633312	1336004	1297308	1260432	634953	625479	47.86
	Total	**56507188**	**29420011**	**27087177**	**7097706**	**3650982**	**3446724**	**12.56**

(Contd...)

1	2	3	4	5	6	7	8
7.	Kokna, Kokni, Kukna	–	2	91	74	165	0.004 Negligible
8.	Koli Dhor, Tokre Koli, Kolcha, Kolgha	–	166	1,075	1,006	2,081	0.059
9.	Mina	1,455,620	1,532,331	1,091,451	995,241	2,086,692	49.88
10.	Naikda, Nayaka, Cholivala Nayaka, Kapadia Nayaka Mota Nayaka, Nana Nayaka	–	32	4,800	4,374	9,174	0.22
11.	Patelia	–	1	931	772	1,703	0.04
12.	Seharia, Sehria, Sahariya	23,299	26,939	20,821	20,124	40,945	0.98
13.	Unspecified	186,740	43,801	3,969	3,494	7,463	0.18

Source:

1. Census of India 1961, Vol. I Part V-A (ii) Special Tables for Scheduled Tribes pp. 40-97 & 186.
2. Census of India, 1971, Social and Cultural Tables (Table vii & viii) part II-C (i) Series-18, Rajasthan pp. 604-693.
3. Census of India, 1981, Series, 18 Part-IX, Special Tables for S.T. pp. 8-15.
4. Mehta, Prakash Chandra; Bharat-ka-Adivasi, Shiva Publishers Distributors, Udaipur, 1993.

APPENDIX—VI

Tribe-wise Population (Census 1961 to 1991)

S. No.	Tribe	1961	1971	1981			Percentage, of total S.T. population
				Male	Female	Person	
1	2	3	4	5	6	7	8
	Rajasthan	2,351,470	3,125,506	2,150, 767	2,032,357	4,183,124	100
1.	Bhil, Bhil Garasia, Dhol Bhil Dungari Garasia, Mewasi Bhil Rawal Bhil, Tadvi Bhil Bhagalia, Bhilala, Pawra Vasava, Vasave	906,705	1,437,937	929,087	911,879	1,840,966	44.01
2.	Bhil-Mina	2,063	17,076	13,766	13,371	27,137	0.65
3.	Damor, Damaria	14,534	14,795	15,937	15,440	31,377	0.75
4.	Dhanka, Tadvi, Tetaria, Valvi	–	157	7,378	6,733	14,111	0.34
5.	Garasia (Excluding Rajput Garasia)	62,509	52,268	60,225	58,332	118,757	2.84
6.	Kathodi, Katkari, Dhor Kathodi, Dhor Katkri, Son Kathodi, Son Katkari	1	1,236	1,137	2,553	0.06	

APPENDIX—VII

Tribe-wise Population (Census 1991)

S. No.	Tribe		Population		
			Total	Males	Females
1	2	3	4	5	6
	Rajasthan	Total	54,74,881	28,37,014	26,37,867
		Rural	52,20,549	26,96,437	25,24,112
		Urban	2,54,332	1,40,577	1,13,755
1.	Bhil, Bhil, Garasia, Dholi Bhil Dungri Garasia, Mewari Bhil Rawal Bhil, Tadvi Bhil, Bhagalia Bhailala, Buvara, Vasava, Vasave	Total	23,05,982	11,77,865	11,28,117
		Rural	22,28,487	11,36,860	10,91,627
		Urban	77,495	41,005	36,490
2.	Bhil-Mina	Total	32,592	16,678	15,914
		Rural	28,733	14,562	14,171
		Urban	3,859	2,116	1,743
3.	Damor, Damaria	Total	43,612	21,801	21,811
		Rural	42,525	21,189	21,336
		Urban	1,087	612	475
4.	Dhanka, Tadvi, Tetaria, Valvi	Total	33,844	17,990	15,854
		Rural	14,493	7,742	6,751
		Urban	19,351	10,248	9,103

(Contd...)

1	2	3	4	5	6
5.	Garasia (excluding Rajput Garasia)	Total	1,48,197	75,899	72,298
		Rural	1,47,303	75,332	71,971
		Urban	894	567	327
6.	Kothodi, Katkari, Dhor Kathodi, Dhor Katkari Son Kathodi, Son Katkari	Total	2,984	1,498	1,486
		Rural	2,893	1,444	1,449
		Urban	91	54	37
7.	Kokna, Kokni, Kukna	Total	710	378	332
		Rural	609	322	287
		Urban	101	56	45
8.	Koli Dhor, Tokre Koli, Koleha, Kolgha	Total	2,973	1,576	1,397
		Rural	2,549	1,339	1,210
		Urban	424	237	187
9.	Mina	Total	27,99,167	14,69,158	13,30,000
		Rural	26,58,344	13,89,085	12,69,250
		Urban	1,40,823	80,073	60,750
10.	Naikda, Nayaka, Cholivala, Nayaka, Kapadia Nayaka, Mota Nayaka, Nana Nayaka	Total	11,627	6,272	5,355
		Rural	7,859	4,177	3,682
		Urban	3,768	2,095	1,673

(Contd...)

1	2	3	4	5	6
11.	Patelia	Total	2,554	1,074	1,480
		Rural	1,977	763	1,214
		Urban	577	311	266
12.	Seharia, Saharia, Sahariya	Total	59,810	30,555	29,255
		Rural	58,749	30,011	28,738
		Urban	1,061	544	517
13.	Unclassified	Total	30,829	16,270	14,559
		Rural	26,028	13,611	12,417
		Urban	4,801	2,659	2,142

2

Commissions and Committees on Development of Indian Tribes

Dr. V.K. Srivastava

The role of commission and committees appointed from time to time has been of great importance, specially in the context of tribal development. In other words, the reports of Tribal Commissioners, Commissions and Committees, Study Groups and Working Groups are since qua non for and indepth understanding of tribal situation in India as well as in the states. The commissioner's and committee's reports have been viewed as a very valuable source of authoritative importance in the policy information process. The role of tribal Commissions has a different perspective as compared to the other Enquiry commissions. The valuable recommendations and suggestions have been quoted, wherever, found necessary in support of the arguments given in this paper and also the views expressed and emphasis laid down by them to illustrate the drawbacks/short comings/negligence towards the protection and development of the Scheduled Tribes.

The Articles 338 (1), 339 (1) and 340 (1) have special say regarding the appointments of commissions to investigate and evaluate the implementation of constitutional responsibility towards the production and development of Scheduled Tribes at the national level as well as in the states. Article 338 has been amended in 1990 and a permanent Scheduled Castes and Scheduled Tribes Commission has been set up.

Dhebar Commission

In persuance of Article 339 (1) only one Commission could be appointed till 18th July, 2002. The President of India appointed on 28 April, 1960 the Scheduled Areas and Schedule Tribes Commission under the chairmanship of late U.N. Dhebar. The terms of reference of the commission inter alia were to report on:

(a) the administration of the Scheduled Areas under the fifth schedule to the constitution and in particular as to:

(i) the functioning of the Tribes Advisory Councils;

(ii) the laws applicable to the Scheduled Areas and the exercise by the Governors concerned of powers under paragraph 5 of the fifth schedule; and

(iii) the principles to be followed in declaring any territory to be, or to form part of, a Scheduled Area, or directing that any territory shall cease to be, or cease to form part of a Scheduled Area.

The Commission submitted its report on 30th October, 1961. The most important recommendation of the Commission was that "in view of the changes that have taken place since the inception of the constitution, we feel that it is no longer necessary to pursue the question whether a tribal area should be declared Scheduled or a Scheduled Area should be descheduled. The Fifth Schedule was conceived as a temporary expedient and its objectives can be achieved by our alternative approach, which is simply that Govt. should undertake a plan which would protect the Scheduled Tribes and ensure development of the tribal areas within a stated period. The State Govts. should undertake general legislation applicable throughout the Scheduled and Non-scheduled areas for protection of the rights of tribals in land and forests, and protection from exploitation by money lenders and this legislation should be implemented within a period of ten years. Pending enactment of such general legislation, the regulatory powers of the Governor under paragraph 5 (2) of the Fifth Schedule may be utilised for the promulgation of corresponding regulations for the Scheduled Areas. Simultaneously all tribal areas should be grouped under tribal development blocks so that the bulk of the tribal population is brought under intensive development schemes. The blocks should concentrate on the following four activities—economic development, education, health and communications and should have specific targets. With fulfilment of the targets in all tribal development blocks and the passing and implementation of protective legislation, the objects of the fifth scheduled would have been achieved and it could conveniently be abrogated".

Special Committees

In pursuance of the special responsibility which the Indian Constitution enjoins on the States, a systematic review of the tribal development programmes was taken up from time to time by appointing expert committees. The following committees appointed by the centre deserve a mention:

S. No.	*Name of the Committee*	*Chairman*	*Reported on*
1	2	3	4
1.	Backward Classes Commission	Kaka Kalelkar	March, 1955
2.	Study Team on Social Welfare & Welfare on Backward Classes	Renuka Ray	July, 1959
3.	Committee on Special Multipurpose Tribal Blocks	Verrier Elwin	March, 1960
4.	Special Working Group on Co-Operation for Backward Classes	M.P. Bhargava	September, 1962
5.	Report of the Advisory Committee on the revision of the lists of Scheduled Castes and Scheduled Tribes	B.N. Lokur	August 25, 1965
6.	Committee on Tribal Economy in Forest Areas	Hari Singh	December, 1967
7.	National Commission on Labour	Gajendra Gadkar	August 28, 1969
8.	Expert Committee on Tribal Development	S.C. Dube	October, 1972
9.	Committee on relief of indebtedness, land alienation and restoration of tribal development agency	P.S. Appu	October 12, 1972

(Contd...)

1	2	3	4
10.	Study Team on Tribal Development Programmes (All India Report)	P. Shilu Ao	September, 1969
11.	Committee on Co-operatives in Tribal Development Projects	K.S. Bawa	September 24, 1973
12.	National Commission on Agriculture		1976
13.	Working Group on Tribal Development during Medium Term Plan 1978-83	O.L. Mandal	September, 1969
14.	Committee on Administrative Arrangements and Personnel Policies in Tribal Areas	Maheshwar Prasad	October 17, 1979
15.	Committee on Forests and Tribals in India	Prof. B.K. Roy Burman	September, 1982
16.	Committee on Forestry Programmes for Alleviation of Poverty	C.L. Bhatia	
17.	National Forest Policy Resolution		December, 1988
18.	Report of the Study Group Land Holding System in Tribal Areas.	Prof. B.K. Roy Burman	1990

In addition, the Commissioner for Scheduled Castes and the Scheduled Tribes in its annual reports to the President and the Parliamentary Committee on the Welfare by the Scheduled Castes and Scheduled Tribes (a Standing Committee constituted by the Parliament in December, 1968) have reviewed the problems and the programmes for the Scheduled Tribes in regular manner.

These Commissions and Committees have been setup by the Central Govt. time to time to fulfil the constitutional committees and to assess the tribal problems, development scenario and accordingly to provide guidelines/suggestions to the Central and State Governments to formulate the tribal development strategies and approaches after independence. But a few committees constituted during the pre-independence period and after independence while preparing the draft of the Indian Constitution have also given valuable suggestions which are relevant even today in the context of tribal development in the country as well as in the state. The names of these Committees and recommendations given by them would be worthwhile to mention here as under:

1. Report of the starte Committee appointed to enquire into the educational, economic and social conditions of depressed classes (untouchables)· and the Aboriginal tribes in the Bombay Presidency, 1930.
2. D. Symingtion Committee appointed on March, 1937 to enquire "Partially Excluded Areas: Measures for improvement of conditions of Bhils and other Aboriginal and Hill Tribes.
3. A.V. Thakkar Sub-committee appointed to report on the Excluded and Partially Excluded areas August, 18, 1947.

The purpose of these reports was as Verrier Elwin put it "to try to assess what has been done and whether it has been done in the right way."[2] In the successive paras the recommendations and suggestions given by these Committees and Commissions have been reviewed in brief to ascertain the reasons for not being followed by the politicians, academicians, planners and administrators who have been responsible to convert them into action in the context of tribal development.

Starte Committee

The Starte Committee was appointed on 5th November, 1928 in acceptance of the resolution moved by Dr. P.G. Solanki and passed by the legislative council with following terms of reference:

"To enquire into the educational, economic and social condition of depressed classes (untouchables) and of the Aboriginal Tribes in the Bombay Presidency and to recommend measures for their uplift".[3]

Starte committee's report is the oldest reports on the Aboriginal Tribes and a historical land mark. He understood the problems of Aboriginal Tribes and advocated for the opening and exposure of Aboriginal to bring them in the mainstream of life. It observed "the problem is due to geographical difficulties combined with lack of desire to avail themselves of such opportunities combined with lack of desire to avail themselves of such opportunities. The problems of Aboriginal Tribes have not been brought before the public in any definite form ... whatever their own desires may be, the march of civilization inevitably bring the Aboriginal Tribes into contact with others. If they remain in their present condition, they will become more and more the prey of the unscrupulous from among the more educated communities. The problem of them is to implant a desire for education to breakdown their exclusiveness and to enable them to take part in the national life benefiting their members".[4] The committee has given several recommendations for educational development and economic and social upliftment of Aboriginal Tribes. But these recommendations in majority remained on paper. Thus, no attention was paid to the problems of aboriginals on the lines of recommendations of Starte Committee.

D. Symigton Committee

D. Symigton Committee (March 31, 1938) identified the problems of Aborginal Tribes from different angles as seen by the Starte Committee. In his opinion isolation was no problem to the Aboriginal Tribes, but their contact with the outsiders and their exploitation. Symigton observed that traders and liquor contractors were the main culprits for the exploitation of Aborginals. So he recommended for stringent restrictions on 'Sowcars' (traders) and eradication of 'Sowcar system and replacing it with credit and sale societies' which could not be done even today by all means. Symigton had observed, "The problem of the Aborginal and hill tribes arose from their isolation from the main body of the community. This is a view with which, it is to be taken at the face value, profoundly disagree. If of course there were no isolation, cultural, economic or otherwise there would be no problem, but such a proposition merely begs the question and can hardly be attributed to the Starte Committee". "...The state ought to now to take an entirely new view of the problem of the Aborginal and instead of relying on the force of time...should adopt active measures designed both to free him from the tentacles of his exploiters and to educate him up to becoming an intelligent and useful members of the community...for next generation, we must regard the Aborginal as being in the nursery. Like a child he must be protected from outside interference and victimization and like a child he must taught how to hold his own. In short the State attitude must be paternal. Section 9 of the current Govt. of India Act make special provision for the administration by means of regulations the Partially Excluded Areas. The section is, I believe, founded the apprehension that the population of the tribal areas are not equipped to take their share in the scheme of democratic Govt. There will not be many dissentions from the first of this belief". "...If we accept that the present 'Sahucari' system is an evil to be eradicated, then a substitute credit structure is essential. Conversely if an improved system of credit, and sale societies as grain depots is to be success then the 'Sahucar' must be hold in check, otherwise our system will fail".[5]

The observations of D. Symigton committee seem to be relevant even today. After forty four years of adoption of the Indian Constitution, and under its provision the fifth scheduled providing the special provision for the grace and good Govt., is now becoming a history.

A.V. Thakkar Sub-Committee

Thakkar Sub-Committee (August 18, 1947) was one of the first, earliest among all important Committees setup to advise on 'Excluded and Partially Excluded Areas'. This Committee is the first which used the term 'Scheduled Areas' and that was incorporated in the constitution and similarly the concept of Tribes Advisory Council was also adopted. But the recommendation of the committee regarding the delineation of 'Scheduled Areas' could not be followed in the state of Madhya Pradesh. Bhanage N.P. has mentioned (1993: 431 & 432) "The basic concepts of tribal life and tribal welfare administration have been most clearly stated by this Committee. The Committee was at pains to note that even after the demacrations of these areas no tangible results in the sphere of economic development has been achieved. The term 'Scheduled Areas' was used with clarity in this report for the first time, and subsequently the same term was adopted in our Constitution. The committee has emphatically stated that the laws passed by the legislature could not automatically be applied to the scheduled Areas, if the Tribes Advisory Council does not consider them suitable for tribal areas".

"The Committee laid down the criterion for declaring the Scheduled Areas by stating that the tribal population should have the preponderance i.e. it should be above 66.6 per cent. The extent of the area was determined on practical and administrative grounds after taking into consideration homogeneity of the area and the contiguity of the territory. We find subsequently that some lacunae have occurred because some of the districts having sizeable tribal population have not been included in these areas. The Committee also gave consideration to the fact that of 'the stage of development' and degree of 'assimilation of tribal people' with general population in our country".

The Thakkar Sub-Committee had clearly mentioned in its report that "the object of special administration has thus not been achieved."[6] This has also been seen and experienced even after the creation of special administration machinery for Scheduled Area.

Kaka Kalelkar Commission

Kaka Kalelkar Commission (March 30, 1955) had also considered the problems of Scheduled Tribes. One of the terms of reference was to examine the list of Scheduled Caste and Scheduled Tribe as already published under the orders and to suggest any revision of those lists, if on enquiry it was found that such a revision was necessary. The Commission suggested certain changes. Besides, the Commission also commented on certain issues and set up viz. administrative machinery, Five Year Plan and land policy. The commission's observation on revision of lists of Scheduled Tribes:

(i) General member of Scheduled Castes and Scheduled Tribes when they go from one state to another should receive the amount of their help that is given to the backward classes in the State where they have gone to reside.

(ii) The whole State should be one unit for purpose of help to Scheduled Tribes and the help offered to tribal people should be given to them irrespective of their shifting from one area to another in the State."[7]

Commission's observation on Five Year Plan and administration; "the economic policy and ideology behind Five Year Plan do not inspire sufficient confidence. It is felt that even the policies enunciated in Five Year Plans have not properly implemented. The administrative set up entrusted with the test implementing the Welfare measures requires a complete reorientation."[8]

Commission's observations on land policy; "The land legislation must be simple and easily understandable by the rural population. There should be no loop holes in such a legislation that might lead to social conflict. Too many and frequent changes in land legislation creates confusion difficulty and often lead to endless litigation and exploitation".[9]

Overall, the report of the commission dealt with the list of Scheduled Tribes and recommendations were made for devising the ways and means for their economic development. But this report has been criticised on the ground that it suffers from the great flaws of methodology and it is also full of "serious internal contradictions".[10]

Renuka Ray Committee

The study team on social welfare and welfare of backward classes was constituted under the Chairmanship of Renuka Ray on July 9, 1959 on Plan Projects. This Study Team submitted its report on 7.9.1959 to late Govind Vallabh Pant, who was the Chairman of the Committee on Plan Projects."[11] In brief the terms of reference of this Committee were:

1. to study the programmes of work relating to social welfare, included in the plan in the central and state sectors keeping in view the modifications necessary in the context of the programmes, the changes required in the methods of works adopted for the implementation of the programme, quality of the personnel engaged upon the implementation of the programmes and training scheme, assessment of the success of programmes and the functions and involvement of the voluntary organisations;
2. to assess the working of the welfare projects related to STs and STs; and
3. to make recommendations on the necessity and feasibility of evaluation machinery of a continuous nature for both types of projects and on methods adopted for reporting upon the results of the programmes.

The recommendations of this Committee were of great importance and suggestions given were pragmatic and feasible. The most important recommendations and suggestions of the committee were related to integration of development programmes. Integrated plans approach, economic criteria, administrative set up, people's participation, training of personnel's evaluation, role of voluntary organisations and overall policy formulation for the development of Scheduled Tribes.

Renuka Ray Committee was the first committee which touched all the important spheres of tribal life. The committee straight way observed that integration of Welfare programme should be taken as 'social objective'. The Committee was against the segregation of programmes in the context of tribals. The committee observed, "In regards the schemes for Scheduled Castes and Scheduled Tribes we find that although the central purpose is to bring them up to the level of the rest of the community, some of the programmes are infact worked out in such a manner that segregation is accentuated. We have therefore, recommended that separate hostels or separate colonies for Scheduled Castes and Scheduled Tribes should be avoided. In all states, there should be general hostels for students where adequate arrangements are made for the children of the Scheduled Castes and Scheduled Tribes. Even where hostels are provided in the scheduled areas, they should be opened to the children of other communities as well and should be termed as 'General Hostels."[12]

Regarding the economic criteria of assistance the committee had clearly mentioned that, "The central idea is to introduce a gradation in the pattern of assistance. So as to make sure that those economically less advanced among them get proportions proportionately higher benefits than those who are some what better off".[13]

The Committee found that no integrated plan approach was asserted to development schemes. It argued to lay broad priorities considering the primary needs of the Scheduled Tribes as under:

1. Economic Development and Communication;
2. Education; and
3. Public Health

The specific priorities for each area and each community should be ascertained before launching any programmes. On these issues Committee observed that "we have noticed a lack of proper synchronisation of the various schemes have failed to register progress owing to delays in the implementation of other complementary schemes. We have also found that the execution of schemes has not been preceded by a period of careful planning. This has led to shortfall in expenditure and has created a sense of frustration in the people. This features have been noticed by us in many of multipurpose blocks for tribals where actual work had started much later than the initiation of the programme due to delay in setting the preliminaries. Our recommendations, therefore, been directed towards a synchronisation of the schemes of the development and required period of pre-planning".[14]

Regarding the administrative setup and the approach, the committee had observed that "our recommendations on administrative setup are build around the concept that the welfare services need and integrated an planned approach. The present distribution of welfare subjects over various Ministries and Deptts. at both the control and state levels have not been conductive to economy and efficiency in the utilisation of resource, ... we are also aware that, in the present circumstances in India, it is not immediate possible to insist on a high qualitative standard. We have limited financial resources as also paucity of right type of personnel. Our studies have convinced us that a mere multiplication of schemes and projects without regard for their quality is harmful. They might indicate progress in statistical terms without maintaining the minimum standard of quality. This creates a sense of frustration among the people and draws them away from participating in future programme, despite all efforts. Basically we have to remember that the progress in the plans would acquire a full meaning and significance only if there is a palpable evidence of growing prosperity in the people whom the plans are meant to serve.[15]

The committee was also critical about the extensive method adopted in the tribal areas and also about the tribal bias. The Committee observed that, "the schemes operating in the tribal areas have not been able to catch the people's imagination. The lack of a suitable adoption of the general extension methods was the main cause of failure."[16]

The Committee was of the view that the traditional tribal institutions should have been actively associated in the planning and execution of the tribal development programmes which could not be done. The administration had thrust upon the programmes on the tribals. The tribals were not taken into confidence through their traditional institutions. The Committee observed, "Associating traditional tribal institutions with planning and execution will have a two fold benefit. In the first instance, the plans will become mere realistic if they reflect the popular needs as represented by traditional tribal institutions. Secondly, once these representative bodies are convinced of efficiency of a programme the whole hearted co-operation of the entire tribal community would follow ipso/facto .... These institutions are still active and have potentialities of being invested with a new vitality that can be directed towards the current needs. If they are harnessed towards planning and execution of developmental and welfare programmes they will be infused with a new message and a new mission which will once again make them the architects of their own destiny. The development programme also stands to gain in being smoother and speedier than it can ever hope to be with purely official efforts".[17]

Further the committee accentuated on the simplicity in planning in tribal welfare and gave its recommendations and suggestions on all sorts of sectoral programmes viz. agriculture and allied sectors, human resource sectors (education and health), forestry and its management, housing and build up of teachers. The Committee regarding housing programme had considered that housing for tribals "need not receive high priority in the schemes for tribal development" and had envisaged only three situations in which it would required. These were:

(a) When tribals carrying on JHUMING cultivation are allotted land or permanent settlement;

(b) When nomadic tribes have to be settled permanently at a particular place; and

(c) When tribals have deprived of their house sites, house and land on account of the construction of dams, industrial plans or other development projects.[18]

The committee also put great emphasis on the role of central and State Tribal Research Institutions and suggested to recognise them.

Dr. Verrier Elwin Committee

A Committee was appointed under the Chairmanship of Verrier Elwin on 1st May, 1959 by Ministry of Home Affairs, G.O.I. The terms of reference of the Committee were simple, but covered a wide range. They were as under:

(i) To study the working of the special multipurpose Tribal Blocks; and

(ii) To advice the Govt. of India on how to implement the intensive development programmes of the blocks more effectively and give the programme a proper tribal bias.

The report of the Committee was submitted on 30.3.1960 by Dr. Verrier Elwin to Shri Govind Vallabh Pant, the then Home Minister, G.O.I. The report of this Committee had more or less talked about the philosophy of tribal life. The report very much advocated the doctrine of 'Panchsheel' given by Late Prime Minister, Pt. Jawahar Lal Nehru. Elwin Committee Report emphatically stated, "we feel that if any development is to be done in the tribal areas, it may be done well that people must be brought out of their long isolation as soon as possible, Tribal touch or the tribal bias, means that we must look at the things through tribal's eyes from the tribal point of views."

The Committee's recommendations and suggestions have been dealt in other chapter of this study. But some of the facts on which the Committee gave its views and suggestions and needed the action then by the Centre and the State Governments are to be also seen. The Committee had strongly recommended that clear cut decision on certain principles should be taken to benefit the tribals, specially in the principles should be taken to benefit the tribals, specially in the forestry sector. The Committee observed that, "...The first of these is that in predominantly tribal areas, the forest must be managed not basically for profit or for conservation, but with a view to further tribal interest. ... It means that revenue will not be the most important factor nor conservation itself. It means that where the demand for land for cultivation is acute, land more suitable for cultivation than for forest will have to be excised and given for cultivation. This point is a rather tricky one and unless individual decision are very carefully considered, there is danger to the tribal as well as the state".

"Refusal to give forest land for cultivation, even though it is contiguous to existing cultivation and eminently suited for the purpose, arouses the bitterest resentment among the tribals. Also, such refusal defeats its own purpose because the tribal invariably proclaim or illicitly feels the forests adjoining the cultivated area until practically nothing exists. Our experiences is that when this occurs the Forest Deptt. withdraws its objection and the land is ultimately allotted to cultivation. Naturally such things further encourages the tribal to adopt undesirable methods for getting land".

"The second principle which we would offer for consideration is that the tribal must have a direct share in the profits of the forest. Unless this is done, he can not identify his interests with those of the forests. There are several ways whereby this can be achieved. One way of doing this is to relate wages to profits, another is to reserve really remunerative camps for allotment to tribal co-operative societies on fixed upset price, which should be calculated so as to allow a substantial margin of profit. The co-operative society should be confined to tribals and no outsiders should be permitted to become members".[19]

These suggested principles related to forestry did not catch attention of the State Govt. No such decisions have yet taken in the State, except in case of Tendu Patta Policy. The net result is that the forests have reduced in the state and a substantial amount of forest areas have been encroached by the tribals in long course of time and that has become problem to the administration at both the levels, Centre and State.

Similarly, on the problem of indebtedness, the Committee had shown its great concern. The Committee observed that, "The problem of indebtedness among the tribals is a major cause of their exploitation. The tribal is so much in debt. to the money lenders that he may stake his own life and the life of the family in his service for long period of time. ... Today tribal falls into debt for his daily requirements of life such as seed, food, salt, clothing and so on and in order to fulfil social obligations such as marriage, festivals and death ceremonies. There are also long standing ancestral debt to be paid. In spite of hazards that he has to face at the hands of money lenders, he continues to associate with him because he acts as helper all the times...All these factors make the tribal remain under obligation to the money lenders from generation to generation... The present efforts to improve his economic earnings through the development programmes has not resulted in achieving this".[20] The Committee had recommended five sided approach:

1. Enactment of social legislation and effective enforcement of it, to prevent money lenders practising their profession among the tribals, at least in the Scheduled Areas;
2. Effective legislation for liquidation of tribal debts of more than 3 years standings;
3. Effective machinery for conciliation and settlement even under the existing legislation;
4. An effective system of giving credit to the tribals, both for production as well as non-productive purposes; and
5. Effective promotion of social education among the tribals to encourage thrift, to preserve their earnings through small scale savings to look ahead.

Out of the above recommendations made, legislations have been made in the state, but effective system of giving credit, effective machinery for conciliation and effective promotion of social education have not been done in the state.

The Committee was highly critical about the schematic budgetary system for the Tribal Blocks and found that no endeavour was made in this direction. The committee observed that, "The schematic Budget has in practice, proved an obstacle to the adoption of the programme to urgent tribal needs. Although the state Govt. have been empowered to funds from one, head to another within the same block in any manner they consider necessary to meet local requirements. This power has not been used with sufficient imagination and knowledge. The schematic budget tends to set a rigid pattern, which results in lopsided expenditure. ... What may be called a psychological paralysis has been created by the very existence of a 'schematic budget'. The Committee has quoted the comment of a senior officer regarding the status of working of the Multipurpose Block. "One Development Commissioner in the course of discussion about the Multipurpose Blocks, explained that they were marked by too much misguided good will, too, much money, not enough care in drawing up programmes, excessive zeal, theoretical and immateurish pressure from the top, and distruction of self reliance. Are we, he asked simply to spend money in a hurry or do we really want to fulfil our basic aims".[21]

At least, while concluding the reports, the committee put the responsibility of the administrators and planners not to improve the condition of the tribals, but driven them away from their real culture and the treasures, they possessed.[22]

Bhargava Committee

What role co-operation can play in the economic rehabilitation of the Scheduled Tribes and the Scheduled Castes, the Ministry of Home Affairs, setup a Special Working Group in June 1961 under the Chairmanship of M.P. Bhargava, to study the progress of backward classes, particularly the Scheduled Tribes, in the field of Co-operation during the First and Second Plans. The terms of reference of the Committee were:

1. To examine the extent to which the backward classes generally, and the Scheduled Tribes in particular, have benefited from the development of the co-operative movement during first and second plans;
2. To consider as to how the backward classes can be enabled to derive full advantage from the development of co-operation under the third plan;
3. In particular to suggest any special kind of co-operative organisation, any amendment of the normal rules by laws, and orders in respect of subsidy etc.; and
4. To make recommendations regarding special assistance to the provided from the Ministry of Home Affairs plan for the welfare of backward classes to supplement provision from the general allocation for co-operation.

The Committee reviewed the progress made in first and second plans and observed that, "...as a result of the efforts made in the First and Second Plans some useful experience has been acquired in the organisation and working of co-operative societies in the tribal areas. The experience, however, is generally limited to few types of activities, forest co-operatives, grain banks, consumer stores etc. No systematic and planned attempts have so far been made in the tribal areas to develop co-operatives in an integrated manner. The progress of co-operatives in the tribal areas cannot be viewed in isolation, but has to be considered in the wide context of the development of co-operative movement as a whole".

"The progress of the co-operative movement in the eastern region has been very slow and has caused considerable anxiety in recent years. 74 per cent of the tribal belt, the eastern part of Madhya Pradesh and the adjoining northern-fringe of Andhra Pradesh which fall in this region. The unsatisfactory progress of co-operatives in the tribal areas of this region, is, therefore, a reflection of the lower level of development of co-operation movement as a whole".

"Many factors have led to the slow and lop sided development of co-operation in the tribal areas. Broadly, this is due to the structural weakness, operational defects, management problems and faulty procedures."[23]

After studying the basic structure and social economic characteristics of the tribal way of life and tribal areas, the Committee recommended, "formation of an integrated service co-operative at the 'Hat' level. The society should serve all the villages covered by the 'Hat'. To begin with there should be a minimum of 100 members. A phased programme for increasing membership should be formulated. The objective should be to extend membership to 60 per cent of the total population during the Third Plan. The service co-operative should have 4 sections; (i) Grain section; (ii) Cash loan section; (iii) Marketing section; and (iv) Consumers grade section."[24]

Further to solve the problem of indebtedness, the Committee recommended to adopt regulation under fifth schedule of the Constitution and suggested the measures. The Committee recommended, "under the Fifth schedule of the Constitution, all states should frame regulations to regulate money lending in scheduled areas. For regulating money lending in areas outside the scheduled areas having considerable tribal population. The State Govt. should enact legislation on the lines of the regulations framed under the Fifth Schedule".

"Every moneylender and trade operating in the scheduled areas should be required to obtain a licence which should be issued after a thorough inquiry into the dealings. The rate of interest admissible under the regulations should not be so low that it might lead to evasion".

The responsibility for issuing licence to money lenders and carrying out its inspection and supervision should visit with the registration of co-operative societies. There should be one whole time inspector per tehsil for this work. The Ministry of Home Affairs should bear the cost of the additional staff. The past debts of the tribals may be scaled down on the following basis:—

	Principal (%)	*Interest* (%)
If the debts was incurred before 31st December 1950	50	50
If the debts was incurred after 31st December 1950 but on or before 31st December 1958	40	40

There may be one Debt Relief Court per tehsil. The cost of the staff should be met by the Ministry of Home Affairs.

"Support of tribal leaders, panchayats, Tribal Advisory Councils and social workers should be enlisted to bring home to the tribals that a matter of justice and equally thing are entitled to get relief in their debts issued on unconscionable rates of interest".

"Special debt relief regulation should be introduced in scheduled areas in all states under the Fifth Schedule. Similar/ legislation should be enacted by the State Govt".[25]

The recommendations/suggestions of the Committee were not transferred into action. No co-operative structure to provide the services related to credit and marketing could be created at the 'Hat' level in the State, except certain Multipurpose Co-operation and Mandies could be established for the collection and sale of grains/ cereals after 2nd plan. No. systematic arrangements could be made in the tribal areas at the 'Hat' level. Similarly the use of Fifth Schedule could also not be made to regulate or eradicate the money lending operations in the tribal areas. Only Debt Relief Act/Rules were promulgated in the Third Plan. Under the Act, 105 temporary Debt Relief Mobile Courts were made for the redemption of debt in the tribal areas of the State. The structural weaknesses, operational defects, management problems and faulty procedures have become the permanent features in the cooperative sector in the state. LAMPS formed in Fifth Plan and onwards have been failed to provide services to the tribals.

Lokhur Committee

The Advisory Committee on the revision of lists of Scheduled Castes and Scheduled Tribes was Constituted under the Chairmanship of Shri B.N. Lokhur, Secretary to G.O.I. on 1st July, 1965 with following terms of reference:—

1. To advise on the proposals received by Govt. for revision of the existing lists of Scheduled Castes and Scheduled Tribes.
2. To advise whether, where a caste or tribe is listed as a Scheduled Caste and Scheduled Tribes in relation to a particular area in a State or Union Territory, members of that caste or tribe residing:
   (i) in other areas within the same State or Union Territory, members of that castes or
   (ii) in other States or Union Territory, should be recognised as belonging to the Scheduled Castes or Scheduled Tribes as the case may be.

During the period 1950 to 1956, under the provisions made in the Article 342, several orders related to Scheduled Castes and Scheduled Tribes list were issued by the President of India to revise the lists of Scheduled Castes and Scheduled Tribes. The list of Scheduled Caste and Scheduled Tribes appearing in the various orders came up for criticism on a number of occasions both in Parliament, outside on the ground that they were not rational and contained several anomolies. To examine them Lokhur Committee was set up with the terms of reference mentioned above. In the Third Chapter of this study, the observations, recommendations and suggestions have been examined and discussed in details. However, the task before the Committee was to advise the Govt. on the revision in a scientific and rational manner of lists of Schedule Castes and Scheduled Tribes. The Committee remarked, "Every tribal need not be regarded as requiring a special treatment. We have considered that tribals who have mixed with general population are not eligible to be in the list of Scheduled Tribes."[26] On these lines the Committee suggested to include certain tribes or part of the group in the list of Scheduled Tribes and to exclude certain group or part of group of tribal communities from the list (detail is given in Chapter III). While during such exercise i.e. scientific grouping of communities, the Committee observed that, "Hitherto, no systematic attempt appears to have been made to list castes and tribes in the schedule according to generic name, synonyms and sub-groups, with the co-operation of the office of the Registrar-General of Census, the State Govt., Tribal Research Institute and some other who appeared before us, we have been able to rearrange the lists of individual states scientifically; an attempt has also been made to ensure that lists of neighbouring states follow a co-ordinated and scientific pattern."[27] While doing so, the Committee was critical of the lists of Scheduled Castes and Scheduled Tribes, because the list had not been prepared taking into consideration the total status of a tribe that too by examining the regional differences.[28]

Lokhur Committee was of the view that the advance Scheduled Tribes Communities included in the list of Scheduled Tribes should be descheduled and gradually such weeding out process would help to integrate these communities in the main stream of Indian life.[29] To do this, the Committee suggested that periodic survey should be done to assess economically, socially and educationally advanced communities.[30]

"We feel that time has come when the question of the descheduling relatively of the advance communities should receive serious and urgent consideration."[31] On the "Area Restriction', the

Committee had commented that "No person can legally be regarded as a member of Scheduled Caste and Scheduled Tribes for the purpose of consideration unless he belonged to the listed castes or tribes and also resides in the specified localities within the aforesaid state."[32]

The irony is that Lokhur Committee Report was not accepted by the Central government.

M.T. Raju Committee

The important feature of the planning process in the Third Plan Period was the appointment of a High Level Committee headed by Shri M.T. Raju in 1965 to suggest equitable distribution of Community Development (C.D.) funds and delineate blocks as viable units of development, so that existing development imbalances are wiped out and economy is achieved by reducing the administrative overheads.

However, the number and existing boundaries of the Tribal Development Blocks were not altered by the Committee. But in C.D. Fund allocation, the T.D. Blocks were given the most preferred treatment. For the purpose of allocation of funds, the Committee classified the Blocks into advanced, ordinary, backward and trial based on the levels of their development. This classification of Blocks was based on the following indicators of developments with weightages indicated against each:

S. No.	*Particulars*	*Weightage*
(a)	Per capita land revenue assessed in the Block	15
(b)	Per cent of irrigated area to cultivated area	25
(c)	per cent of children of the age group of 6-11 attending schools	10
(d)	Literacy—Districtwise	10
(e)	Districtwise national income	15
(f)	Road mileage per 100 Sq. miles within the Block	25
		100

A composite index of development was compiled for each block based on the above indicators and taking the State average position as 100. All blocks whose indices of development were nearer to the State average as backward and those far above the State average as advanced. The Tribal Blocks were those which were so declared by the State Govt. ... The allocation of funds were suggested on the basis of the following ratio:

Advanced	3/4
Ordinary	1
Backward	3/2
Tribal	2

Thus, if an ordinary block could get Re. 1.00 per capita, a tribal block could secure Rs. 2.00 per capita, while the advanced and backward blocks could get 0.75 paise and Rs. 1.50 respectively. The classification helped the tribal blocks in securing enhanced per capita allocation from C.D. funds instead of the previous practice of distributing funds equally on per capita basis along with other blocks and securing less C.D. grant due to sparse distribution of population.

The land marks in planning process during Third Five Year Plan period were thus coverage of tribal population and are through the opening up of a number of T.D. Blocks, introduction of Panchayati Raj as instrumentality of tribal development and classification of blocks as advanced ordinary, backward and tribal for affording C.D. allocation on the basis of level of development of each block. By the end of Third Five Year Plan development strategy took a clear shape and firm foundation was laid for institutionalising the development process.

Dr. Gajendra Gadkar Commission

The National Commission on Labour was appointed by the Ministry of Labour, Employment and Rehabilitation on December 24, 1966 under the Chairmanship of Dr. Gajendra Gadkar.

The report was signed on August 28, 1969. The terms of reference of the Commission were:

1. To review the changes in condition of labour after independence and to report on existing condition of the labour.

2. To review the existing legislative and other provisions intended to protect the interest of labour, to access their working and to advice how far their provisions serve to implement the Directive Principles of State Policy in the Constitution on labour matters and the national objectives of establishing a socialistic society.

The report of the Commission dealt with the economy of the labour, labour situation position of employment/unemployment, bonded labour, tribal labour, forest labour and other types of labour viz. migratory labour, unorganised labour etc.

Some of the observations and recommendations of the commission were as under:

"On the issue of tribal labour the Commission has observed that, "the mergence of tribal labour in a sizeable proportion for industrial work is an aspect which is acquiring significance in the country. The process started with the exploitation of forest wealth and minerals..."

"The first consequence of change is "urbanisation" of tribal areas... Isolated homogeneous "adiwasi" communities which being acquired for industrial use and a new environment being built with substantial investment flowing in with such monetisation in the area. The traditional institution...the tribal panchayat could help them no longer... The tribal youth who managed to get absorbed in non agricultural employment gradually changed his way of life. This have multiplier effect. Families uprooted as a result of their lands being acquired for developing industrial complexes were no longer satisfied with a compensation received...".[33] The Commission further observed (p. 206-207) that the question of preference to local population in the matter of employment within the local area was not as complex before independence as it is today. 'Sons of the soil should be given their rightful share'. About the bonded labour the Commission had observed (p. 208-209) that, "Bonded labour can best be described as debt-bondage fixed for a time for a lifetime on hereditary, descending from father to son in some cases. The system grew out of acute indigen or helplessness of tribal and semi-tribal communities in the grip of precarious subsistence economy".

"This only emphasis that mere legislation is no remedy for difficulties raising out of economic compulsions. With slow improvement in economic conditions, enforcement of tenancy, security of tenure and opportunity for employment, the systems has shown signs of disintegration. Growing monetisation of agricultural economy, development of agriculture, availability of institutional credit, spread of education and greater awareness have also somewhat mitigated the evils of this system".[34]

About the forest labour, the Commission had observed (p. 209) that, "Forestry is an important industry in the public sector, about 90 per cent of it being State owned. According to 1961 census labour engaged in forestry, fishing and livestock constituted about 6.4 million out of the working force of 137.5 millions in the agricultural sector. Forestry and logging are a primary source of livelihood for a retively small but significant sector of workers in rural areas."[35]

"Forest labour ordinarily employed in:

1. State Forest Department on departmental works like afforestation, protection, coups etc.
2. Forest Contractors— (a) individuals and partnership firms, (b) Forest Labour Societies; (c) Quasi Govt. Corporation".

"They have to give preference to forest villagers. Forest labour can be divided into three categories (1) Local Labour, (2) Migratory Labour, (3) Labour from forest villages."

The problems faced by the forest workers in regard to employment wages and working conditions have not been systematically tackled. It has by and large remained unorganised. Various pieces of labour legislation did not cover forest labour e.g. Minimum Wages Act, 1948 did not cover forest labour. Seasonal operations did not assure full time employment to the forest workers all the year round. Shortage of labour was experienced during agriculture seasons. These factors have explained the difficulties in building up a 'specialised and stable' labour force for forest operations.

Conditions of work in forest operations are not satisfactory. Labour has to work in remote areas, away from home, under difficult conditions. Accommodation at worksite limited medical facilities, transport and ration were also inadequate.[36] These were the specific remarks of the Commission.

Regarding the un-organised labour, the Commission had observed (p. 211) that, "This is a group of workers who cannot be identified by definition, but could be described as those who have not been able to organise in pursuing a common objective because of constraints such as: (1) Casual nature of employment; (2) Ignorance of illiteracy; (3) Small size of establishments with low capital investment per person employed; (4) Scattered nature of establishment; and (5) Superior strength of employer.

The categories are numerous scattered through. The Commission had taken only those where number of workers were large. The Commission had considered only illustrative categories and one of them was the group of tribal labour.

"Beyond mention in the 1946, policy statement, Govt. had paid inadequate attention to these workers".

"It is common complaint that the benefits of labour legislation have not reached rural and urorganised, had weak bargaining power and had been deprived of reasonable wage and working condition."[37]

From the point of view of actual benefits and effects they produce on tribal labour. Tribals have demanded certain privileges and rights and opportunities as "sons of soil" these demands cannot be brushed aside because the tribals have lost their lands which have been acquired from the development and have suffered on many counts to facilitate industrial undertaking to come up".

At last Commission recommended that, "We recommend evolving a consistent and integrated policy towards involving members of backward communities in the industrial process at work around them, but mere reservation of posts will not any longer help, if steps are not taken to make them fit for the jobs which are likely to be available. Steps should be taken to ensure that local tribal labour especially the displaced labour gets reasonable opportunities for recruitment to unskilled and semi-skilled jobs."[38]

P. Shilu AO Committee

Under the Chairmanship of Shri P. Shilu AO, Govt. of India, Planning Commission, set up a study team on Tribal Development Programmes on Plan Projects on 26.10.1966. This Committee on Plan Projects had set up a study team to acquaint itself first hand with the problems and needs of tribal communities in each State, appraise the working of tribal development programmes, especially during the Third Five Year Plan and make detailed and specific recommendations regarding programmes of development to be carried out during the Fourth Five Year Plan. The Committee had to suggest in the light of past experiences the schemes formulated unable the tribal communities to secures an adequate share in the benefits of general development programmes and spread up their economic and social advancement.

The Committee prepared 20 reports on individual State/ Union Territories after a detailed study of the problems in each State. Over all the committees observed (p. 215), "the drawback in the approach to tribal development in the past has been for action to lag behind even the weighty recommendations made by high level bodies to safeguard the interests of the tribals and promote their welfare. In review of the obligations cast of the State by the Constitution to promote the welfare of the tribal communities we hope that vigorous action will be taken to implement the recommendations made by us. We also trust that the reports will help the state authorities to avoid the pitfalls of the past of the formulation of future programmes of tribal development and enable them to make the maximum use of resources.[39]

The Committee gave its recommendations/suggestions on tribal welfare policy, classification of tribes, programmes performances, protective measures and administrations and institutional set ups at the level of Govt. of India as well as the State. In regard to tribal welfare policy, the committee suggested that, "the main aim of tribal welfare should be reviewing as the progressive advancement of the tribals with a view to their integration with the rest of the community on a footing of equality within a reasonable distance of time.[40]

"Regarding the classification of tribes the Committee observed that, "certain anomolies have come to notice of the team which even after the appointment of Advisory Committee for revision of lists of Scheduled Caste and Scheduled Tribes, continue to persist. These anomolies have arisen largely because of the absence of clearly defined principles or criteria governing the classification of tribals."[41]

"As the present even obvious mistakes in classification cannot be corrected except by legislation, it will be for Parliament to consider whether provision should not be made in the proposed legislation to set up a suitable machinery for the speedy rectification of palpable anomolies and mistakes in the classification of Scheduled Tribes. As it is of the utmost importance that the Parliament should have reasoned and objective advice while considering the inclusion of any community from the list of Scheduled Tribes, the study team suggests that a High Powered Commission, consisting amongst others, of Anthropologists, Social Workers, Administrators and Legislators may be appointed as and when necessary to draw up a revised list of Scheduled Tribes on a scientific basis for consideration and approval by the Parliament. The commission may also assist the Parliament in rectifying the anomolies and mistakes which may have crept into the approved list of scheduled tribes."[42]

In short the recommendations/suggestions of P. Shilu AO report can be summarised as under:

"Report took the historical review of the development policy in the First and Third Five Year Plans. It observed that while some advances have been made, the expectation that substantial outlays in the Tribal Development Blocks themselves would have proportionate favourable impact was belied. In fact, revelation was that the amount earmarked for tribals have been diverted for non-tribals beneficiaries."[43]

The findings of Shilu AO Committee made it clear once again that it was necessary to adopt the flexible policy for the development of tribals. At the end, the team observed that the achievements under the programmes had generally fallen short of expectations, nevertheless the programmes had helped "to bring about the psychological change in the outlook of the tribals".[44] The "Area

Approach" and also "adopting to the felt needs of the areas" were the main recommendations of the Shilu AO Committee. This study Team had a realistic approach to the tribal situation when they commented that the task of assimilation of tribal by the Scheduled Castes and Scheduled Tribes Commission with the goal of total assimilation should be reached by the end of the Fourth Five Year Plan was some what optimistic. "To assume that social and economic advance can be accelerated so as to reach the goal within 5 or 10 years would be too far simplifying the problems".[45]

Prof. L.P. Vidhyarthi Committee

The Planning Commission setup a Task Force on "Development of Tribal Areas on April 5, 1972 under the Chairmanship of Prof. L.P. Vidhyarthi, with the following terms and references:

1. To review the nature and level of development, identify the present bottlenecks and weakness in politics and programme and suggest corrective measures;
2. To suggest a perspective of development from 1973-74 to 1988-89 in the light of the overall development perspective envisaged in the Fourth Plan;
3. To formulate proposals for the Fifth Plan in the light of the perspective indicating priorities, polices programmes and outlays. As far as possible contents of programmes with geographical coverage should be outlined.

Vidhyarthi Committee overall reviewed the past efforts made during First to Fourth Five Year Plans and for the Fifth Five Year Plan suggested that the tribal areas may be categorised as extremely backward on the basis of the following criterias:

1. density of tribal population in relation to arable land;
2. position of literacy (less than 5 per cent or less than 50 per cent literacy of the district/state average);
3. arable land, forest resources, irrigation facilities etc.;
4. occupation of the tribals, like hunting, fishing, food gathering etc.,

5. availability of agricultural infrastructure land reforms, agricultural outputs, credit and marketing, warehousing etc.; and
6. development of infrastructure (facilities like schooling, medical facilities, communications and transport etc.)

The Committee reviewed the tribal scenario and observed that, "The administrative structure for implementation of area development programmes will have to be evolved in a simplistic manner with limited number of functionaries who could undertake multiple jobs. Various services offered by functionaries both engaged in regulatory and development work, will need to be integrated. Most important point to keep in mind while administering tribal areas is to gain confidence of the tribal people and establish a rapport with them. In this matter service of experts in tribal culture would be necessary to have a better comprehension of the overall developmental problems of tribal areas".[46]

Regarding the approach under the Fifth Plan, the Committee suggested that, "a policy of integrated development for tribal areas may be emphasised. As pointed out, block area is too small for comprehensive developmental programmes. Therefore, ... in marking/out during tribal development areas be ... undertakes T.D. Blocks and other areas with high concentration of tribal population. Such tribal areas may be macro areas which give general correspondence to a sizeable scheduled areas, Meso area may be ... with district or teluka (tahsil) boundaries and micro area may be a Tribal Development Block. A part from Macro, Mesho and Micro areas there are small pockets of tribal population throughout the country. This community has to be attained and their development will necessarily have to be given priority in multi level planning at district level".[47] Regarding the plan programme and administrative and personnel policies, the committee observed that, "on the whole there is need to rationalise the entire administrative machinery in tribal areas. The administrative structure in these areas require to be simplified to be within the comprehension of tribal, whom the administration intends to serve. The tribals should be required to deal with limited number of persons who should have their confidence. The administrative structure has to be integrated at an appropriate level so that regulatory and developmental functionaries work in a coordinated manner for speedier economic development. It is also felt that, too much of specialisation in services in these areas create unfilled vacancies or conflicts. There is need to have a high level officer who can attend to numerous narrow specialisations in a broad group and who can be assisted by suitable staff. Specific accountability should be built-in the administrative system so that quick decision could be taken at field level. There should also be adequate mechanism for evaluation and feedback so that corrective steps are taken in time."[48]

The recommendations of Prof. L.P. Vidyarthi Committee have strong say in the formulation of Tribal Sub-plan strategy adopted on the eve of Fifth Five Year Plan.

Dr. S.C. Dube Committee

The Education Minister, G.O.I., has constituted an expert committee under the chairmanship of Dr. S.C. Dube for advising of formulation of new strategy for tribal development during the Fifth Five Year Plan on October 10, 1972.

This Committee observed that, "the problem of tribal development has reached a critical stage and has assumed an added significance in the context of the high priority accorded to social justice in the new planning efforts. Some of the tribal groups have remained completely untouched by the process of development and some have been adversely affected by it. This cannot be allowed to continue. It is proposed therefore, to take a fresh look at the tribal situation in the country, review the strategy of development, and define the total needed national efforts with a view to making tribal communities equal partners in all spheres of national life as early as possible. It is also proposed to take up some key programme on a time bound basis immediately and start preparatory work for the Fifth Five Year Plan."

"In the light of the past experience the Fourth Five Year Plan came to the conclusion that the problem of the Scheduled Tribes living, in concept areas is essentially that of economic development of those area and of integrating their economies with that of the rest of the country. Development plans must be formulated to suit the specific potentialities and levels of development of separate regions or areas."

"Area development by itself will not be sufficient, area development must proceed in consonance with the development of the people of those regions. No section of any community should be allowed to be exposed to exploitation, and the benefits of development must diffuse as widely as possible. The task of tribal development can be defined, therefore, as social and economic development of the tribal people through phased and time bound integration area development and other programmes suiting the genius and the economic situation of the people, ensuring a move towards the goal of equality and justice. This should enable them to join the mainstream of national life as equal partners, enriching its variety and giving it a new strength. For achieving this objective it will be necessary to articulate the objectives in terms of definite policies, administrative actions, and socio-economic programmes."[49]

"The committee reviewed the tribal scenario and suggested the strategy for the tribal development and protective measures, strengthening of tribal traditional institutions, preparing digests of Civil Courts and four categories of economic development programme:

1. traditional sector;
2. building of infrastructure;
3. modern sector; and
4. isolated small tribal communities.

"The Committee highly emphasised the administrating tribal development which included the personnel policy, re-structuring of administration at all levels, voluntary organisation and financing aspects of tribal developments. On this issue, the committee observed (p. 271-273) that, "it is not financial resources which prove critical in tribal development, administrative structure and personnel hold the key to success of planning in these areas. Action on two fronts is necessary."[50]

THE OTHER IMPORTANT RECOMMENDATIONS

Personnel Policy

"Posting of better officers in tribal areas has been an accepted policy of Govt. However, it has not been implemented satisfactorily in all cases. Posting in tribal areas does involved an element of hardship and, therefore, it is necessary to compensate adequately those working in these regions.

Service rendered in tribal areas should be specially recognised for promotion, preference should be given to those who complete their tenure satisfactorily for posting in better stations, there should be adequate reservations in good schools for children of these employees, special leave rules may be framed for more difficult areas and so on. Special state level and national level awards should also be instituted for recognising service rendered in tribal areas."

Restructuring of Administration

"The tribal area have been treated generally at par with other area and sophistication has been introduced in administrative system with considerable specialisation of functions. Further, some institutions have been created for meeting the special problems of tribal areas which added to the multiplicity of organisations. This has resulted in high over-head administrative expenditure".[51]

"The social situation in tribal areas is much too simple. The tribal should be required to deal with a limited number of persons with whom a confidence relationship can be developed. Therefore, all services, viz. credit both for consumption and productive purposes, agricultural inputs, facilities for marketing of forest and agricultural produce, supply of essential consumer goods and food grains etc. should be provided at one point and a single agency should be responsible for their handling".[52]

Hamlet

"The first basic departure from the prevalent practice should be to treat Hamlet, instead of a revenue village, as the unit of development effort. In a number of tribal areas a village does not represent anything except a conglomeration of Hamlets for revenue purposes. Treating village as a basic unit for collection of data is responsible for unsatisfactory statistics and non-disclosure of relevant facts."[53]

Voluntary Organisations

"Voluntary efforts can pay rich dividend in tribal development. Voluntary organisations should be encouraged to undertake specific projects so that the results can be evaluated and a spirit of healthy competition can be inculcated. Specific projects should be treated as a part of the total effort in that particular areas and its expenses may be met from the normal development budget".[54]

Financial Implications

"In the Fifth Plan, a Higher Central Sector Plan and some weightage on prorata share in sectoral and state plans will be essential to mobilise necessary resources for tribal development."

"At present T.D. Blocks have been started generally in areas having 2/3 or more tribal concentration. Those blocks, which have 50 per cent or more tribal concentration should be covered in the Fifth Five Year Plan.

"It will be necessary to spell out the nature of special scheme for extremely backward areas also. Area development plans, when ready, will take into account the requirements of each area. However, the first priority should be given to the extremely backward areas."

"Thus, the total national efforts for the tribal areas will be of the order of Rs. 1,600 crores which will mean a per capita outlay of about Rs. 400 during the Fifth Five Year Plan period. However, much of this investment will be in the form of building up of infrastructure, education and minimum amenities which are so essential for quickening the pace of growth in these backward regions."

Advance Action

"Urgency is the key note of the new strategy of Tribal Development Programmes have to be time bound. Therefore, preparatory exercises must be started immediately and advance action should be taken for a number of programmes without losing any time".[55]

The tribal sub-plan strategy more or less has been formulated on the lines of recommendations/suggestions given by Prof. S.C. Dube Committee in India as well as in the State of Madhya Pradesh on the eve of Fifth Five Year Plan.

P.S. Appu Committee

A Study Group to report on the Relief of Indebtedness Land Allienation and Restoration of Tribal Development Agency (TDA)

Area, under the Chairmanship of Shri P.S. Appu was appointed by Govt. of India on October 12, 1972. The basic objective behind the appointment of this study group was to review the integration of the tribals with the rest of the community, on a footing of equality within a reasonable time. In Madhya Pradesh two Pilot Tribal Development Agencies viz. Dantewara and Konta were created. The terms of reference of the Study Group were:

1. To consider the existing legislation, available in the concerned states, for debt redemption and land restoration and to suggest necessary modifications/ improvements to make them more effective and purposeful;
2. To consider the necessity of a model bill to be made available to the concerned State Govts. to handle the twin problems mentioned above;
3. To make an accurate estimate as possible of the amount that would be required for debt redemption in the project areas/districts and to advise on the need for and extent to which the loans should be scaled down; and
4. To recommend necessary steps for having minimum land records so that the credit programmes can be effectively put through in the project areas.

The recommendations of the Committee in brief were that, "for debt relief the legislation made in Andhra Pradesh and Madhya Pradesh for scaling down of debt may be adopted on the lines method adopted in Madhya Pradesh for setting up a Debt Relief Court and appointments of Debt Relief Inspectors can be emulated for relief of indebtedness in tribal development agency areas and the appointment of staff may be made on the lines of M.P. pattern".[56] Further the Committee also gave its recommendations on maintenance of land record and to deal with the problems of land alienation in the agency areas. In this regard the committee recommend that, "in order to avoid dilatary litigation, it is suggested that legislation designed for the benefit of tribals should be made to secure the protective umbrella of Article 313 of the Constitution". This, if Ninth Schedule of the Constitution were to be so enlarge in scope as to include important items of legislation protecting the interest of tribals .... Further, it would be useful if the juridiction of the ordinary Civil Court were to be completely excluded in the matters relating to the implementation of laws protecting the interests of tribals."[57]

Dr. R.N. Haldipur Committee

The Planning Commission constituted a Task Force on Development of Tribal Areas under the Chairmanship of Dr. R.N. Haldipur on November 27, 1972 with the following terms of references:

1. To review the nature and level of development, identify the present bottlenecks and weaknesses in policies and programmes and suggest corrective measures;
2. To suggest a perspective of development from 1973-74 to 1988-89 in the light of the overall development perspective envisaged in the Fourth Plan; and
3. To formulate proposals for the Fifth Plan in the light of the perspective indicating priorities, policies, programme and outlays.

The committee reviewed the tribal situation of the tribals predominantly settled including Madhya Pradesh and the administrative structure of tribal areas of those States which including monetary incentives, personnel in the field level cadres, qualification for recruitment, training, knowledge of local dialects and institutional frame for implementing personnel policies.

In its conclusion, the Committee recommended a single line of administrative system for tribal areas. The Committee was also of this view that, "the personnel policies for tribal areas have not been properly formulated and they are at a critical stage. Because new projects and programmes for the social and economic development of the tribals have been taken in tribal areas very fast. This has added numerical strength of the personnels working in the tribal areas. Therefore, the personnel structure as well as the policy has to be diverted in the tribal areas to deal with the situation."[58]

K.S. Bawa Committee

Since the importance of cooperatives was gaining its root in the tribal areas, the Ministry of Agriculture appointed a Committee under the Chairmanship of Shri K.S. Bawa on December 6, 1971. The Committee gave its report on September 1973. The terms of reference of the Committee were:

1. To examine the working of the cooperative organisations in the concerned States with particular reference to the project areas and to give its recommendations for strengthening the cooperative structure in these project areas; and
2. To examine if, in the interest of speddy and efficient implementation of the tribal programmes, some specialised agencies could be setup/utilised to channelise credit to the tribals and to link marketing functions with it.

The basic approach of the Committee was firstly to suggest a package of services having credit-production the main component as well as consumption credit and secondly, the tribal should not be required to approach too many institutions for assistance.

The Committee studied reference wise finances for the programmes, contribution from tribals, assistance from Tribal Development Agencies, State Govt. and Institutional Finances. The Committee recommended that, "for effective implementation of various cooperative programme in the project areas, it is important that adequate administrative arrangements, should be made. We have considered the following specific aspects in this regard:

(a) Constitution of the Board of Management;

(b) Chief Executive and staff of Co-operatives; and

(c) Arrangements for coordinating the activities of various developmental and financial agencies in the project areas."[59]

National Commission on Agriculture

The National Commission on Agriculture was constituted in 1976 to study and recommend the forest policy, production and social policy, minor forest produce, forest ecology and wild life management, forest protection and law and forest planning, research, and education.

The summary of the recommendations given by the Commission includes so many aspects related to forestry sector, specially the minor forest produce. The Commission recommended that minor forest produce should be classified to facilitate the availability of minor forest produce in the possible manner to the tribals. The Commission also gave its recommendations for nistar and grazing facilities, employment and rights and concessions. A clear cut areawise Nister policy yet to be framed in Madhya Pradesh.

Maheshwar Prasad Committee

After the adoption of Tribal sub-plan strategy on the eve of Fifth Five Year Plan, it was realised that due to heavy outlay made for tribal sub-plan areas, it was essential to assess the benefits accruing to the tribals. The personnel policy could not be visualised and the concept could not become the full reality in the States. With the result the employees posted in tribal areas showed disinclination towards their working in tribal areas. Though in the past two Committee (both under R.N. Haldipur) gave the detailed guidelines on the personnel policy, but even then it was realised that detailed guidelines and directions that required to be issued to the State Govt. could remain to be adopted by States. In order to prepare a comprehensive personnel policy and the administrative structure in the tribal areas a Committee under the Chairmanship of Shri Maheshwar Prasad was constituted on October 17, 1978 with the following of references:

1. Administrative arrangements in the Centre and the States for implementation of tribal development programmes;
2. Improvement in the administrative structure, personnel policies including creation of sub-cadres, ensuring continuity of tenture at different levels of administration, recruitment of local candidates etc.;
3. Placement policies in tribal areas ensuring proper selection and training of right quality of personnel; and
4. Formalising the systems of standing Committees at project, states and centre level to review the implementation of personnel policies in the sub-plan areas.

The Committee observed that, "it is necessary that the administrative structure at the block level becomes an integral part of the chain. The plans for the blocks should be prepared within the over all framework of the ITDP, since the ITDP represents the total investment in the area including the outlays which may be specifically meant for each block. Logically speaking therefore, the ITDP plans have to be built up from below on the basis of the block plans."

"The state of Madhya Pradesh has done well to place development blocks in line under the ITDP, implying that BDO is under the control and supervision of Project Administrator of the ITDP. This is not the case in Orissa and hence the Project Administrators find it difficult to get the tribal programmes executed in the field through the block agency. For the administrative structure to function smoothly, transfer of control of development blocks to the Tribal Welfare Departments in States is desirable".

"As indicated, in the field the unit of Planning and supervision is the ITDP, it is desirable that tribal representation should be secured in the planning forums for expression of the tribal point of view."

On the basis of above observations the Committee recommended that, "State level, division level and district level screening committees may be setup for making selection of persons to be posted in tribal areas."

"As a part of non-monetary incentives, recognition of service in tribal areas can be given by making an appropriate entry for each year of service rendered in the tribal areas in the record of the officer".

"The State Govt. might consider weightage for each year of service rendered in the tribal areas, reckonable for promotion."

"Recognition of service in tribal areas should be done by grant of suitable awards."

"Tribal areas should be graded for grant of monetary incentives and persons posted in the remoter areas should receive a bigger package of compensatory incentives than those posted in less difficult areas. The element of the package should have a self-liquidating character and disappear progressively with the creation of the concerned facilities."

"Grant of the Seventh Finance Commission for construction of residential buildings in tribal areas should be fully utilised. Where there is insufficiency of residential accommodation, suitable house rent allowance should be permissible."

"The award of the Commission in respect of compensatory allowance for employees posted in tribal areas should similarly be made full use of for payment at the rate of 20 per cent to 50 per cent of basic pay."

"Children Education allowance be given on the lines of the Central Scheme thereof. State Govt. might consider the proposal of M.P. for grant of these concessions to the children of grassroot workers like teachers VLWs as are available to tribal children."

"In the matter of entitlement of causal leave, one day for every two months of service in tribal areas may be allowed over and above the normal. Further, an additional day or two as necessary may be allowed once a year to an employee proceeding on leave to enable him to reach the nearest railway station from his place of duty as well as on return."

"Liberalised leave travel concession should be allowed and the restriction on enticement in result of the initial 400 kms. distance should be removed if it exists."

B. Sivaraman Committee

National Commission on Development of Backward Areas

This Committee was constituted in June 1981 to review the tribal development scenario at the national level. The Committee reviewed the tribal development scenario specially, after the adoption of tribal sub-plan strategy and certain important observations of the committee are as under:

1. Effective and sensitive administration for tribal development was sought to be established as a part of the sub-plan strategy. Some frame has been created but there is lack of effectiveness because a clear unity of command had not emerged;
2. The strategy for tribal development should underline measures for building the inner strength of the

community, so that they are able to face as quickly as possible, the new system on term of equality;

3. The tribal areas are passing through a stage when the individual is facing the situation of basic conceptual change in relation to property, ownership of natural resources etc. economic infrastructure in this context should comprise stabilisation of their de facto rights in a form of acceptable in the new system;
4. Exploiting elements who do not contribute to the local economy, have to be put down with a heavy hand. Elimination of exploitation has to be a priority item on the agenda;
5. Administrative unpreparedness has appeared to be an important constraint in purposive utilisation of resources. There have been savings even in the limited resources allocation for the sub-plan areas and funds have not been fully utilised. Suitable arrangements for effective implementation are urgently required, least unregulated expenditure becomes counter productive;
6. There has been no conscious approach to train the tribals in the new skills which would be needed for new programmes;
7. There is lack of a systematic and continuous appraisal of the situation with reference to the clear policy frame and administrative goals which may be set in this regard. There is a critical gap in the Constitutional Scheme which makes it virtually in operative. This gap can be filled only if the executive keeps the Governor and the President informed about the situation in the tribal areas and the development of the tribal communities.[62]

Reports of Commissioner Scheduled Caste and Scheduled Tribes

Commissioner for scheduled Castes and Schedule Tribes under the constitutional provision (Article 338), has so far submitted 29th reports to the President of India during the last 43 years. All these reports have critically examined the tribal development situation in each state throwing light on constitutional provisions effective legislation, local framework, protective and the developmental aspects adopted for Scheduled Tribes. In the 29th report (1987-89), the Commissioner for Schedule Castes and Schedule Tribes has presented a very sad picture of the current status of the tribals and the tribal development programmes in his letter addressed to the President of India. It is quoted from that letter as under (1987-89 : V & VI).

(i) "The honour and dignity of a persons is dependent on his right to manage the system. The condition of the members of the ... Scheduled Tribes on all these counts was deplorable from the very beginning. Hard work fell in their share, while command over resources was enjoyed by others. But after independence these people were rendered still more helpless and vulnerable in the face of unholy collusion between the system and the more powerful groups";

(ii) "The biggest irony with regard to dignity and prestige of a people in our country is that the condition of the tribal communities who are most conscious about self-respect and honour, is the worst. These communities have become completely helpless in the face of the omnipotent system on account of the 'criminalisation' of their social and economic system itself, denial of their rights over resources and non-recognition of their traditional self governing systems. The forests are the property of the State, therefore, it is an offence for the tribal who has been living in those very forests for the ages to make a living from these forests. His very presence in the forests is against the law. If a tribal enters the forest with his bow and arrows, it is an offence. If his cattle as usual graze in the forest they are taken to a kine house. If he takes his traditional brew after worshipping his Gods or in social functions according to his tradition he still becomes a law breaker. He is branded as an offender in all matters concerning his social and economic life only because the law is against him. The criminalisation of the entire communities in the tribal areas is the darkest plot on the liberal tradition of our country."

(iii) "And the saddest thing is that all this has happened and is happening in the name of principles, claiming authority from the Constitution and the law. That is not all, this is being done by a system, which considers itself to be a symbol of justice, rationality and modernity. Those who have been given the responsibility under the constitution for correcting this anomolious situation have almost no realisation about that responsibility. The first attempt of the system ordinarily is to assert its own position as right and to prove that the others are on the wrong. It is expected that the tribal society should change and adopt itself in accordance with the frame on the modern system. And, finally an attempt is made to convince the people that this is what development really is."

(iv) "Thus, firstly no action has been taken to correct this basic anomaly and even if some action is initiated one can never be sure as to where it might get stuck."

Planning Commission Working Group Report

After the adoption of tribal sub-plan strategy for the overall development of Schedule Tribes, the Planning Commission constituted its first Working Group for the period of 1978-83 and also for succeeding Sixth and Seventh Five Year Plans. These Working Groups have made assessment of tribal development for the period they have been constituted and gave guidelines, suggestions, recommendations to the Central Ministries of the Central Govt. and the State Govts. regarding strategy, administrative mechanism, financial framework, development programmes, protection and anti-exploitation measures, development of primitive tribal groups, priorities under the various sectoral programmes and the involvement of voluntary organisations for the task of tribal development.

State Committees and Commission

In the state of Madhya Pradesh to review the activities of tribal development, the following Commission/Council on the lines of the constitutional provision and under the agies of tribal development administration have been set up.

Tribal Advisory Council (TAC)

This Council has always been constituted under the Chairmanship of Chief Minister for the period of the State Assembly constitutionally functioned. The Minister, incharge Tribal Welfare Deptt. have acted as Vice-Chairman of the Council. Two third member of TAC belonged to Scheduled Tribes. The Principal Secretary/ Secretary of Tribal Welfare Deptt. have acted as Secretary. On matters related to the Scheduled Tribes of the state were referred to TAC by the State Governor. But in practice, constitutionally laid down procedure has never been followed in the State. Similarly, the Cabinet perhaps has ever given serious consideration to the recommendations of the TAC, but implemented in a adhock manner. Several examples can be quoted (Given in Chapter III).

Scheduled Caste and Scheduled Tribes Welfare Vidhan Sabha Samiti

This Samiti is constituted under the Chairmanship of a Member of Legislative Assembly (MLA) appointed by the Speaker of the State Assembly for the period the state assembly remains in existence constitutionally. The Samiti reviews the various policies framed for the welfare, development, and protection of the Scheduled Caste and Scheduled Tribes in the State. Besides, it also tours the tribal areas of the State and gives its recommendations on various policies, problems and programmes.

Since 1978 to 1990 the Committee has given twelve reports which contains several hundred recommendations related to the various departments of the State Govt. These recommendations cover variety of subjects related to the protection and development of Scheduled Tribes in the State. All the reports have been kept before the State Assembly. The First Report of the Committee was placed before the Assembly on 7th September 1978 and the last Report in 1990. In each Report, the Committee has reviewed the administrative working of those departments which have been important for the development of Scheduled Tribes viz.Agriculture and Allied Sectors, Education, Drinking Water, Health, Reservation of Posts, Veterinary, Rural Industry, Land Revenue, Road, Electricity, Home Panchayat and Social Welfare, Tribal Welfare, Excise, Cooperation and Housing and Environment. The Committee has also considered the various kind of problems faced by the development departments, while implementing the programmes in the tribal areas. The recommendations of the Committee more or less have contained the suggestions related to the problem operative and functional aspects of the department concerned, which may be summarised as under:

1. The major recommendations of the SC and ST Commission, G.O.I. made in the context of Scheduled Tribes of Madhya Pradesh should be placed before the State Assembly by the State Govt. (Tribal Welfare Deptt.) and appraise the State Assembly about the development programme, so that member of assembly could give their suggestions on the line of recommendations (First Report of the Committee 1978).
2. How and in what manner the educational programmes are to be implemented and how these programmes should be made attractive and inspiring to the Scheduled Tribes? (First Report—1978).
3. How to promote health and nutritional programmes in the tribal areas? (First Report—1978)?
4. Reservation in Services—What should be the proportion of posts to be reserved for Scheduled Tribes for various categories of posts in Govt. (Second Report—1982);
5. Distribution of Agricultural Lands to the Scheduled Tribes, programmes to get rid of indebtedness, atrocities, rehabilitation of displaced Scheduled Tribes and mode of payment of compensation (Third Report—1982);
6. Percentage flow to TSP from the State Plan, problem of employment, increase in rate of scholarship and stipend in the context of price escalation (Fourth Report—1983);
7. In its 11th Report (1987) the Committee has observed that:
   (a) State Govt. is not paying attention towards, the filling of reserved posts from the candidates of Schedule Tribes. The Committee took evidence of the Secretaries of Forest, School Education, Higher Education, Health Public Works, Housing &

Environment, Excise, Cooperation and Electricity Departments and found that several posts in all the categories are lying vacant. The Committee has expressed its displeasure over the carelessness of the departments.

(b) The Committee has been critical about the replies given by the departments. It has observed that assurances had been given by the departments to fetch the information in time required by the committee, but failed.

Over all the review of the performances of the Committee reveals that this Committee has not been effective. The departments have taken the recommendations of the Committee in a routine manner.

Adivasi Vikas Neet Nirdharan Ayog: (High Power Commission)

In May, 1966 a tribal revolt took place in Baster district of the State, Maharaja of Bastar, The Senior Bhanjdeo, (The priest of Danteshwari Devi and beloved king of Erstwhile Bastar State) had developed political enimity with the State Govt. and became the victim of political controversy emerged at that time. A stage came when Bhanjdeo organised the tribal force to defend his life and in a police encounter, he was killed. State Govt. constituted a Commission under the Chairmanship of Justice B.L. Pandey to enquire this episode. The Commission realised that the tribal unrest should be dealt with care and approach to tribal development should be well thought of. Therefore, the Commission recommended that the State Tribal Development Policy should be re-examined in the context of Bastar revolt and the tribal scenario of the State and the programme formulated and tribal administration should be re-structured accordingly. In the persuance of such recommendation, the State Govt. constituted a six member Commission known as Adivasi Vikas Neet Nirdharan Ayog in the year 1971-72. Finally Late Shiv Kumar Pagare was made the Chairman of the Ayog (popularly known as Pagare Commission). The main objective of this Commission was to suggest a policy for tribal development covering the protective and anti-exploitive measures and the developmental aspects of the Scheduled Tribes and Scheduled Areas of the State.

The Pagare Commission submitted its Report in 1973 to the State Govt. But the recommendations of this Commission never saw the light of the day and thus, the Constitution of the Commission proved invain.

The Madhya Pradesh Anusuchit Jati, Anusuchit Janjati Tatha Pichhada Varg Ayog

The Madhya Pradesh Anusuchit Jati, Anusuchit Janjati Tatha Pichhada Varg Ayog, Adhiniyam, 1983 was promulgated. This Act came into force on the 16th of August, 1983. For the purpose of the Act, the State Govt. has constituted the Madhya Pradesh Anusuchit Jati, Anusuchit Janjati Tatha Pichhada Varg Ayog in 1984 constituting of five members of whom, at least one has been from the Scheduled Tribes, Scheduled Castes and Backward Classes. The one of the members of the Commission has been appointed as the Chairman of the Commission for the period of three years. This is a permanent State Commission under the administrative control of the State General Administration Deptt. (G.A.D.)

Under the Act, the function and duties of the Commission have been laid down. The main function of the Commission is to "act as Watch-Dog for the protection afforded to the member of SC, ST and OBC under the Constitution". Besides, inbrief, the Commission is to see:

(i) proper and timely implementation of programmes as envisaged in the 'Twenty Point Programmes' for SC, ST and BC announced by the Prime Minister of India on 14th January 1982;

(ii) to suggest improvement in programmes and plans of the State Govt. for upliftment of SC, ST and BC;

(iii) to entertain complaints as to the improper implementation of enactments, programmes, plans and in matter of reservation of seats;

(iv) to submit a report to the State Govt. containing a detailed account of its activities in a year at the end of the financial year.

Regarding the duties of the Commission, it is laid down in the Act, "It shall be the duty of the Commission at such intervals as may be prescribed to investigate the manner in which the protections in relation to Scheduled Castes, Scheduled Tribes and Backward Classes have been implemented and the benefits which have accrued to the member of such Castes, Tribes or Classes thereby and to make report thereof to the State Government.

Under the Act, the Commission has been given two wide powers:

(a) Commission may call information and report from the State Development Department;

(b) Commission may enquire into and report to the state Government on any matter related to SC, ST and OBC.

The Commission has submitted six reports to the State General Administration Department till 1990. Out of these reports, only first report could be placed before the State Assembly so far. Under the Clause 15(1) and (2) of the Act, the State Govt. have not taken action and given guidelines to the concerned. No effective steps and measures have been taken on the recommendations of the report. The remaining reports are also lying ineffective. The State General Administration Deptt. had sent all the recommendations of each report to the concerned development deptts. for comments.

In real sense the enactment of the Madhya Pradesh Anusuchit Jati, Anusuchit Janjati Tatha Pichhda Varg Ayog Act, 1983 has been proved dormant. It appears that for the fulfilment of the political commitment, this Act and the Commission, under the Act have been constituted. It is evident from this fact that the post of the ST members has been remained vacant from 1986 to 1990. Under the clause 17 (1) of the Act, State Govt. have not issued any direction so far on the matter of policy etc.

The study of all the above mentioned reports and comments, thus reveals that during the period 1952 to 1970, the Commission and Committees appointed have tried to review the overall situation of the tribals and tribal areas at the National as well as at the State level. The Commissions/Committees appointed from 1970 and onward have not covered all the spheres of tribals. They have observed change in the pattern of the reporting on tribal development taken place. Full fledge Commissions and Committees for reviewing the entire tribal life and development aspects were not appointed (except Dhebor Commission). But small working groups and study groups have been formulated time to time to investigate and to recommend or suggest on particular aspect of tribal development.

The theme of all the Commission, Committees and the Study Groups has maintained the same wavelength laying focus on the following aspects of tribal development:

1. Official use and implementation of the constitutional provisions in real spirit in the interest of Scheduled Tribes;
2. The lack of political will and the administrative ineffectiveness have been largely responsible for slow pace of tribal development;
3. The relief against indebtedness and restoration of land in the tribals areas;
4. Strengthening the Cooperative and Credit and Marketing structure;
5. Well defined administrative arrangements and personnel policy for tribal areas;
6. Tribal's hold on natural resources: forest and land and with regard to minor forest produce and land holding system; and
7. Suitable development programmes at the grass root.

In case the total recommendations and suggestions would have been implemented in the right context, this could have definitely helped in changing the tribal scenario at the national level as well as in the state of Madhya Pradesh.

In case the total recommendations and suggestions would have implemented in the right context, this could have definitely helped in changing the tribal scenario at the national level as well as in the state of Madhya Pradesh.

In other words, these reports have laid down developmental philosophy for the tribals. The irony of the situation is that nc concerted efforts were made to translate these recommendations and suggestions into action. Even today, they are meaningful and of great use to the administrators and the planners.

REFERENCES

1. Gomango, Girdhar—*Constitutional Provisions for the Sch. Castes and Sch. Tribes*, 1992, p. 24.
2. Bhangage, N.P.—*Tribal Commissions and Committees*, 1993, p. 431.
3. *Ibid*, 1993, p. 405, 406.
4. *Ibid*, 1993, p. 406.
5. *Ibid*, 1993, pp. 412, 413.
6. *Ibid*, 1993, p. 7.
7. *Ibid*, 1993, p. 32.
8. *Ibid*, 1993, p. 26.
9. *Ibid*, 1993, p. 27.
10. *Ibid*, 1993, p. 432.
11. *Ibid*, 1993, p. 34.
12. *Ibid*, 1993, p. 36.
13. Ibid, 1993, p. 36.
14. *Ibid*, 1993, p. 36.
15. *Ibid*, 1993, pp. 38 and 39.
16. *Ibid*, 1993, pp. 44 and 45.
17. *Ibid*, 1993, p. 45.
18. *Ibid*, 1993, p. 79.
19. *Ibid*, 1993, p. 69.
20. *Ibid*, 1993, p. 80.
21. *Ibid*, 1993, p. 94.
22. *Ibid*, 1993, pp. 99 and 100.
23. *Ibid*, 1993, p. 159.
24. *Ibid*, 1993, p. 163.
25. *Ibid*, 1993, pp. 175 and 176.
26. *Ibid*, 1993, p. 433.
27. *Ibid*, 1993, p. 190.
28. *Ibid*, 1993, pp. 190 and 191.
29. *Ibid*, 1993, p. 192.
30. *Ibid*, 1993, p. 433.
31. *Ibid*, 1993, p. 434.

32. *Ibid*, 1993, p. 434.
33. *Ibid*, 1993, p. 206.
34. *Ibid*, 1993, p. 208.
35. *Ibid*, 1993, p. 209.
36. *Ibid*, 1993, p. 209.
37. *Ibid*, 1993, p. 211.
38. *Ibid*, 1993, p. 211.
39. *Ibid*, 1993, p. 215.
40. *Ibid*, 1993, p. 216.
41. *Ibid*, 1993, p. 217.
42. *Ibid*, 1993, pp. 217 and 218.
43. *Ibid*, 1993, p. 227.
44. *Ibid*, 1993, p. 435.
45. *Ibid*, 1993, p. 435.
46. *Ibid*, 1993, p. 252.
47. *Ibid*, 1993, p. 252.
48. *Ibid*, 1993, p. 260.
49. *Ibid*, 1993, p. 271.
50. *Ibid*, 1993, p. 271.
51. *Ibid*, 1993, p. 272.
52. *Ibid*, 1993, p. 272.
53. *Ibid*, 1993, p. 272.
54. *Ibid*, 1993, p. 272.
55. *Ibid*, 1993, p. 273.
56. *Ibid*, 1993, p. 276.
57. *Ibid*, 1993, p. 280.
58. *Ibid*, 1993, p. 287.
59. *Ibid*, 1993, p. 293.
60. *Ibid*, 1993, pp. 320 and 321.
61. *Ibid*, 1993, pp. 322 and 325.
62. *Ibid*, 1993, pp. 327 and 328.

3

Tribal Women and Educational Programmes

Dr. V.K. Srivastava

The importance of education for Tribal women can not be over emphasised. The Govt. of India, the State Governments and all non-Government, Agencies have taken up programmes for education of tribal women. A study has been done to ascertain the impact of these programmes on the literacy of tribal women during the period 1995-96 in Madhya Pradesh including Chhattisgarh by the author. In view of the vastness and lack of development in the tribal areas, the effort involved was great and the study confined to one district in each of the five cultural zones of Madhya Pradesh including Chhattisgarh. These districts have been Jhabua, Dhar, Betul, Bastar and Sarghuja (at present in Chhattisgarh State). A total of 200 families were covered, five in each of the four villages in 2 blocks of each selected district. Although the coverage was thin, yet some very pertinent findings have emerged.

The Philosophy of education advocates the full and balanced development of an individual, his or her personality. In the field of education the problem is most complex because education deals centrally with areas of values, understanding, tradition and habit in which changes are slow to emerge and difficult to demonstrate. Educators who implement the educational programmes have dual role to play in the society, particularly in the tribal society intent on rapid social change. In the first place they must be concerned about the contribution of education to development goals. This includes the analysis of social problems, and rethinking the basic values and structure of the society. It also includes the education and training of young people with the understanding attitudes, critical abilities and skill required to make most appropriate contribution to the rapid development of the society. The second role of educators is related to the first. They must introduce the kind of innovations that will transform educational institutions into dynamic, creative, self-reforming, organisations capable of responding to the development needs of the society and that is known about effective education.

Therefore, the educationist or the educational agencies have to take interest in the environing social, economical, political and democratic forms because of their impact on the individual. The over all progress and development of man and woman is an indicator of educational impact bringing change in their values, attitudes and aspirations. In other words, the effectiveness of the educational programmes can be correlated with success of economic development programmes, because the educational development programme will open the mind of the individual in terms of modern, cultural and traditional way of thinking. Improve the receptivity and awareness of the individual for further linkage.

The tribal scenario of India and particularly of old Madhya Pradesh reveals that education has hardly been a subject of importance for the tribal. During the British rule in India, no serious thinking was given for the educational, and for that matter even social and economic development for the tribal. As per 1931 Census the percentage of literacy amongst the tribal was as low as 0.7 compared to the general literacy rate of 8.3 corresponding figures of literacy amongst the tribal women being 0.2 per cent only as compared to the general female literacy rate 2.3 per cent. The percentage of literacy amongst the tribal of the Central Province and Barar (Present Madhya Pradesh) was only 0.5 and for female literacy was negligible. Because the educational grants for the tribal areas were mearge and with result the number of high schools, middle schools and primary schools were of course, negligible, if not all together zero. The main reason to this negligence was the

British policy which in generally had been providing protection to the tribals through isolation, resulting their exploitation at the hand of money lenders, feudal lords and contractors. The efforts of the Government was to provide smooth administration in the tribal areas than to ameliorating the conditions of the tribals. Though the British Govt. had appointed an officer on special duty Mr. W.G. Grigson in 1940 in then the Province of C.P. and Barar to investigate into the conditions of tribals. He made some useful suggestions viz. opening of schools, hostels, mid day meals and grant of scholarship and stipend, but nothing could be done.

After independence during all Five Year Plans, education in general, and tribal education in particular has been the priority of Central as well as the State Governments. The Constitution of India through Article 45 has laid down Free and compulsory education for all children upto age of 14 years as of the Directive Principles of State policy. The time frame for achieving this goal was mentioned in the Constitution as ten years (i.e. by 1960). Further, the Article 46 particularly lays emphasis for the promotion of educational and economic interest of Scheduled Tribe. Unfortunately, still we are far from reaching this goal.

The overall scenario of educational development emerged during the last fifty-five years reflects gender bias. The educational programmes have not contributed to the desired extent, but whatever have been the achievements, those have been more or less on male side. Females have been incidental in the process of educational planning. The global/national and the State level available information and Data portray that women in general and tribal women in particular are far behind in the educational ladder as compared to their male counterparts. The Draft Declaration Report of United Nations Organisation (1995 : 17) says, "that prevent, their full and equal participation. In a number of countries, the practice of parental sex selection, higher rates of mortality among very young girls and lower rates of school enrolment for girls as compared with boys suggest that 'Son preference' is curtailing the access of girl children to food. Education and health care and even life self'.

For the first time the National Educational Policy (NEP) was framed in 1968, which marked significant step forward in the history of education in post independent India. This policy was framed taking into consideration important aspects, which had been examined in depth by Commissions and Committees over a long period, both before and after independence, culminating in the Education Commission (1964-65). "The policy of 1968 aimed at promoting national progress creating a sense of common citizenship and culture and strengthening national integration. It laid down stress on the need for a radical reconstruction of education to improve its quality at all stages, much greater attention to science and technology, cultivation of moral values and a closer relation between education and the life of the people".

The 1968 National Policy on Education had recommended to review every five year of progress made in its implementation. But such reviews were not made till 1985. The New National Policy of Education was again framed in April 1986. For the first time this National Education Policy (NEP) laid emphasis on empowerment of women in general and educational improvement of Scheduled Tribes. This accorded priorities:

(i) Opening of Primary Schools in Tribal Areas;

(ii) Socio-cultural in the context of Scheduled Tribes;

(iii) Imparting educational training to educated Scheduled Tribes;

(iv) Tribal youth to take up teaching;

(v) Promoting residential issues;

(vi) Introducing incentive schemes;

(vii) Opening of non-formal educational centres; and

(viii) Curricular for Tribal students at all stages of education to create awareness.

The NEP was again reviewed and revised in 1992 laying educational development of Scheduled Tribes and their equalization with the non-Scheduled Tribe population at all stages of development and level of education. Besides, this has envisaged wide ranging action on a variety of issues and problems yet it has sought a convergence of such action to secure a total and co-ordinated impact. It has also reached beyond the education sector to link effectively with other sectors of social development to achieve quick and positive results. But the task of ensuring the effective implementation of the NEP, rested on the following factors:

1. Effective education planning and management system;
2. Effective decentralisation;
3. To evolve priorities and pursue objective oriented programmes;
4. Sound personal management system; and
5. Performance of routine task i.e. supply of text books, conduction of examinations and delivery of educational services etc.

The making the system work, NEP suggested that education needed to be managed in an atmosphere of utmost rigour, seriousness of purpose and at the same time of freedom essential for innovation and creativity, NPE also suggested the following strategies:

(i) a better deal to teachers with greater responsibility;

(ii) provision of improved student services and insistence of observance of acceptable norms of behaviour; and

(iii) provision of better facilities, institutions and creation of a system of performance appraisal of institutions according to the standards and norms set at the national or state level.

Soon after adoption of Programme of Action (POA) 1986, the Central Advisor Board of Education (CABE) had constituted Committees to recommend measures for toning up educational management, these committees prepared draft report for pursuing action with the states and other authorities concerned. However, due to frequent political changes, action could not be pursued on many of these initiatives.

However, in pursuance of this policy and based on the report of the committee appointed by the Human Resource Development (HRD) Ministry, GOI in 1990 and the recommendations of the CABE, minimum level if learning (MLL) have been laid down for the primary stage with the intention of reducing the curriculum load and making it more relevant and functional for those children who have no support for learning at home or outside the schools, who are not likely to avail of the opportunity of education beyond this stage and who must learn here what is required to sustain them throughout their lives and enable them to function in their world as socially useful and contributing individuals. Another important development was the World Conference on Education for All (EFA) held in March, 1990 in Jomtien, Thailand. The conference was organised by UNESCO, United Nations system and Several Donor Agencies. The conference adopted a declaration calling up all Member States and International Agencies to take effective steps for achieving Education for All (EFA) by the year AD 2000. The conference advocated a holistic concept on basic education in lieu of a sectoral approach segregating section like primary schooling, Non-formal education, Adult and continuing education in separate compartments. In order to harness increased donor interest in the basic education, as a result of the conference, it was decided to formulate comprehensive basic education project in educationally backward states. The framework for availing external assistance for basic education was involved at the 46th meeting of the CABE held on 8-9 March, 1991 and reiterated in the 47th Meeting of the CABE held on 5-6 May, 1992.

The fourth World Conference on women, held Beijing, China described the pathetic status of the women in general. The draft Declaration Report (1955 : 17) of United Nation Says, "Since 1975 significant knowledge and information has been generated about the status of women and the conditions which they live. Throughout their entire life cycle. Women's daily existence and long-term aspirations are restricted by discriminatory attitudes, unjust social and economic structure, lack of resource in most countries that prevent and full participation. "Girls of today are the women of tomorrow. The skills, ideas and energy of girls are vital for full attainment of the goals of equality, development and peace, (for girl to develop her full potential she needs to be nurtured in an enabling environment where her needs for survival, protection and development are met and her equal rights safeguarded). If women are to be equal partner with men, now is the time to recognise the human dignity and worth of the girl child and to ensure the full enjoyment of her human right and fundamental" ... "special measure must be taken to ensure that young women have the life skills necessary for action and effective participation in all levels if social cultural, political and economic leadership".

The Constitution Seventy Third (Amendment) Act, 1992 on Panchayat Raj envisages introduction of democratically elected bodies will be responsible for the economic, social and education development of all and have representation of tribal women. In the State of Madhya Pradesh under the State Panchayat Act, 1993 the Panchayat elections have been done in 1994 and accordingly, the administrative and financial powers and schemes of all the developments have been transferred to district, Janpad (Block) and village level.

The status of tribal women in the tribal society vis-à-vis to Indian society is altogether different. In the tribal society, tribal women is a main component of economic, social and magic religious activities. She runs the family. She manages domestic household activities, rear the child and outside the house, she also earns wages, collect fuel wood and minor forest produce, fetch water and look after the domestic animals. Thus, she discharges multiple roles and in overburdened with drudgery. The result of this overburdening is that women has low health status and often totally neglect herself, overall, inadequate attention to biological social and economic functions of tribal women is paid in the micro situation. These factors play important role to determine the status of the tribal woman which in true sense varies from one region to another region and from one tribal community another tribal community in Madhya Pradesh. Overall, the tribal women enjoy two kinds of status; the traditional status they have been given in their society and the status they have earned by upgrading their economic, social and literal achievements under various educational and other development programmes. It is regretting the hardly separate information/data is maintained to distinguish the performance of tribal women, so that one can highlight the socio-economic status of tribal women.

Though all the units of a tribal family contributes economically and socially to maintain the family. But it is the women in the family who is the central theme of whole affairs. There is a division of labour in the tribal society and different types of taboos have been attached to the women folk in day-to-day life. For example a women will not plough the field, during the period of menstruation, she will not touch anything within the walls of the house and does not discharge any of the household and outside activities.

Tribal women share more household, economic and social responsibilities than her male spouse. There are certain functions which are more and more discharged by the tribal women viz. witchcraft, weeding, preparation of seedlings and transplantation etc. In the weekly tribal markets, tribal women of all age groups sell all kinds of commodities in the market. Their exposure to forest, weekly markets and socio-religious functions is maximum. At the societal level, the economic participation of tribal women is maximum to improve the economy of the household. But as regards the inheritance of property of father or husband there is a certain built-in-discrimination against women in tribal society. For example, women are not entitled to any share of their father property. The customary law of some of the tribal communities viz. Pahari Korwa, Bhil, Oraon and Gonds excluded women from inheritance rights. Inheritance rights are restricted to male line. These customs are even enshrined in tenancy laws, wherever enacted and applicable to these community. This discrimination against women has harmful effect on their lives, rendering them economically and socially powerless and driving large of them into destitution.

As per 1991 census, 29.60 per cent Scheduled Tribes are literate in India and out of it, percentage of tribal male literacy is 40.65 and female literacy is 18.19. In Madhya Pradesh percentage of tribal literacy is 21.54 for males and females, it is 32.16 per cent and 10.73 respectively. Thus the level of literacy of tribal women is poor.

The proportional increase in the literacy is poor. The proportion of literates in the state has risen among the tribal during 1971-81 from 7.62 per cent to 10.68 per cent and 21.54 per cent in 1991 census. In case the female literacy is compared to other States, as per 1981 census, Madhya Pradesh has been placed third lowest in the rank. First is Rajasthan (1.20 per cent) and second in Andhra Pradesh (3.04 per cent). Thus, the tribal female literacy has been low in general, but its rural segment is extremely poor. As per 1961 census, the tribal rural female literacy was 0.93 per cent, which rose to 2.05 in 1971 census, 3.4 per cent in 1981 census, and 7.50 per cent in 1991 census. Though during last four decades, the rate of progress of tribal literacy in amongst the female population at the national and in the state of old Madhya Pradesh can be seen from the table given below.

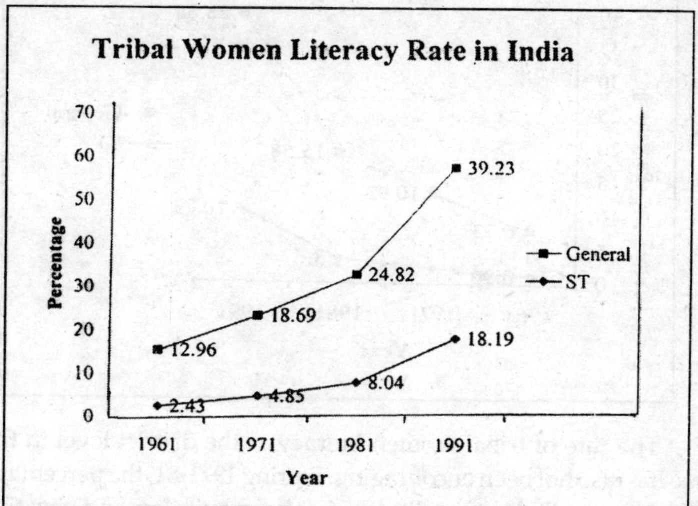

Table—3.1 Tribal Literacy Rate (In Percentage)

S. No.	Year	*India*			*Madhya Pradesh*		
		General	*ST*	*Difference*	*General*	*ST*	*Difference*
1.	1961	24.03	6.28	17.75	17.13	5.11	12.02
	Male	34.45	10.01	24.44	27.03	9.24	17.79
	Female	12.96	2.43	10.53	6.73	0.96	5.77
2.	1971	29.45	11.3	18.15	22.14	7.62	14.52
	Male	39.45	17.63	21.82	32.7	13.05	19.65
	Female	18.69	4.85	13.84	10.92	2.18	8.74
3.	1981	36.23	16.35	19.88	27.87	10.68	17.19
	Male	46.89	24.52	22.37	39.49	17.74	21.75
	Female	24.82	8.04	16.78	15.58	3.6	11.98
4.	1991	52.21	29.6	22.61	44.2	21.54	22.66
	Male	64.13	40.65	23.48	58.42	32.16	26.26
	Female	39.23	18.19	21.04	28.85	10.73	18.12

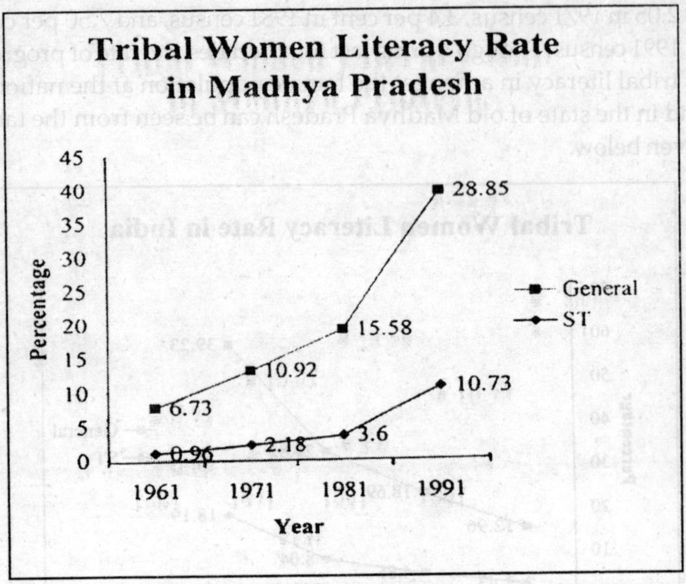

The rate of tribal women literacy at the district level in the state has also not been encouraging. During 1971-81, the percentage difference of tribal women literacy has been quite low and negative in six districts which includes one partial tribal district i.e. Sidhi. Similarly, during 1981-91, the positive difference (above state average i.e. 10.68 per cent) in the rate of tribal districts Balaghat (12.5 per cent) and Chhindwada (11.86 per cent). A District wise percentage of Scheduled Tribe literacy is appended at Appendix No. 1.

Tribe wise literacy rate is available for 1981 census. The rate of literacy of women in tribal community is extremely poor. Average women tribal literacy for the State has been 3.60. The highest tribal women literacy has been in the Andh Tribal Community having few hundred of population. The percentage of women literacy in the tribe has been 13.70 and next to it has been Halba Tribal women. i.e. 13.96 per cent. Among the 8 tribal communities the percentage of tribal women literacy is zero.

In the field of adult education, the position is not encouraging. During the period 1981 to 1990, 42.65 per cent adult population has been found successful in the adult education programme. Out of it, percentage of tribal adults has been only 13.12 per cent and among them, the percentage of female adult has been estimated to 5.50 per cent.

Education in India and in the State of Madhya Pradesh is largely a budget based system where efficiency is rated by ability to 'Consume' budget and to demand more. This is the pattern which has been followed by the State Government. The funds budgeted for the educational programmes have been consumed by the class of urban population. The tribal/rural population could hardly get their full share. Thus, the whole education system, including the curriculum, the text books, the reading materials, the educational group and the management system, is addressed to and focussed on non-tribal middle class urban population which ethnocentrically is called the mainstream. Since the tribals are expected to join the mainstream, education is also conceived as mechanism to enable them to join mainstream and, therefore, incongruity and mismatch between educational system catering to the mainstream and the culture of the tribals is rarely noticed. This however is a very significant factor for low participation of tribal in general and tribal women in particular in total educational process. Therefore, the type of educational ambit created within the limited approach and the paucity of funds, the tribal population lagged behind in the field of education and have subjected to exploitation.

A brief review of the management of the primary educational system in Madhya Pradesh reveals that after the reorganisation of the States in 1956, a common integrated system of education was adopted and the entire system was put under the control of State Education Department. But gradually it was realised that the tribal education needs special focus in order to run the educational programmes in full swing in the vast tribal areas of the State. Therefore, in 1964 a policy decision was taken that the educational institutions located in the tribal areas of the State will be managed by the State Tribal Welfare Department, who will look after the special needs and problems of the tribal population. Since then, school education in the State is managed primarily by the School Education Department for the general areas and Tribal and Scheduled Caste Welfare Department for the tribal areas. Policy matters are decided by the department of School Education headed by a Secretary. Implementation of policies and programmes is done by the Directorate of Public Instruction. About 21 per cent schools in the State are being run by the Tribal Welfare Department headed by the Principal Secretary at the Government level and Commissioner, Tribal Development as Head of Department. About 7.6 per cent of the schools in the State are run by private agencies of which nearly 22 per cent receives grant-in-aid from the State Government and unaided schools follow their own pattern. The Education Department has the power to maintain education standards in these institutions by inspecting them and giving recognition.

There have been in all 71300 primary schools, in the old State of Madhya Pradesh. *The management system of these schools is as under:

Management of Schools

S. No.	*Name of the Department/Management*	*Percentage of Schools*
1.	Schools Education Department	72%
2.	Tribal Welfare Department	21%
3.	Local Bodies but the Employees are Government Servants	13% (include in 72%)
4.	Private Managements	7%
5.	School Receiving aid from the State Government	20% (of the 7%)

Source: School education department.

To associate the local communities with its activities and to have public administration in its development, each school has a School Development Committee. It comprises official and non-official members.

Non formal education programme was taken up in the State in 1975-76 as a part of strategy to achieve the universalisation of Elementary Education. The important features of the programme are:

(*i*) Common syllabus both for formal and non-formal education with condensation of 5 year stage curriculum into 18 units for NFE students;

* At present total number of Govt. Primary School is 55,888 in M.P.

(ii) Common accreditation scheme; and

(iii) Transferability of students from one system to another.

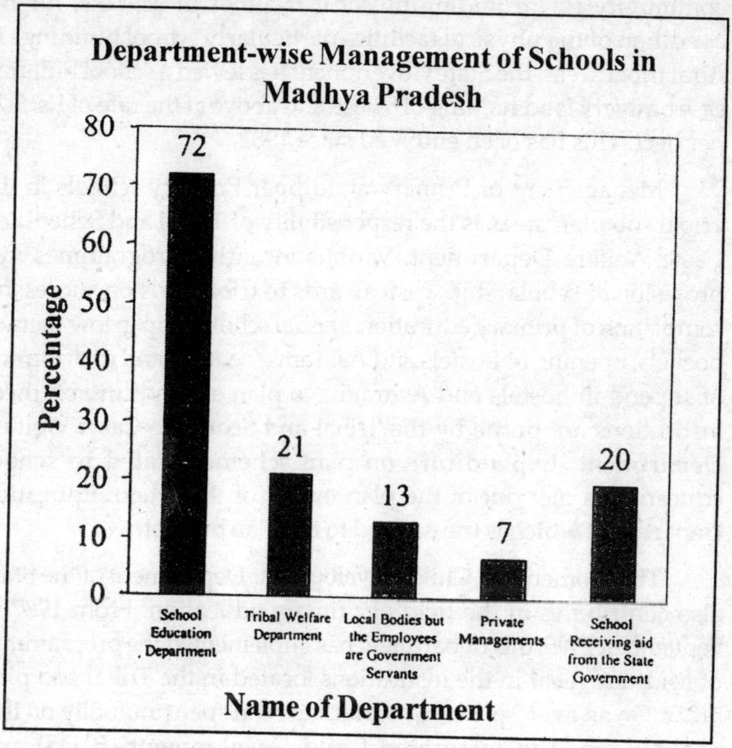

Non-formal centres have been opened in urban slums as well as in rural and tribal areas. About 31230 centres were running in the State in 1994. There are two types of centres, one is exclusively for girls, and other is common for boys and girls.

Common centres are assisted by the Central Government on 40-60 basis, while 70 per cent grant is received from GOI for girls, centres sanctioned exclusively for girls is 16796, while sanctioned number of common centres is 17824. (Source— School Education Department).

About 93.8 per cent of the primary schools in the State are almost fully funded by the Government and only 6.2 per cent are private unaided schools. These unaided schools are concentrated in the urban areas.

The non-official members of School Development Community of each primary school is authorised to collect money from the local community for providing physical facilities in schools, for the condition of the physical facilities particularly school buildings in rural tribal areas, the State Government has levied a school building case on every land holding of 8 hect. and above at the rate of Rs. 3.75 per hect. This has been enforced since 1982.

Management of Primary and upper Primary schools in the Tribal sub plan areas is the responsibility of Tribal and Scheduled Caste Welfare Department. Various incentive programmes viz. provision of scholarship, cash awards to tribal girls on successful completion of primary education, special scholarship in low literacy pockets, opening of hostels and Ashrams/schools and distribution of stipend in hostels and Ashram. No plan expenditure on these institutions are borne by the Tribal and Schedule Caste Welfare Department. Expenditure on plan scheme related to school education is met out of the plan outlay of the school Education Department which is transferred to the plan budget.

The Women and Child Development Department of the State also contributes in the field of primary education. From 1987 to September, 1995, this department has implemented the programmes of Mid-day meal in the institutions located in the Tribal sub plan areas. On an average Rs. 1006 lakh has been spent annually on this programme. The Integrated Child Development (ICDS) and Balwadis are also being run by this department. Now, mid day meal scheme is being implemented by the Panchayats in their respective villages.

Under the scheme of Jawahar Rojgar Yojana, Department of Rural Development, gets funds, some of which are used for the construction of primary school buildings. In 1991-92, 1500 primary school buildings were constructed in rural/tribal areas under this programme. From 2nd October, 1995, the mid-day meal programme is being implemented as per guidelines given by Government of India. The programme is financially assisted by GOI and jointly implemented by the department of Rural Development and Tribal and Scheduled Caste Welfare of the State Government. The position of Department structure relating to Elementary Education and Allied sector in Madhya Pradesh is shown in chart in No. 1.

With the introduction of National Policy of Education (NPE) 1986 many schemes have been launched in the State with the assistance of GOI. Some schemes in the filed of primary education are: (i) Operation Blackboard, (ii) Non-formal Education, (iii) Educational Technology, (iv) Establishment of District Institutes of Education and Training (DIET). Since beginning, Adult Education had been the responsibility of the State Social Welfare Department, from 1994 and onward this responsibility has been given to State School Education Department under the Rajiv Gandhi Literacy Mission.

Under the policy of Universalisation of Primary Education (UPE), an integrated programme of Universalisation of Primary Education (UPE) in 19 districts (seven are tribal districts) of Madhya Pradesh, with the assistance from under their District Primary Education Programme (DPEP) has been launched in 1993. The ratio of State to Central of DPEP has been fixed at 15 : 85, Five more tribal districts have also been included under DPEP.

The Primary and secondary data which have been made available reveals that the Education Management System (EMS) is yet to come up on the lines of Tribal way of life and culture. Because in devising the educational management system in the tribal areas of the State, the model has been adopted of general nature. The irony of the situation is that no suitable educational ambit could be evolved for the tribal communities on the line of their socio-cultural milieu. Therefore, Education for the tribal people, as for any one else in India, has today become a matter of great importance. Among various development schemes of the State and Central Government, Educational schemes are very important from the point of view of the various changes they bring in the life of the tribal community. It is useful for any national as well as State Development plans to know the actual effects it brings about and also to know whether these very one are wanted to have.

The Human Development Report of Madhya Pradesh (1998) has revealed that over all position of female literacy, child infant mortality rate (IMRO), adjusted per capita income and level of rural poverty is poor and needs careful planning and huge investment with effective implementation of the human resource oriented development programmes.

Findings and Recommendations

On the academic forum there has always been hue and cry to pay attention to raise the tribal women's literacy at the national and the State level. Therefore, all the time, it has been thought that it is useful for any national as well as State Education Development plan to know the actual effects they bring about and also to know whether these very one are wanted to have. The overall review of educational scenario at the national as well as in the State of Madhya Pradesh reveals that tribal woman could not be placed on the ladder of higher literacy. Women in general and particularly women in tribal setting have always been side tracked and let behind in the field of education. Tribal women are far behind in the field of education. Tribal women are far behind in the race of literacy. During last five decades, the percentage of tribal women literacy could be raised to 18.19 per cent (1991) at the national level and 10.73 per cent (1991) in the State of Madhya Pradesh. In the context of rural/ tribal areas, it is estimated to be around 12 per cent at the national level and 7 per cent in the State.

References

Several evaluation studies done during last decade have revealed that the impact of education on the growth of tribal literacy, specially the tribal female literacy has been extremely slow (Nail 1969, Rathaiah 1977, Tappò 1979, 1987, Pathy and Satpahty 1989, Reddy 1991). The causation of educational backwardness has been investigated by using secondary sources of data (NIEPA, 1986 and through survey studies focusing on women in general (Upadhya 1983) and tribal women in specific (Chauhan 1989) bringing to the floor the existing social realities acting as barriers to the educability of women in general and tribal women in particular. The 28th report (1988-89) of the Commissioner for SC and ST is also critical about the impact of educational programmes on the ST females. "Scheduled Tribe females have not received the benefit of the educational inputs and also continue of face deprivation of most."

The broad backdrop of the tribal education presents that the tribal areas have been extremely backward. There has been a complete neglect in the position of educational facilities in these areas during the British rule mainly because of their State of relative isolation. The formal education started after independence. But in tribal areas of the State this start delayed due to several constraints. The population is sparse and the habitations are scattered and small with poor communication because of natural barriers like forests, hills and rivers. The Government targets are set in terms of a primary school in every village having a population of 200 or more, when applied in the context of a tribal village, many of which have less than 200 people, a large number are ineligible for a primary school. The content, curricula and textbooks are not related to the local culture, environment and life of tribal people. Another problem related to education of tribal girls is the low enrolment and large number of dropouts. Considering the magnitude of the problem and its effects on the socio-economic life of the tribals, the National Policy of Education (NPE 1968 modified in 1986 and 1992) laid great emphasis on opening and upgrading of educational residential institutions, specially in the context of tribal culture and way of life.

On the eve of Fifth Five Year Plan, the concept of Tribal sub-plan has been introduced and under the tribal sub-plan strategy the tribal education had to be boosted by separating tribal education under the management of Tribal Welfare Department.

Construction of School Buildings has been undertaken on a priority basis under the normal funds for education as well as under the Special Local Development Funds and Tribal Welfare Schemes etc. There has also been stress on residential schools called "Ashram Schools", where education upto middle standard is supposed to be tagged along with intensive vocational training in agriculture, spinning, weaving etc. Various incentives are offered. All education in tribal areas is now free. Two sets of clothes and books. Copies and pencils are supplied. Mid-day meal are also provided free to all primary school children.

"Earn while you learn" schemes have also been started in some schools in bigger villages. The idea has been to allow students to work and earn while studying. They make chalk sticks, mats, small furniture and girls knot woollen pullovers. The students are paid according to the output.

The sub-plan also lays greater emphasis on women education in tribal areas. Some schools are reserved for girls only and there are residential facilities available for girls in bigger villages.

Under "Operation Blackboard" started in Seventh Plan period (1985-1990), the following facilities were to be provided:

(i) Provision of two reasonably large rooms usable in all weathers, with separate toilet facilities for boys and girls.

(ii) Provision of at least two teachers, one of them a woman in every primary schools.

(iii) Provision of complete teaching material including blackboard, maps, charts, toys, library equipments for work experience.

In this background a study was undertaken by the either to ascertain the impact of tribal educational programmes on the development of tribal women's literacy in the State of Madhya Pradesh. The main objectives is to study the various educational programmes and to the extent they have been successful to promote general awareness and rate of literacy among the tribal women. The universe of the study has been 40 villages covering 200 tribal households falling in 10 blocks of 5 tribal districts namely, Jhabua, Dhar, Betul, Bastar and Surguja.

The study reveals that despite all these efforts the coverage of population and area by schools is still inadequate. Primary schools are still not within reach of tribal girls in the tribal girls in the tribal areas. According to the 4th All India Education Survey, only 83 per cent of tribal population has been covered by primary schools with in one kilometer of their habitation. At the secondary level only 51.9 per cent of the ST population has a secondary school available within 8 km. (According to the norms of the Government, there should be a secondary school within a radius of 8 km.) Although the rate of growth of tribal women literacy has increased, it is still far below the State level. Also enrolment amongst tribal girls has not increased with the increase of level of education. It has been found that economic and social factors are primarily responsible for tribal girls not going to school. Despite the fact that several incentives in the form of books, meals, cash payments, scholarships and stipends given, but the implementation of the schemes at the grassroot level is not carried out properly. Often stipends and scholarships are not disbursed till the middle of the session, forcing the poor students (who could not maintain themselves) to drop out. Ashrams/residential schools have been opened to attract large number of tribal girls. However, the rate of stipends/scholarship have been found to be inadequate till 1994. The impact of education has not been felt as it has not led to employment or created scope for self employment to Scheduled Tribe women. This is mainly due to neglect of vocational training i.e. in carpentry, cottage industries etc. which can make the Scheduled Tribes girls skilled for certain trades. This has not been given due importance.

Findings

The major reasons for dropout are:

(a) The girl child being required to help at home;

(b) Lack of interest in education. Economic deprivation of tribals does not allow the smallest investment on education. Teachers who are mostly from non-tribal communities are often indifferent and lack sympathetic attitude towards the tribals. For those tribal children who do attend schools, the quality of education received is of low standard. Little attention has been paid to school buildings, play grounds, libraries and laboratories.

Teachers are found to be insufficiently trained and motivated. Teachers who are, by and large from non-formal areas and urban background, are unwilling to work in tribal areas, where the basic facilities of life which they are so used to are not available. Lack of suitable residential accommodation has been important demotivating factor.

The analysis of the data in the respective chapters of the report based on the secondary data and empirical findings has reflected that specific attention has not been paid towards the development of Scheduled Tribal women's literacy in the State. The tribal women have lost their individual identity in the crowd of general women. The formal education programmes have been implemented in routine manner. Therefore, the literacy of tribal women could not increase to the desired extent. Tribal women has always been incidental in the process. As regards the non-formal education the level of awareness has not reached to that extent that they could earn their livelihood in a better way or approach to the self employment programmes. Still they have been placed at the low key in the process of development. Whatever development programmes are being implemented by various development department, no separate account or data is maintained, which could indicate their level of participation and social alleviation in their society. The employment exchange of all the sample districts have not maintained separate figures giving the information that how many tribal women have been employed in various Government Organisation in the district. Such information is also not available even at the State level.

The sample study has revealed that about 24 per cent tribal women fall in the age group of 18 to 30 years. Out of this female lot, 15 per cent are working as a part time in organisation like. Anganwadi, teachers, and Dai/Medical Educator in Jhabua and Dhar districts. It is observed that in terms of educational and job participations as elsewhere, gender inequalities persists. Gender discrimination in its various facets is at work in putting girls out of schools before they are due to leave. This relative deprivation is a blockade for ST women's access to human development which mainly includes education, health and socio-economic components. The factors responsible are:

1. The high attrition rates for Scheduled Tribe girl students barring them to go for higher education;
2. Attrition in access to education i.e. lowering of levels of awareness on issues such as, medical education which it self is a tool for empowerment and better livelihood; and
3. Gender attrition in education which has implications for women's awareness of their legal and political rights.

Under the total literacy campaign massive efforts have been made to cover the women folk. With the result an atmosphere is being created to the level of consciousness, so that each woman is aroused to the extent that non is left to take benefit of the programmes. To make this campaign successful various kinds of approach and methodology have been developed. For the official and non-official are being involved and a management system is being developed. The District Education Officer is the nodal source of programme implementation and monitoring in the district with regard to all government sponsored education activities. The total literacy programme and District Primary Education Programme (DPEP) are at starting point. The results could be seen after five years.

The newly created Three-Tier Panchayat Raj System is being geared up in the State by transferring certain official powers and schemes at district, Janpad (Block) and Gram Panchayat levels. But the whole process is at the formative stage. It will take its own time to time give results.

In brief, the study indicates that the impact of formal and non-formal mode of education on the development of tribal women's literacy could not be displayed in-terms of functional output i.e. satisfactory growth of literacy rate, participants in development programmes, employment, higher income and enterprising output etc. Thus, the following trends have been emerged out of this study:

1. All the villages and habitations do not have schools within reasonable walking distance;
2. Small sparsely populated hilly and different areas of habitation make access more difficult;
3. Inadequate participation due to illiteracy of parents;
4. Education being not related to nee of tribal women's life style. Education Management System (EMS) has yet to come up to have positive impact on tribal women's literacy;
5. Due to lack of proper and effective educational monitoring system, the achievement are low;
6. Economic constraints—presents being economically weak do not like to part with their female children by

sending them to schools, instead they prefer to engage them in house hold works, viz. agriculture operations and collections of forest produce. They also feel difficulty in purchasing, books, stationery uniform and arranging transport facilities for the school going children;

7. Malnutrition and frequent intermittent illness of tribal girls leads to continuous absenteeism from schools;
8. Socio-cultural factors: Linguistic differences, gender disparity and lack of sensitiveness towards education; and
9. Non-formal system being not flexible to fix learning hours in accordance with the facility of learners.

Recommendations

1. To develop region and tribal community wise educational programmes looking to the regional disparities and response of each tribal community living at different socio-economic stages in the state.
2. To improve the implementation of existing incentives scheme for tribal girls by proving adequate funds and strength to education management system.
3. Providing educational opportunities within a reasonable distance to all the tribal girls and illiterate tribal women.
4. Alternative arrangements are necessary for those tribal girls who cannot come to schools because of physical barriers.
5. It must be ensured that every girl child gets as easy access to school or alternative education system.
6. Local Youth and adults preferable women should be entrusted with the responsibility for/of looking after the educational needs of the village. They should be managed and looked after preferably by a locally selected tribal women worker and in some cases by a male workers.
7. Non-formal education centres should be set up in areas where opening of new schools is not possible.

8. The system of peripatetic teacher can also be adopted at such places where there are no facilities of education or where people want to learnt at the place their work.
9. Girl's Ashram Schools should be opened in more numbers for sparsely populated areas.
10. Appropriate arrangements for the migratory tribal population should be made Location wise non-formal centres can be more useful methods for such communities. Specially trained teachers and self-learning models can be developed for migratory tribal populations.
11. The curriculum for the age group 4-11 should be based on skills and joyful activities to attract tribal girls for coming to school/NFE centres.
12. The system of continuing education to upgrade skills of tribal girls and knowledge should be created.
13. Curriculum for middle and secondary level should be redesigned with greater emphasis on vocational education.
14. Schools hours and vacations to be determined according to local requirements.
15. Participation and involvement of the community in deciding locations of schools, ensuring enrolment, retention of tribal girls of school going age group and resource management.

At last it can be concluded by quoting the observations made by late Dr. S. Radha Krishnan, the former President of India and eminent educationist that if general education had to be limited to men and women than opportunity should be given to women, because that it would pass on to the next generation. Our future strategy for improving the literacy and education of tribal women should, therefore, aim at attacking the tribal Women's Literacy as its first priority.

APPENDIX—I

Statement Showing Districtwise Literacy in the Old State of Madhya Pradesh including Chhattisgarh During 1971, 1981 and 1991

(Ftg. in Percentage)

Name of State/ District	Scheduled Tribe									Percentage Difference					
	Male	Female	Total	Male	Female	Total	Male	Female	Total	Year – 1981-1971			Year – 1991-1981		
	1971			1981			1991			Male	Female	Total	Male	Female	Total
1	2	3	4	5	6	7	8	9	10	11	12	13	14	15	16
M.P.	13.05	2.18	7.62	17.74	3.60	10.68	32.16	10.73	21.54	4.69	1.42	3.06	14.42	7.13	10.86
Morena	3.43	0.13	1.84	5.29	0.46	2.94	12.11	1.43	7.02	1.86	0.33	1.10	6.82	0.97	4.08
Bhind	14.82	0.96	8.38	25.69	2.89	15.19	44.38	14.14	30.99	10.87	1.93	6.81	18.69	11.25	15.80
Gwalior	6.01	0.27	3.24	13.14	4.31	8.88	27.57	10.07	19.45	7.13	4.04	5.64	14.43	5.76	10.57
Datia	2.70	0.00	1.38	5.53	0.84	3.32	18.49	6.60	13.05	2.83	0.84	1.94	12.96	5.76	9.73
Shivpuri	2.76	0.16	1.49	4.52	0.20	2.41	11.28	1.55	6.57	1.76	0.04	0.92	6.76	1.35	4.16
Guna	2.16	0.03	1.16	4.46	0.25	2.43	11.20	1.94	6.79	2.30	0.22	1.27	6.74	1.69	4.36
Tikamgarh	8.69	0.50	4.75	5.07	0.32	2.77	19.10	6.40	13.03	-3.62	-0.18	-1.98	14.03	6.08	10.26
Chhatarpur	2.42	0.34	1.41	4.19	0.39	2.37	15.05	3.41	9.54	1.77	0.05	0.96	10.86	3.02	7.17
Panna	6.15	0.54	3.38	8.48	0.77	4.69	17.75	4.36	11.26	2.33	0.23	1.31	9.27	3.59	6.57
Satna	6.50	0.49	3.51	8.96	0.62	4.89	21.37	3.89	12.96	2.46	0.13	1.38	12.41	3.27	8.07

(Contd...)

1	2	3	4	5	6	7	8	9	10	11	12	13	14	15	16
Rewa	4.96	0.29	2.67	7.26	0.43	3.92	22.98	3.88	13.89	2.30	0.14	1.25	15.72	3.45	9.97
Shahdol	11.55	1.02	6.32	13.90	1.34	7.56	28.44	6.32	17.55	2.35	0.32	1.34	14.54	4.98	9.89
Sidhi	7.59	0.70	4.19	9.42	0.54	5.05	21.07	3.23	12.49	1.83	-0.16	0.86	11.65	2.69	7.44
Mandsaur	3.93	0.61	2.34	9.63	1.07	5.54	26.11	5.61	16.29	5.70	0.46	3.20	16.48	4.54	10.75
Ratlam	4.01	0.71	2.37	8.63	0.98	4.85	20.54	4.50	12.66	4.62	0.27	2.48	11.91	3.52	7.81
Ujjain	17.69	4.58	11.25	22.71	3.57	13.44	38.41	11.68	25.69	5.02	-1.01	2.19	15.70	8.11	12.25
Jhabua	4.41	0.60	2.53	6.84	1.38	4.11	16.95	4.68	10.87	2.43	0.78	1.58	10.11	3.30	6.76
Dhar	9.04	0.64	4.88	9.83	1.19	5.53	24.75	7.38	16.17	0.79	0.55	0.65	14.92	6.19	10.64
Indore	19.19	6.70	13.70	16.93	5.12	11.32	35.39	15.55	26.04	-2.26	-1.58	-2.38	18.46	10.43	14.72
Dewas	7.39	0.12	3.84	9.56	0.87	5.31	24.53	6.11	15.53	2.17	0.75	1.47	14.97	5.24	10.22
Khargone	7.73	0.82	4.32	10.73	1.82	6.32	20.94	7.05	14.12	3.00	1.00	2.00	10.21	5.23	7.80
Khandwa	10.06	0.77	5.47	13.96	1.83	8.01	26.01	6.31	16.37	3.90	1.06	2.54	12.05	4.48	8.36
Shajapur	7.00	1.14	3.90	17.47	1.71	9.98	39.08	8.94	24.90	10.47	0.57	6.08	21.61	7.23	14.92
Rajgarh	11.37	0.80	6.40	13.46	0.94	7.44	32.96	6.65	20.35	2.09	0.14	1.04	19.50	5.71	12.91

Statement Showing Districtwise Literacy in the Old State of Madhya Pradesh including Chhattisgarh During 1971, 1981 and 1991

(Ftg. in Percentage)

Name of State/ District	Scheduled Tribe									Percentage Difference					
	Male	Female	Total	Male	Female	Total	Male	Female	Total	Year – 1981-1971			Year – 1991-1981		
	1971			1981			1991			Male	Female	Total	Male	Female	Total
1	2	3	4	5	6	7	8	9	10	11	12	13	14	15	16
Vidisha	5.11	0.18	2.71	7.00	0.63	3.91	20.41	5.72	13.43	1.89	0.45	1.20	13.41	5.09	9.52
Sehore	8.36	0.87	4.49	10.95	1.05	6.15	25.52	6.68	16.50	2.59	0.18	1.66	14.57	5.63	10.35
Raisen	8.65	3.28	6.04	10.46	1.32	5.96	22.95	5.99	14.89	1.81	-1.96	-0.08	12.49	4.67	8.93
Hoshangabad	14.97	2.01	8.59	16.06	2.92	9.65	30.44	10.03	20.63	1.09	0.91	1.06	14.38	7.11	10.98
Betul	7.75	1.62	4.66	13.72	2.09	7.37	26.09	8.35	17.21	4.97	0.47	2.71	13.37	6.26	9.84
Sagar	0.00	0.00	0.00	13.69	2.02	8.03	29.38	9.93	20.07	13.69	2.02	8.03	15.69	7.91	12.04
Damoh	0.00	0.00	0.00	19.79	2.90	11.43	32.67	10.51	21.89	19.79	2.90	11.43	12.88	7.61	10.46
Jabalpur	9.12	16.49	9.12	22.01	4.10	13.13	39.41	13.33	26.64	12.89	-12.39	4.01	17.40	9.23	13.51
Narsinghpur	16.55	2.93	9.87	15.56	4.73	12.20	42.63	18.40	30.79	-0.99	1.80	2.33	27.07	13.67	18.59
Mandla	18.49	4.23	10.99	24.88	4.58	14.60	41.61	13.01	27.18	6.39	0.35	3.61	16.73	8.43	12.58
Chhindwara	12.00	2.94	7.40	17.95	3.85	10.85	31.51	15.71	23.62	5.95	0.91	3.45	13.56	11.86	12.77

(Contd...)

1	2	3	4	5	6	7	8	9	10	11	12	13	14	15	16
Seoni	17.48	2.80	10.10	22.36	4.37	13.28	38.92	14.42	26.59	4.88	1.57	3.18	16.56	10.05	13.31
Balaghat	18.96	3.93	11.44	32.61	9.03	20.64	48.90	21.58	35.06	13.65	5.10	9.20	16.29	12.55	14.42
Sarguja	13.26	2.01	7.68	15.95	2.88	9.47	29.62	8.98	19.45	2.69	0.87	1.79	13.67	6.10	9.96
Raigarh	24.21	6.40	15.21	30.45	9.95	20.10	46.13	19.85	32.82	6.24	3.55	4.89	15.68	9.90	12.72
Bilaspur	21.46	2.82	12.08	28.00	4.52	16.17	46.42	13.44	29.89	6.54	1.70	4.09	18.42	8.92	13.72
Durg	31.06	6.36	18.44	44.16	13.34	28.47	68.71	32.94	50.64	13.10	6.98	10.03	24.55	19.60	22.17
Rajnandgaon	0.00	0.00	0.00	31.20	6.84	18.76	51.83	20.15	35.60	31.20	6.64	18.76	20.63	13.31	16.84
Raipur	25.55	4.02	14.51	32.87	7.23	19.79	54.83	17.24	35.74	7.32	3.21	5.28	21.96	10.01	15.95
Bastar	7.53	0.98	4.23	12.53	2.41	7.43	23.82	7.23	15.45	5.00	1.43	3.20	11.29	4.82	8.02

REFERENCES

1. Angustine S., *Indian Family in Transition*, Vikas Publishing House. New Delhi.

2. Baig, Tara Ali, *India's Women Power*, S. Chand & Co., New Delhi.

3. Buch. M.N. & Pathak Pushpa, *The Role of The Informal Sector in the Development of Small and Intermediate Cities of India*.

4. Buch. M.N., *Planning The Indian City*, Vikas Publishers, New Delhi.

5. Chattopodhya Kamla Debi, *Indian Women's Battle for Freedom*, Abhinav Publications, New Delhi.

6. Census of India (1991) and Madhya Pradesh (1991) and District Census Hand Book of Jhabua, Dhar, Betul and Surguja.

7. District Statistical Book of Jhabua, Dhar, Betul, Bastar and Surguja.

8. Das Veena, *Indian Women Work, Power and Status*, Vikas Publication House, New Delhi.

9. Desai Neera and Krishna Raj Maithrey, *Women and Society in India*, Ajanta Publications, New Delhi.

10. Dasai, Neera, *Women in Modern India*, Vora and Co. Publishers, Bombay.

11. Desai, Neera and Patel Vibhuti, *Indian Women Change and Challenge in the International Decade 1975-85*, Popular Prakashan, Bombay.

12. Dayal Rekha (Editor), *Resource Book on Women's Development 1987*.

13. D.P.E.P. Report of M.P. — 1994.

14. Everrtt, Jana, Matson, *Women & Social Change in India*, Heritage Publisher, New Delhi.

15. *40 Years of Social Welfare and Development Papers* Written for Souvenir 89 of Indian Council of Social Welfare.

16. Gill H.S. Squatters of Delhi, *Issues and Perspectives*, Discussion Paper.

17. M.P. Human Development Report—1995.

18. Jain Devaki (Ed) India. *Indian Women Government of India*.

19. Dr. Kopadekar H.D. *Role of Local Self Govt. In Programmes for Alleviation of Urban Poverty*.

20. Kapoor Promilla, *Marriage and the Working Women in India*, Vikas Publishers, New Delhi.

21. Kanhere P.R., *Housing, Shelter, Access to Land and House Types with Reference to the Urban Poor*.

22. Khanna Amod, *Government Intervention in Informal Sector for Alleviation of Urban Poverty*.

23. Lal A.K., *Status of Women in Urban Settling—An Analysis of Role in the Family Differentiation*.

24. Lev Wood Stromberg Gontik and Sage (Eds) *Women and Work, An Annual Review, Volume-I* — London.

25. Mann, *Tribal Women in A Changing Society*, Ariltal Publication, New Delhi.

26. Mukherjee Prabhat, *Hindu Women Normative Models*, Orient Longman Ltd., New Delhi.

27. Majumdar Vina, *Symbol of Power Women in Changing Society*, Allied.

4

Development of Tribals in Madhya Pradesh

Dr. V.K. Srivastava

After independence, special attention has been given to the tribal people and the areas by the politicians, planners, and the administrators to bring them in the mainstream of national life. "It has been envisaged to telescope the process of tribal development ordinarily spanning a few centuries into a few decades without at the same time blowing the tribal communities off their feet."[1] This problem has been considered in detail by the constitution makers. Because during the pre-independence era, a policy of isolation than of development and assimilation was generally followed.[2] It is in this context that the Constitution provides a reasonably flexible frame for the administration and development of these areas and the communities.[3] Through its various articles, specially under the Fifth Schedule, the executives have been given powers for adopting various laws of the State/unions. The Constitution, thus has given a wide enough frame for enabling the fast socio-economic development of the tribal areas and the tribal communities.[4]

The intention of the Constitution is to bring tribal population of India in the mainstream of national life. In keeping with this spirit earliest opportunity has been taken to bestow special attention to their problems. State of Madhya Pradesh being the biggest State and having the largest chunk of tribal population of India owns the tribal problems maximum.[5] The Tribal Scenario of this State is

Unique. The Scheduled Tribe population in the state is 96.82 lakhs (1991 census), which is 19.93 per cent of the total population (485.66 lakhs) of the State.* (It is about 14.62 per cent of the ST population of the country) The predominant Scheduled Tribe population occupies about 30.19 per cent geographical areas of the State.[6]

The assessment of the political consciousness developed, the policy of compensatory positive discrimination adopted and the administrative mechanism evolved from the First Five Year Plan to Eighth Five Year Plan for the Tribal upliftment/welfare/development reveals that these efforts/factors due to some reasons, however, have not allowed a broader perspective of tribal development to emerge at the national level.[7] Because the tribal development has been viewed/understood in isolation from the wider contexts of the themes and the strategies operating in the national life.[8]

It is the demand of the time that the above discussed situation is examined and analysed to attract the attention of the academicians, politicians, administrators and the planners. In other words it is to examine critically the whole situation and pace of development of the tribals and the tribal areas in Madhya Pradesh to discuss and highlight the tribal situation and efforts made with gives a *Mosaic Presentation* of Tribal life and culture. This is a revealing fact that tribal people are emerging as unified social category not only at the State level, but at the national level also. Therefore in this paper an attempt has been made to discuss and highlight of the tribal situation prevailed during the Pre and Post independent period and the system of governance developed to administer the tribal areas by formulating/adopting various policies, strategies and programmes for their development and protection, specially in the State of Madhya Pradesh.

---

* The Chhatisgarh region of M.P. has been carved out on 1st November 2000 and has been declared (as Chhatishgarh State. Due to separation of Chhatisgarh (the Eastern part of M.P.), the ST population and its percentage has been reduced to 96.82 lakh (19.93 per cent), while it was 153.99 lakh (1991) before separation of Chhatisgarh for whole of M.P. In 2001 census, the ST population has increased to 122.33 lakh, which is 20.3 per cent of the total population (603.48 lakh) of M.P.

Conceptual Framework: It is inevitable to define the word *'Tribe'* the, *Tribal Areas* and *Development* conceptually, so that all the arguments/logics regarding welfare/development acculturation could be taken at least in the right context. The Indian Constitution aims to bring the Tribal Communities in the *Mainstream* of the National life with adequate safeguards. Hence, the broad meaning of *Mainstream* of the national life needs to be highlighted, what does it convey when it is talked in the context of Tribal Development?

There are conflicting definitions given about the tribe. The anthropologist have been seen the tribes from various angles and have defined them accordingly. These definitions add to their cultural traits, habitats, living conditions, and functional as well as operational merits of the life. Therefore, since beginning of the human civilization, various names have been given to the tribes. The tribes are called "Adivasis". The Sanskrit meaning of it is 'Original Inhabitants' and refers to the original people, who were the earliest settlers of the sub-continents. They are also called 'Aadimjati' (Primitive Tribe) — age old caste (Jati) dwelling on the land. Since they lived on hills and in the midst of forest—close to nature, they are called "Vanvasi" (Jungle Tribe) by the people of plains. The British rulers called them "Aboriginals". This word was used for the tribals when the Christian civilization advanced, condemning the civilization of the regions as uncivilized and backward.

After independence, the Constitution of India for the first time in the administration of Tribal people, place the responsibility for their welfare on the popular Government through the President and Governors of the States. The term 'Tribe' has not been given anywhere. However, according to the Constitution, the Tribal communities are 'scheduled' in the specific Areas for each State. The difficulty in setting out formal criteria for defining tribes arises from the fact that the tribes in India are, and have been for some decades in transition. The first serious attempt to list "Primitive Tribes" was as in case of 'Depressed Castes' made in 1931 census. Subsequently under the Govt. of India Act 1935, a list of "Backward Tribes" was specified for the provinces of India. The list of Scheduled Tribes was prepared in 1950 by making addition to the list of backward tribes under the Govt. of India Act 1935. In considering the fresh proposal for inclusion in the list, "It was noted that care was necessary in drawing up the schedule in order to ensure the communities which had been assimilated in the general population were not at this stage invested with an artificial destructiveness as tribes and the communities which might be regarded as tribes by reason of their social organisation and general way of life, but which were really not primitive should not be treated as primitive."[9]

The tribes recognised by the Central and the State Governments had been included in the President's Scheduled Tribes Order, 1950. This order was revised on the recommendations made by the Backward Classes (B.C.) Commission (1953). The B.C. Commission stated that the Scheduled Tribes lead a separate excluded existence and are not fully assimilated in the main body of the people. Scheduled Tribes may belong to any religion. They are listed as Scheduled Tribes because of the kind of life led by them.[10] On the recommendations of the Backward Class Commission (1953) and reorganisation of the Status in 1956, a substantial Tribal Population in these State was recognised only in some districts. In 1976 the position has been rationalised with the enforcement of Scheduled Caste and Scheduled Tribes (Amendment) Act, 1976. All Tribal Communities are now recognised through out the territory of a State unless specially mentioned otherwise.[11]

The International Labour Organisation (ILO) has classified such people as "Indigenous". As adopted in the International Convention under the aegis of the ILO, "The main purpose of the recognition of Tribal and Semi-Tribal Population by the political community is to bring such populations at par with the other sectors of the natives and integrate them in the national policy. It therefore, logically follows that communities which are considered to be such as would require special measure for being integrated with the national policy and for being brought on par with other sections of the nation should for operational purposes be recognised as "Scheduled Tribes".[12]

The areas inhabited by a Scheduled Tribes have been declared as Scheduled Areas. The President issued order the Scheduled Area Order, 1950 declaring certain tribal areas Scheduled Areas in the State of Andhra Pradesh, Madhya Pradesh, Maharashtra, Gujarat, Orissa, Punjab, Madras and Rajasthan. This order has been revised three times, once in 1956-1975 and in 1976 to make the distribution of Scheduled Areas extensive and rational, and in 2003. Madhya Pradesh, in its present form, came into existence on the November 1st, 2000 following its bifurcation to create a new state Chhatisgarh. So, again the Scheduled Areas have been notified for the state of M.P. by Govt. of India in 2003 (vide orders No. 192 dated 20.3.2003). Now the notified Scheduled Areas in the State is 0.68 lakh sq. km. which is 22.07 per cent of the total geographical area (308 lakh sq. km.) of the State.

After reorganisation of the State (1956) the former Madhya Pradesh Government had taken decision that wherever, the concentrated population of the tribals (as per given in the Scheduled Tribes List, 1956) was 20 per cent or above, they should be regarded as Scheduled Tribes, but those vary tribals in areas where they were less than 20 per cent should be regarded as Backward Classes. The criterion for the Scheduled Areas was laid down that the tracks were the concentrated population of tribals was 50 per cent or above that would be under Scheduled Areas, the tehsil being unit.[13]

In the context of the present paper the concept of *Development* is needed to be defined. Because it is generally confused with modernisation. It is accepted that development is the process leads to modernisation. Modernisation is achieved through development, so development is a tool to modernisation. Development has been categorised viz. under developed and developed. Thus, this process goes on starting from tradition to the stage of modernisation, but in the sociological perspective, development is seen as a process of social change takes place, through social process. Social change is treated equivalent by some social scientist to 'development' and progress.[14] This, Dumout (1964, p. 10) says amount to justification of the social order being found not in what it is, but in what supposedly becoming in such circumstances a great and increasing social pressure is brought upon those who in the public estimation should know about social change.[15] B.D. Sharma (1978, p. 2) observes social process of change as "Secular Change". By Secular Change, he means the change "from the tribal form of social organisation to village communities and from the village society to the modern industrial system..."[16]

Neil J. Smelser (1965, p. 100) has observed that social process, segmentation and structural change are associated empirically.[17] While taking about sociological aspect of economic growth and analysing the relation between economic growth and social structure, he says, "it is possible to isolate the effects of interrelated technical, economic nd ecological process frequently accompanying developn ent:

1. In Technology, the change from simple and traditionalised techniques toward the application of scientific knowledge;
2. In Agriculture, the evolution from subsistence farming toward commercial production of agricultural goods. This means specialisation in cash crops purchases of non-agricultural products in market, and frequently agricultural wage labour;
3. In Industry the transition from the use of human and animal power toward industrialisation proper or man aggregated at power-driven machines working for monetary returns, with the produces of the manufacturing process entering, into a market based, on a network of exchanged relation; and
4. In Ecological arrangements, the movements from the farm and village toward urban centres. These several process often occur simultaneously. However, certain technological improvements e.g. the use of improved seeds can be introduced without automatically producing organisational change, agriculture may be commercialised without accompanying industrialisation.

Therefore, on the basis of above facts it is observed that at the societal level, conceptually development is an indication directing the social process taking place in the society from traditional stage to the development stage. However, in the modern society, development is seen in terms of Gross National Product (G.N.P.) growth and industrialisation. The use of high technology, technical know how, rich material culture and per capita income and investment are taken as indicators of development. But the experiences gained in the past have given sense of realisation that qualitative development is essential through the process of change which means to provide input to the aesthetic and basic needs of life to the people in the society. So here development means to bring qualitative growth in the life of the last man belonging to the Scheduled Tribe Community.

The various provisions of the Indian Constitution have provided the powers to the Executive. Both at the Centre and in the State to bring the tribal communities in the 'mainstream of the national life'. Its meaning is to draw the tribal communities within the fold of Indian territorial unit, democracy, secularism and modern life. Prof. Niharranjan has elaborated the concept of 'Mainstream of National Life' in the Indian context. According to him, "From our point of view, these four, namely the territorial unit of India, democracy, secularism and planned economy of which industrialisation is the means and socialism is the goal are the four tributaries that constitute the mainstream of contemporary Indian Life.* He further says, "Any citizen of India who is still standing a side, or away from the mainstream or who is thinking in such terms should be drawn into it and with a sense of participation that would engender in him a sense of involvement. The above concept has been taken into consideration in this paper.

The planning process and the administrative mechanism evolved in India, and in the State of Madhya Pradesh can be broadly divided into pre-independence and post-independence periods. In both the periods, the approach adopted and policies framed are based on the various situations emerged and events taken place in the tribal areas of the country. Over all the approaches adopted and the policies framed during these two periods can be broadly characterised as amelioration and welfare/development oriented taking the basic objectives and measures introduced.

* A seminar was held under the Chairmanship of Prof. Niharranjan Ray, Director, Indian Institute of Advance Study on "The Tribal Situation in India" under the aegis of Indian Institute of Advance Study, Simla in collaboration with the Dept. of Sociology, Delhi University at Simla, from the 6th-19th July, 1969. In that Seminar Prof. Niharranjan Roy, spoke on INTEGRATION.

Pre-independence Period: Emergence of Tribal Group—Man is known from his history. The history of man as a social being begins in small tribal groups. Scholars have given various theories about the original homes of these tribal groups.[19] The brief survey of the Indian History reveals that since the early days there has been continuous in flow of people from neighbouring and even distant countries in India. This process has resulted a constant and often enriching process of interaction and fusion of cultures.[20] The conflict between the force of integration and those of disintegration continued up to the period that cannot be specified. Thus, in long course of time, the stronger group of immigrants—stronger physically, numerically, organisationally tried to impose either to surrender to complete absorption or to escape to inaccessible areas. Even in the 'Vadic Age' the 'tribe known by various names originally meant human being' but due to enmity and conflict with the Aryans, came to mean alien, hostile or savage men. Later on, these names became terms of opprobrium and abuse which led to attribution of evil characters to these people (p. 254, ch. xix, Applied Anthropology in India). In this process, the communities passed through prolonged phase of new struggle for existence against the elements of nature and other denizens.[21] Gradually, these communities started displaying their distinct characteristic and got separated from the main society by the rulers of the time.

Colonial Transformation of Tribal Society: The ethnographers have described the pre-colonial tribal situation as 'Static'. In this direction, the historical evidence however, suggests three trends: First, the situation as 'Static'. In this direction, the historical evidence however, suggests three trends: First, the Mughal Rulers encouraged the peasant caste to reclaim the lands and may incentives were given to them for this purpose, or by other categories of immigrants. Trades or strategic routs passing through the Jungle regions acquired a new significance with result 'JHARKHAND' and 'GONDVANA' emerged as historical regions in the medieval period. Secondly, many tribal communities such as Gonds, Bhils and Oraons were recognised as dominant communities by the Mughal Empires. Thirdly, and most important of all was the rise of State either out of the tribal matrix as in the case of the Gonds and as the result of the imposition on the tribal system of the authority of the Rajputs and other caste which established their power in the high lands of Middle India (12th Century A.D.). Thus, the formation of such States created a new situation. Such States acted as the agents of 'Sanskritization', but they also strengthened the sense of the tribal identity, "All in all, a complex social economic system had emerged in certain parts of tribal middle India the colonial system was established there.[22]

The role of British empire was decisive in this direction. The British rules separated the tribal population in the administrative sphere from rest of the society. Thus, in course of past two centuries, the so called tribal societies came into existence with the result, a large section of the society (tribal) has fallen behind the main section in the march of civilization.[23] It was due to colonial transformation of the tribal society in the middle India. The tribal communities—a sub-system of the Hindu system were sought to be enclaved by the Colonial system under the British Rule, K.S. Singh—an administrator cum anthropologist opines, "The tribal communities living in relative isolation and were sensitive to exogenous influence. Their society has generally being described as peripheral to the large society, but in many ways. The first is the matrix of the Indian Social system and its study provides valuable insight into evolution of social formation".[24]

British Administrative Mechanism and Model of Tribal Development/Exploitation—These so called uncivilized tribal communities living in the remote hills, dense forest and almost cut off with the mainstream of life for many centuries, led a life of their own, unaffected by the general level of development. The British administration kept them as they were thus isolated them. The entry of missionaries who acted as the protectors of tribal against the non-tribals (as the myth has been built up) however, diverted the attention of the administration towards them. But the contact of the administrative officers were superficial and of no use to the tribals. The people of plains were administrative officers were superficial and of no use of the tribals. The people of plains were completely ignorant about their life style and culture, because they (tribal) were kept away from the purview of the legislation. It can be said that the British Administration could contribute to the difficulties of tribal people by its policy of isolation and detachment and the people of plains attributed to the problem by their direct or indirect neglect.[25]

The British policy of isolation gave encouragement to exploitation. The Zamindars landlords, money lenders and contractors exploited the tribals to the maximum. Their rights on forests and land were snatched by conserving and preserving the forests. Beside, the entry of missionaries, land allotted to retired soldiers at the foot of hills in order to make ring fence of royal military men to encircle the tribals, forced the tribal communities to agitate against the British administration. Series of disturbances took place in 1789, 1801, 1807, 1832 and during the period of 1869-1897 in different tribal areas of the country. The emergence of this new situation compelled the British Administrators to setup a special administrative mechanism in the tribal areas in the later half of the 18th century in order to check the tribal unrest and safeguard them.

A large part of area of tribal concentration caused disturbances were enclaved and integrated with in the administration of the province of British India. The most important administrative reform was Regulation XIII of 1833, as a result of which the Chhota Nagpur was declared a non-regulated area. These reforms and administrative step however, more of less remained on the paper as the tribals were totally un-informed about them. The British resident kept a watch on the tribal situation and in some situation, even acted as the agent of the tribal regions. It was in those enclave that the concept of protection of the tribes as an ethnic community developed in stages. Its main feature were:

1. The paternalistic rule of the district officers means the tribes needed a government by men not by a system;
2. Keeping tribal areas out of the operation of the Regulation, laws etc. which were alien to tribal ethos and undermined it;
3. Laying down a set of simple rules to settle dispute and restriction on the jurisdiction of the of the courts which enforced normal laws and exclusion of the lawyers from courts;
4. Special agrarian laws were made;
5. Regulation of the entry of the aliens into tribal areas; and
6. Strengthening tribal institutions and traditional leadership.[26]

An agency system was established with the objectives of quelling rebellions. This was the earliest mode of protective administration. Such four agencies were established viz. one agency to pacify the Bhils (1825), another in Chotanagpur, the south west frontier Agency (1833), a third in the Mariah (1839). These agencies settled tribes, opened up the tribal world, laid lines of communicators established, 'chatries' along high ways and set up cantonment and centres of administration and trades. But, these efforts could not perish the tribal rebellions and the pace of colonization of the tribal region had began earlier, was accelerated. The process of immigration speeded up. For example, alone in Chhota Nagpur region between 1871 and 1931, the incidence of immigration rose from 96,000 to 307,000.[27]

"Thus the colonial system ended the relative isolation of the tribal society, brought it into the main stream of new administrative set up, policy and programmes, put an end to political dominance of the tribals in the region and roped the tribal communities by their States into a new system of production relation. The colonial system, as elsewhere, followed the dual policy of strengthening the feudal crust of the tribal societies, formed by the 'Rajas' chiefs and zamindars and simultaneously creating conditions in which their economy and political system were undermined by the rampaging market forces.[28]

In this way, the colonial system bore harshly on the tribal communities and with the result, several tribal socio-economic cum religious movements took place viz. Santhol/Kol and Munda movements in due course of time which were taken into cognigance in late forties by the anthropologist, sociologist and reformists.

The British administration declared the tribal areas as 'Scheduled District' and their administration was conducted in accordance to the Scheduled District Act XIV of 1874.[29] By promulgating the Scheduled District Act, 1874, wide powers of legislation were vested in the Executive. The tribal areas were separately administered from the rest provinces. They were removed from the purview of the legislature and divided into two categories; "Wholly Excluded Areas and Partially Excluded Areas". Further a number of Acts were enforced from time to time and certain territories were declared "Backward district under the G.O.I. Act 1919. The areas were more of less same, as those of "Scheduled Districts" with certain addition and alternations. This was the result of the reforms suggested by Montague and Chelmsford in their report. Again "Excluded Areas" were created under the Govt. of India Act 1935, as per the recommendations of the Simon Commission (1928). The Govt. of India (Excluded & Partially Excluded) Order, 1936, contained the list of these areas. On the whole the provision of such areas largely left the situation as it was in 1874, barring only certain areas on frontier positions. Thus, in the name of safeguarding the tribals from the consequences of incursions of the fellow non-tribals, the British administration made them cut off from the main current of Indian social and economic life.[30]

Social Stratification

The sociological of the tribal situation of British India reveals that the British way of administration and well knitted colonial system created and strengthened a three fold division with the feudatory chief/zamindars at top, the well to do headman, in the middle and the general mass at bottom. As per the district settlement reports, a rich stratum of buyers of tribal land emerged at the that time. But this internal differentiation did not grow to a point of complete alienation of one stratum from another. The Bonds of Kinship and ethnicity and the appreciation of the political advantages of the continuation of the tribe as an entity after 1920 became stronger. This inhibited the development of intra-tribe contradiction which was also overshadowed by the confrontation between tribals and non-tribes.[31]

The land management system developed shows that the land system in the tribal areas was integrated within the two broad systems of land tenure, the Zamindari and Ryotwari system. The tribal regions of eastern part of central province, Bengal and Bihar to the first and those in western parts of Central Provinces, Bombay and Gujarat to the second category. In both the systems there were primeval survivals of the communal mode of production. The tribal land laws, framed in the background of the rebellious, incorporated new agrarian concept. For instance, the idea of the prevention of alienation of tenure/land could be traced to the Wilkinson Rules

(1833). The Chhota Nagpur Tenancy Act (1908) innovated many provisions to give protection to the aboriginal tenants and became a piece of model legislation and the central province legislation (1916). While these laws and give a measure of protection, they could not prevent, as a Chhota Nagpur survey in the 1920 showed, either alienation of usury on a large scale.[32]

The most striking feature of this period, in the central province was the break down of the communal mode of production and the emergence of private right in land. This was related generally to the technology of hunting and food gathering, the slash—and burn cultivation which were again associated with the system of communal ownership/control of land and use of collective labour. The peasantry coming up from plains introduced the concept of agricultural season and new crops, implements and practices related to both wet and dry farming. The tribes also developed indigenous technology suited to them. But the transition from the tribal to the peasant system was however, neither uniform or complete. Factors responsible for this were: (1) small land holding continuously encroached upon all sides; (2) poor quality of soil; (3) low agricultural yield. Dependence on forest as source of food, shelter and occupation was still crucial in many ways. Though by and large, some of the major tribes like Gonds, Bhils, Oragons and Mundas were emerging as a community of peasants while the most of the tribes still depended on the forest.[33]

A further state in the development of the peasant system was the penetration of the tribal economy by market. The colonial system created a demand for money in largely non-money economics to pay land revenue and other levies. Even the most primitive economics came gradually within the operation of the weekly market system, or seasonal fairs which enabled the tribals to barter their produce. With the market came the middle men, merchants and the money lenders. The tribals were evicted from their lands, specially from the lands which were brought under the cash crops.[34]

The process of peasantisation and depeasantisation were at work simultaneously and rate of land alienation increased. The tribal handicraft declined. The out migration increased. For example out migration from Chhotanagapur alone was 330000 in 1891,

707000 in 1911 and 947000 in 1921. The tribals went out to work in the tea garden, on plantation as industrial labour, or the form of bonded labour in the regions peripheral to their home land. The process of depesantisation was faster in the eastern areas of Central Provinces and Barars and Chhota Nagpur. This can be seen in the context of and as an example of the development of under development at the micro-level, while the development of the industries made tribal areas large ahead in terms of the indicators of modern development.[35]

The foregoing analysing shows that a trend of moving closer to the peasant/caste system emerged in the tribal society. This again reflects the process of upward mobility/sanskritisation which had been restricted to family/group of persons in the pre-colonial situation. It is somewhat clear that under the colonial impact, the process of sanskritisation cropped up and started taking a shape of movement encompassing tribes and sub-tribes. The Oraons of erstwhile States of Surguja and Rajgarh embraced Christianity, the Santhol of Chhota Nagpur put on the sacred thread and claimed the status of the Kshatriya, Gonds of Mahakeshol region adopted the 'Hindu Karm kand' rituals customs and ceremonies.

Role of Christian Missionaries

A close link between Christianity and colonialism existed. The Christianity moved to civilise the aboriginals. The Aborigines Protective Society established in 1836, exercised a powerful influence on the colonial policy of administration. For example, the official policy of social neutrality and non-interference in religious matter as proclaimed in November, 1858 was not acted upon. Sir Richar Temple, observed: "I may remained you of the fortunate fact that in India out of 200 million British subjects (Exclusive of native stock) 18 millions are of aboriginal rates, and 9 millions are no caste at all. Thus, 2.7 million are beyond the pale of the principal oriental religions and their minds present a 'Tabula Rosa' on which Christianity may work.[36] In the initial phase, the missionary activities were disruptive of the tribal system. The missionary imposed a puritical ethnic on the permissive tribal society, through the approaches of various denominations to social questions markedly varied depending on the exigencies of the situation. The strategy of proselytization was carefully worked out to cover the distant and sensitive regions, major tribal communities and particularly upper strata.[37]

Mr. J.P. Mills I.C.S. in his book 'The Nagas' has remarked about the missionaries" ... by preventing the converted Nagas from attending the dormitories, the Baptist missionaries made them run the risk of cultural disintegration."[38]

As far as literacy was concerned the conditions of the tribal people was worse than that of the Scheduled Castes. The census figure of 1931 disclose that among the tribals the literacy percentages was as low as 0.7 as compared to the general literacy rate of 8.3 per cent some details of a few States are given in the Table 4.1.

Table—4.1 State-wise Literacy Rate

Province	*Tribal's population*	*Tribal literate*	*Percentage*
Assam	992390	14094	1.4%
Bengal	528037	3874	0.7%
Bihar & Orissa	2048809	11834	0.5%
Central Province	1351615	6769	0.5%

Source: Report of Scheduled Areas and Scheduled Tribes, Commission 1961, page no. 29.

Late Shri A.V. Thakkar observed in 1941 that "Education grants to aboriginal areas have been meager and inadequate hitherto. Middle School, High School and College Education among the adivasis is of course negligible, if not altogether zero. We can find a few aboriginals who have received or now are receiving university education among the Khasis of Assam and the Mundas of Oraons of Chhota Nagpur. At present many Christian mission organisation and a few non-Christian Indian Bodies are conducting schools for aborigines with Government aid in most cases. Their work more commendable as it appears to be only a drop in the ocean."[39]

Some Observations

The important British Administrator like J.H. Hutten and Social thinkers like G.S. Ghurya and S.C. Roy have commented on the impact of British rules made for the tribals. Their writings reflect real condition of the aboriginals, Dr. J.H. Hutten says "Far from being of immediate benefit to the primitive tribes the establishment of the British rule in India did most of them much more harm than good ... It may be said that the early days of British Administration did very great detriment to the economic position of the tribes through ignorance and neglect of their rights and customs many changes have been caused incidentally by the penetration tribal country, the opening up of communications, the protection of forests and the establishment of schools, to say nothing of the opening given in this way to Christian Missions. Many of the result of these changes have caused acute discomforts to the tribals". Adding to this professor G.S. Ghuryas says, "The acuteness of the discomfort was very often so great that it led to apathy, indifference, moral deterioration and even a decline in population." On the administration of justice in the tribal areas, S.C. Roy remarks, "The British system of law and administration has further tended to impair the social solidarity of those tribes and has weakened the tribal authority, the social heads of Panchayats and the respect formally they commended. Until recently when rules against alienation of ancestral lands were promulgated by government, the ancient tribal custom against such alienation was utterly disregarded".[40]

The British administration did not want that the wave of India's freedom struggle movement should touch the tribals. They deliberately tried to isolate the tribals from political contagion. The Indian Statutory Commission's (Simon Commission) recommendations regarding the development of the tribal areas were also examined by Government of India (G.O.I.) and the Government's decision on the recommendations of the Simon Commission (1928) were embodied in the Government of India Act, 1935; Section, 91 and 92 of the Act provided for the declaration by an Order—in Council of 'Excluded Areas' and 'Partially Excluded Areas'. Any act of the Federal or the Provincial legislature would apply to these areas only on the direction of the Governor, who was empowered to make such exceptions and modifications, as he considered necessary. It also authorised the Governor to make regulations for the peace and good Government of the areas with the approval of the Governor General. The expenditure in regard to

"Excluded Areas was non-votable and in case of 'Partially Excluded Areas', the demand was to be invariably voted by the legislature. Reservation of seats for tribals was made in the legislature of Madras, Bombay, Bihar. The Central Province, Assam and Orissa. In drawing up the schemes, it was indicated that the areas to be placed in the category of 'Excluded Areas', must be as limited as possible. In regard to areas classified as Partially Excluded", and area having a preponderance of tribals sufficient to make possible the application of special legislation and administrative treatment was to be included. Accordingly, the frontier and border regions in Assam, the Laccadive and Minicoy Islands and Lahul and Spiti areas in the Punjab were declared "Excluded Areas", and huge tribal tracts in the provinces of Madras, Bombay, Bengal, United Province, Bihar, Central Province and Orissa were made "Partially Excluded Area".[41]

Due to pressure built by the popular Ministries in 1937, a committee was appointed in the provinces of Bihar, the Central Province, Orissa, Bombay and Madras to enquire the socio-economic condition of the tribals, specially of those of partially 'Excluded Areas', Central Province Govt. appointed a committee under the Chairmanship of Sri W.V. Grigson in 1940 to enquire and report on the (C.P.) and suggest ways and means to improve them a lot. Grigson submitted the report in 1944. The recommendations, however, could not be acted upon due to exigency of the World War II.[42] But efforts were made to open number of primary schools for the tribals. Special hostels were also established and a scheme for ranting scholarship to the tribal students instituted. Arrangements for mid day refreshments for boys and girls were also made. In 1946, when the Congress Ministry returned to the power a committee headed by Shri A.V. Thakkar was appointed to submit to the Government of India (G.O.I.) a plan for Tribal Welfare. Thakkar Bapa submitted a Five Year Plan for Tribal Welfare in Madhya Pradesh in 1947 which chalked out an over all social, economic and cultural development of tribals of the State. But the plan could not see the light of the day.[43]

It is clear from the above investigations of the historical facts that the approach and strategy of the British Administration towards the tribals were not positive. Thus, the policy of isolation adopted on the name of development and protection was nothing more than a maintenance of 'status quo' as has been observed by the Scheduled Areas and Scheduled Tribes Commission (1961) it resulted in reducing the tribals to a state of penury in most part of India."[44] The efforts made by the British Govt. for the amelioration of the tribals could be summarised as under:

1. The colonial system separated the tribal communities from the mainstream of life by keeping them away from the purview of the administration;
2. The enactment a few Act were ineffective. The Scheduled District Act, 1874 divided the tribal areas into two categories—Excluded Areas and Partially Excluded Areas. That continued till last;
3. Degree of exploitation of tribals increased by land lords, money lenders, contractors, Christian missionaries and revenue/forest officials;
4. Traditional rights of the tribal communities on their customs and economy were ignored;
5. The authority of traditional panchayat was weakened;
6. The recommendations of the Indian statutory Commission (Simon Commission) were not executed by the administration; and
7. Traditional rights to brew the liquor and prepare rice bear were snatched through Excise Act, 1915.

POST INDEPENDENCE SCENARIO

Approach to Development

The network of British Administration was as such that the tribals had to remain at the mercy of petty official; and nothing positive by way of rehabilitation and development was achieved. Thus, the British policy provided for a sort of protection achieved largely through isolation. It was only after attainment of the independence of India, a consciousness was developed towards the tribals and the Constituent Assembly appointed a sub-committee with A.V. Thakkar as its Chairman (1947). This sub-committee examined the overall situation of the tribals and recommended that on the basis of past experience, it is necessary to provide statutory safeguard measures to protect the economic life of the tribals and their traditional customs and institutions. The sub-committee urged that any scheme which confined attention to the tribals living in

Excluded or Partially Excluded Areas would be inadequate and that all tribals wherever, they were found should be brought within the contemplated framework of the Constitutional arrangements. This was significant change from the policy hitherto pursued and focused the attention of Govt. on the necessity of viewing the tribal problem as whole.[46] Under the Constitutional provisions the Integration of the tribes to get the benefit of the progress. They were given Constitutional identity and formally recognised under Article 342 of the constitution and referred to as Scheduled Tribes, and the areas where substantial Scheduled Tribes population resided were declared 'Scheduled Areas' under the Article 244 (1) and Fifth Schedule, besides, through various Articles, special provisions were incorporated in various parts of the Constitution of India to provide specific safeguards to Scheduled Tribes. Thus, the main objective of the framers of the Constitution was to give adequate protection to the tribal groups, to provide specific funds and development programmes for their welfare. The Commissioner Scheduled Caste and Schedule Tribe was used directly responsible for the Scheduled Areas of respective States.

A number of anthropologist, social thinker, politicians were advocating different approach and social process regarding the upliftment of the tribal communities. It needs special mention here that in 1931, Dr. J.H. Hutten had expressed his views on the approach towards the tribals. The solution of the problems according to him was to create self governing tribal areas with free powers of self determination in regard to surrounding or adjacent unit (Hutten 1936: 04–507) Dr. Varier Elwin in his famous monograph on 'Baigas' published in 1939, criticised the over-hasty and unregulated process of upliftment and civilization. He advocated the establishment of 'National Park', to protect the tribals, not being satisfied with provision made under the G.O.I. Act, 1935 for excluding wholly or partially certain areas from the operation of legislative control. Later, his support for isolationism became even stronger. He affirmed that the tribal population could be divided into three groups:

1. Those who through continuous and intimate contact were assimilated in the Hindu hierarchy;
2. Those who were partially Hinduised and had thus suffered moral decay as a result or contact; and

3. Those who live mostly in inaccessible hills and remained free from being de-tribalised."[47]

The national Park would according to him, provide refuge to the second group and protection to the third. The administration was to be so adjusted as to allow 'Tribesmen' to live their life with utmost possible happiness and freedom. The missionaries of any sort were to be allowed to break the tribal life. Their (the tribals) contact with the outside world were to be reduced to the minimum.[48]

However, Elwin himself declared later on that the policy of isolation was no longer necessary after independence. He further stated, "Isolation in the modern world is impossible; it would not be desirable even if it was possible. The old controversy about zoos and museums has long been dead ... To try to preserve and develop the best elements of tribal art, religions and culture is something very different from wishing to keep the people in a Zoo."[49]

The policy of assimilation was advocated very much contrast to isolationism by sociologist like Dr. G. S. Ghurya and Social Worker A.V. Thakkar. But both differed in degree and approach. Ghurya was of the view that the aborigines were nothing but "Backward Hindus". On this he has given a very scholarly exposition in his book. 'The Aborigines so called and their Future' (1943). In the various sense beginning from 1891, the tribal people were classified separately as animist. Yet a few Census Commissioners such as J.B. Baines (1891), E.A. Gait (1911) J.T. Merten (1921) and J.H. Hutton (1931) felt that there was very little difference between Hinduism as practised by the lower caste and the tribal region. Hence, Ghurya maintained that the assimilation of the tribal people into Hindu, society should be easy and almost natural.[50] On the other hand A.V. Thakkar was against constitutional provision that would wholly or partially separate the tribal areas from the rest of the country (R.R. Kale Memorial Lecture delivered in 1941). He maintained that "the tribals should form a part of the civilized communities, not for the purpose of swelling the figures of the followers of a particular religion, but to share the privilege on equal terms in the general social and political life of the country. Separation and isolation seemed to this dangerous theories which strike at the root of national solidarity."[51]

The policy of isolation and assimilation, both were not considered suitable to benefits and uplift the tribals. It was envisaged that the tribal communities were at the various stages of cultural life and socio-economic conditions, as classified by Dr. Majumdar, Dr. V. Elwin, Dr. S.C. Dube and Tribal Welfare Committee constituted by the Indian Conference of Social Work, 1952 all these classifications indicated that the tribal problems vary in degree and magnitude.

Considering the various stages of tribal situations, it was decided that the major aim of tribal welfare programme should be to solve the various problems arising out of 'isolation' of tribals i.e. uncontrolled, haphazard and at time disastrous culture contact, to provide amenities of modern life and to create conditions of their systematic integration into the mainstream of Indian Society. For that broadly three approaches were suggested as under:

1. Classical approach;
2. Voluntary organisation approach; and
3. Nehru's approach

Dr. Huton, Dr. Elwin, Dr. Ghurya were the relief exponent as mentioned above who advocated the classical approach. Voluntary organisation approach was also attached due importance. During the pre-independence period, Servant Society of India was the only organisation which served for the benefit of the tribals. Role of Christian missionary was of a great length which did a lot of ameliorative services, specially in the field of education and medicine.[52]

Pandit Nehru, the then Prime Minister of India in his speech delivered at the opening session of the Scheduled Tribes and Scheduled Area Conference in June, 1952 said, "Tribal people of India are virile people who are naturally went astray sometimes". He was of this view that distinctive life styles of Tribals should not be disturbed and deprived of their simple joys of life. Nothing was to be gained by imposing on them a drab and uniform pattern. It was in this context that he enunciated his famous 'Punchsheel' for the tribes, that is Five Fundamental Principles for the upliftment of the tribals mentioned as under:

1. People should develop along the lines of their own genius and we should avoid imposing anything on them. We should try to encourage in every way their own traditional arts and culture;
2. Tribal rights to land and forest should be respected;
3. We should try to train and build up team of their own people to do the work of administration and development. Some technical personnel from outside will, no doubt, be needed, especially in the beginning. We should avoid introducing too many outsiders into tribal territory;
4. We should not over administer their areas or overwhelm them with a muplicity of schemes. We should rather work through, and in the rivalry to, their own social and cultural institutions; and
5. We should judge results, not by statistics or the amount of money spent, but by the quality of human character evolved.

According to Pt. Nehru, the first priority in the tribal areas was road and communications and next were schools, health relief and cottage industries etc. .

Thus, in the wake of new thinking and dispensation every effort was to be made to preserve the distinctive life style and the vitality of the tribal people and at the same time to extend them the benefits of the development. Therefore, in the National Policy there was a shift from 'Protective Discrimination' to Compensatory Discrimination, bestowing certain special benefits to the tribal communities, for a stipulated period.

While emphasising this policy specially, the execution part certain economist like K.L. Mehta had observed' ... We must be cleared in our minds about what we are trying to do, unless in fact we have a philosophy behind all our activities we spend."[53] Further K.K. Lenva observed, "Whether we wish or not, but in view of the rapidity with which the development programme is being executed it may not be possible for the Scheduled Tribes to stick to their own way of life which is bound to be interfered. The Excise Laws, Forest Laws and other arms of administration can be cited in this support".[54]

The Indian Constitution adopted by the Constituent Assembly on 26th January, 1950 advocated the Policy of 'progressive Acculturation' through compensatory discrimination for the protective and positive development of the tribals. The question of segregation or isolation thus ended for ever. To bring the desired goal the mechanism of Five Year Plan was evolved. In the Five Year Plan of India, planning was described as essentially "A way of organising and utilising resources to maximum advantage in terms of defined social ends.[55] "In Indian Planning, the social ends were visualised at the national as well as regional and local levels. At the national level, the social ends were set in the 'Directive Principles of the State Policy' of the Constitution. All the components of standard of living as indicated by the U.N. Statistical Commission are covered by these Directive Principle'. Further, it has been laid down interilia that the State shall strive to promote the welfare of the people by securing and protecting as effectively as it may a social order in which justice—social, economic and political shall inform all the institutions of national life.[56]

The general principles were given more precision, by the Indian Parliament in December 1954. The parliament adopted the 'Socialistic pattern of society' as the objectives of social and economic policy. Essentially, this means, "that the basic criterion for determining the lines of advance must not be private property, but social gain, and that the pattern of development and the structure of socio-economic relation should be so planned that they result not only in appreciable increases in national income and employment, but greater equality in income and wealth. It has further been stated that the socialist pattern of society is not to be regarded as some fixed or rigid pattern. It is not rooted in any doctrine of dogma. Each country has to develop according to its own genus or tradition.[57]

How precisely this socialist pattern of society has been attained to at the national, regional and micro-level through Five Year Plans, specially in the context of tribal development is to be examined. Because in the dynamic society the events/developments are not determined by traditional or genius only but, also in the context of the interplay of administrative, technological and economic factors on the one hand and cultural and social factors on the other. None of these factors can be over emphasised alone, because each one has its own importance.[58]

While examining the pace of socio-techno-economic development, it is also necessary to examine the pace of development of non-economic developmental aspect of the tribals. Social values and cultural aspect play significant roles in the development of tribal communities. First, the value system determine the broad response of the community in the development programme. Same time, it plays crucial role in determining the broad strategy of the programme, secondly the specific belief and practice influence the specific of the community to the specific items of the programme. Thirdly, there is mid range influence, which is a combination of strategy and tactics, and which is more important for planning.[59]

During the 1st Five Year Plan, the upliftment of tribal communities was started in the form of community development programme. In the 2nd Five Year Plan the word 'Upliftment was replaced by welfare. The programmes of the tribal areas of the State were covered under this approach. The tribal areas were more difficult, sparsely populated undulated, and poor in infrastructure including the institutional infrastructure. Therefore, efforts for the development of the tribal areas were made for intensive supplementation by starting a few Special Multi-Purpose Tribal (SMPT) Blocks in the year 1954. (10 such SMPTBS were identified in Madhya Pradesh). But, the magnitude of tribal problems on the economic as well as social fronts could not be envisaged on the realistic parameters. Considering these facts, the working of SMPT blocks was reviewed towards the end of the 2nd Five Year Plan period, and the concept of Tribal Development (TD) Blocks was evolved. Since then the 'Welfare' terminology was replaced and conceived as 'Tribal Development'. By the end of 3rd Five Year Plan, there were 127 Tribal Development blocks in Madhya Pradesh. But the experience revealed that tribal and backward communities could not be benefited to the desired extent. The gap between the tribals and the developed lots persisted, and though the T.D. Block strategy was an improvement over the general C.D. approach, it did not prove effective to the desired level.

During the Fourth Five Plan, to make the development approach more realistic and to enhance the area coverage, special programmes were formulated for various tribal areas in the form of Tribal Development Agencies on pilot basis. Such two agencies were registered in the State of Madhya Pradesh during the year 1971-72. But these Tribal Development Agencies proved to be partial success only.

Review of the past efforts done from time to time from the First to Fourth Five Year Plan for the upliftment, welfare and development of tribal communities reveals that nothing tangible could be achieved to bring the tribal community at par with the general communities in Madhya Pradesh. The total investment made was meager looking to the vastness of the Tribal problems and the manner the money spent was rather unsystematic. The reasons are many. The magnitude of the problems of tribals was recognised, but the priorities set were elite-biased. The programmes were formulated in an adhoc manner without necessary perspective and were more in the nature of Welfare Schemes. Whatever programmes were taken up in the field of agriculture and allied sectors, education, drinking water, public health and administration lacked proper strategy, insight and planning process. Consequently, the tribals received very little benefit of these programmes. Many unwanted reforms were thrust on the tribal people and their pressing and felt-needs were overlooked.

The financial review of the pre-Fifth Five Year Plans reveals that the total expenditure incurred on tribal welfare in the State during the four plan periods was Rs. 35.65 crores (including the expenditure figures of Central and States Government both). Planwise total expenditure and per capita expenditure incurred are shown in the Table—4.2.

Table—4.2 Financial Investment in India/M.P. Level and Per Capita Investment Made From 1st Plan to 4th Plan

(Rs. in Crores)

Plan period	*India*		*Madhya Pradesh*	
	Total outlay	*Expenditure on TDP (%)*	*Expenditure TDP (%)*	*Investment per capita Rs.*
1	*2*	*3*	*4*	*5*
1st	1,960	17.37 (0.88)	3.48 (20.03)	7.01
2nd	4,672	40.49 (0.86)	4.849 (12.31)	7.33
3rd (Including Annual Plans 66-69)	8,577	116.32 (1.35)	10.216 (11.82)	15.29
4th	16,160	84.20 (0.52)	17.060 (20.6)	20.34
Total	**31,160**	**258.38 (0.82%)**	**35.655 (15.56%)**	

Source: Occasional Paper No. 28, Ministry of Welfare, G.O.I.

It is clear from the above table that the amount spent on the tribal development in the country (0.82 per cent) as well as in Madhya Pradesh (15.56 per cent) was quite meager. In the First and Second Five Year Plans the per capita investment on the tribals was almost same i.e. Rs. 7.01 and 7.33. In the subsequent Third and Fourth Five Year Plans, it rose to Rs. 15.29 and 20.34 in Madhya Pradesh.

The overall analysis reveals that whatsoever efforts were made they did not take the 'human element of the local matrix into consideration, the tribals therefore, became incidental' in the whole process. There was no system. The net result was that under the tribal welfare programme, there was schematic outlay for special programmes which no where had the level of 'tribal development'.

Thus, the pre-fifth year plan efforts failed to provide protective measures and positive all round development programmes. The tribal communities remained in the State of penury in almost all the regions of the State. In other words the strategy and approach adopted could not permit realistic appraisal of tribal problems in different cultural context, not only in Madhya Pradesh, but also, at the national level.

The stock of the past efforts made for tribal development was critically reviewed at the national level on the eve of Fifth Five Year Plan, keeping in view the recommendations of Scheduled Areas and Scheduled Tribes Commission Report (1961), Renuka Ray Committee (1959), Shilu AO Committee (1969) and expert committee headed by Dr. S.C. Dube (1972) to spell out the strategy of tribal development on the eve of Fifth Five Year Plan. At the end of Fourth Five Year Plan, it became clear that no single solution (T.D. Block approach) can be expected to have universal applicability to the entire tribal areas since the situation in terms of resources, people, social constraints, infrastructure development, local priorities was entirely different in different regions.

Tribal Sub-Plan Approach

The Fifth Five Year Plan presented a special policy frame for the development of the tribals and the tribal areas in the form of a Tribal Sub-plan (TSP). The strategy of Tribal Sub-plan (TSP) envisaged a total picture of 'development'. The Guidelines of Planning Commission clearly stated that all the activities of the Government and Semi-Government Organisations, financing and credit institutions and special sectoral programmes may be fully integrated. A wider frame encompassing all aspects of tribal life was, therefore, provided. It was, in fact, an attempt to articulate the constitutional provisions in terms of specific programme. The policy-frame of the new strategy emphasised that approach to tribal development should not be bound by precedent or a rigid normative formula. The actual condition of the tribal area should be the determining factor. Hence, it was suggested that the entire legal, administrative and institutional frame as also intersectoral priorities should be reviewed keeping the primary focus on the welfare and the development of the tribal people.[60]

Late Prime Minister Smt. Indira Gandhi spelt out the special responsibility of the Union Government as ordained by the Constitution and pointed out that Centre has not exercised by this authority enough. In actual practice its role has been confined to making grants to states for tribal development. With the new sub-plan strategy the Central assistance has been increased manifold and therefore, she directed that the concerned ministries must assume a more positive role on the basis of a clear cut policy.[61]

The economic programmes announced by the Prime Minister on the 1st of July, 1974 was a new deal for the weaker section, the tribal communities found a special place in this programme. In her message to the Nation, she condemned the barbarous practice of bonded labour and directed that it should be abolished. Liquidation of rural indebtedness is one of the crucial programme for the weaker section have to be pursued with a renewed vigour. After announcing the new programme, the Prime Minister lost no time and specially addressed the Chief Ministers about tribal development (Compendium of Circulars on/Tribal Development, G.O.I. MOW, 1990).

A plan for the development of tribal areas within the State plan was coined and called the 'Tribal Sub-Plan'. This new strategy of tribal development under the new concept of sub-plan, envisaged the problems of tribal development in Madhya Pradesh during Fifth Five Year Plan period in:

1. Areas of Tribal Concentration i.e., having more than 50 per cent tribal concentration and the Scheduled Areas at the tehsil level, and in some cases at the Block level;
2. Areas of primitive tribal communities at pre-agricultural level of technology (identified as special group); and
3. Dispersed tribal.

Thus, the identification of areas of Tribal concentration and the Special Primitive Tribal Groups (SPTG) was done as the first exercise. Such identified area were termed as 'Tribal Sub-Plan Areas'. This areas was further divided into 42 viable Integrated Tribal Project (ITDP) areas, taking into consideration, the administrative boundaries, topography, level of economic development, ethnic composition, natural resources and potentials for development. These identified ITDPs on the basis of area and population (31 major and 11 medium ITDPs).

Objectives of Tribal Sub-Plan

The Tribal Development scene was, thus critically examined and strategy of Tribal Sub-Plan evolved. The long term objectives were defined as:

1. To narrow the gap between the level of development of tribal and other areas; and
2. To improve the quality of life of the tribal communities.

The immediate objectives were to eliminate the exploitation of tribals in various forms, speeding up the process of their social and economic development, building-up the inner strength of the tribal people and improving organisational capabilities.

The problem of tribal development was broadly classified into two categories:

1. Areas of tribal concentration including primitive tribes; and
2. Dispersed tribals.

The first categories were covered under Tribal Sub-Plan Areas. The problem of dispersed tribals i.e. outside the areas of Tribal Sub-Plan (TSP) could not be taken up in a planned manner during the Fifth Five Year Plan as well as the Sixth Plan periods. Family oriented programmes of economic existence were decided for this group, since no area programme could effectively be taken up for them.

Resources for Tribal Sub-Plan

The resource availability for the Tribal Sub-Plan (TSP) was assessed to arrive at first order projection with regard to the level of investment from various sources in the Tribal region during the Fifth Plan Period. All sectors including the financing institutions and autonomous organisations were given higher priority for programmes in these areas. The resources of sub-plan mainly comprised of:

(i) State Plan outlay;

(ii) Sectoral outlay in the central ministries for tribal areas (centrally sponsored and central sector);

(iii) Institutional finance.

It was decided in principal that the basic frame for the economic development of tribal communities and these areas would be provided by an appropriate share in the allocation of State plan. The outlays from the other sources would only be additive and supplemental. The quantum of outlay in the State plan (State flow equal to the percentage of Scheduled Tribe population in the State) for Tribal Sub-Plan (TSP) area would be fixed, keeping in view:

(a) Total population percentage of tribals;

(b) Geographical area;

(c) Comparative level of development; and

(d) State of social services available in TSP areas.

The State plan outlays would distinctly be divided into four sectors. Infrastructure sector, social services sectors and direct economic benefiting sectors and other sectors. These sectors could again be divided into divisible and non-divisible pools; the divisible sectors being those from which, quantified flow of funds from the State plan could not only be possible, but the positively beneficial also to the tribal families. The flow of institutional finance would be determined, keeping in view the total ceiling for the State and the special problems, if any, including its flow to the tribal region. On getting an idea about the central sector programmes, the likely flow of benefits from these programmes to the tribal areas would also be quantified. The special Central Assistance for the Tribal sub-plan from the Central Government would supplement the total resources which could be mobilised by the State, Central Ministries and the Financing Institutions.

First Tribal Sub-Plan (V^{th} Five Year Plan)

The First Tribal Sub-Plan document of the State was prepared on the above lines, within the broad framework of the State's Fifth Five Year Plan, highlighting the problems of the tribal areas as well as the specific problems of different regions in the Sub-Plan areas. Thus, the broad parameters of developmental programmes were chalked-out and the action plans for each tribal development project (ITDP) also were prepared within the broad framework of the sub-plan document. Separate development plans were proposed for each of the identified Special Primitive Tribal Groups (SPTG) along with the project reports of ITDP's. Under the First Tribal Sub-Plan the structural base could be created, but implementation, planning and administrative set up could not be geared up. Besides, the sectoral coordination, financial discipline could not be streamlined. Hence, effective delivery system and better efficiency could not be provided to the tribal problems during the Fifth Five Year Plan period.

Before the land mark of Sixth Five Year Plan, a mid term tribal sub-plan was proposed for the period of 1978-83, which included the Action Plan for the year 1979-80, this mid-term sub-plan followed almost same strategy and priorities, which were laid down for the first Tribal Sub-Plan. Education, health services and full employment were some of the specific programmes that were given high priority. Besides accepting the need for consolidation of protective measures initiated during the Fifth Plan.

Second Tribal Sub-Plan (VIth Five Year Plan)

The Second Tribal Sub-Plan was prepared on the eve of Sixth Five Year Plan for the period 1980-85, the process initiated in the Fifth Five Year Plan with the preparation of the sub-plan, continued in the Sixth Five Year Plan also. Thus, the broad approach of the Tribal Sub-Plan strategy continued during the Sixth Plan laying emphasis on the following specific objectives:

1. Covering the entire tribal population living in the areas of tribal concentration or outside, by suitable developmental programme;
2. Raising the productivity level in the several fields of the tribal activities with a view to enable a targeted number of families to cross the poverty line;
3. Developing the human resources and improving the educational standard;
4. Elimination of exploitation of tribals in the fields of land alienation, money lending, bonded-labour, excise and forest; and
5. Development of adequate infrastructure.

During the Second Tribal Sub-Plan of the State, further areas of tribal concentration under the MADA (known as modified areas development approach) group of village (pockets) having a total population not less than 10,000 (between 10,000 and 50,000) with 50 per cent ST population were included in the sub-plan area. That increased the TSP area as well as the population, Twenty (20) new viable ITDP's were formulated out of the MADA pockets. Thus, the total Tribal sub plan area in the State consisted 62 (42 old + 20 new) ITDP's of which 38 major 8 medium and 16 were minor. These ITDP's were categorised on the basis of population and areas into major, medium and minor. The vastly varying socio-economic situation in each ITDP area required specific solution. The ITDP's provided a reasonable frame in which the problems of the area were broadly identified and programme priorities were fixed accordingly. The annual plans were prepared to project level, and within the broad policy-frame provided at the project level, as well as at the State level. In these plans, greater emphasis was laid on the family-oriented and beneficiary-oriented schemes to achieve the desire goals.

Periodical review of the developmental sectoral schemes implemented by the respective departments were taken up to assess the progress at the Block, Projects, Division and the State level by various committees constituted at these levels. The administrative structure was strengthened and monitoring system was developed to achieve the targets. The financial and administrative procedure were rationalised by creating separate Budget-Grants to focus special attention to the investments made and to ensure utilisation of funds earmarked for tribal sub plan, thereby eliminating possibility of diversion of allocations to non TSP areas. New personnel policy, forest policy, excise and revenue policies were formulated to check and eliminate the exploitation of Scheduled Tribes in these fields. Besides Revenue Dept. relief and other acts were also amended to restore the tribal lands and remove indebtedness etc.

All possible efforts were made to bring the various tribal communities near the development programmes with the aim to benefit them directly under the TSP strategy. A target of 6.18 lakhs ST families was fixed to raise them above poverty line. Though the

TSP financial outlay, was raised to 16.55 per cent (State plan), but nothing could be done for the dispersed tribal communities (32 per cent population) and less could be done for the development of the Special Primitive Tribal Groups (SPTG). Because the development plan prepared for the 6 SPTG by the State Government was so late that they could be finalised by the GOI in the middle of Sixth Five Year Plan (1983-84). This was one of the main reasons that the fund earmarked for SPTG could not be utilised.[62]

Third Tribal Sub-Plan (VIIth Five Year Plan)

Sixth Five Year Plan was the formative period for TSP in the State. The administrative structure, planning process, implementation machinery and monitoring system were streamlined. Sectoral programming were linked and priorities were decided considering the local needs of the people and the area. Quantification of funds was raised. Financial and budgetary mechanism was evolved. To prepare the Third Tribal Sub-Plan of the State, as per the recommendations of the working group constituted by the Planning Commission, so that the planning from below implying realistic and integrated effort could be reflected in the sectoral plans.

The TSP coverage was enhanced to cover more and more dispersed tribals, with the result the whole of TSP area was reorganised (1988) in order to make the administrative units more viable and make the delivery system effective. With a view to streamlining the administrative structure and sectoral programmes, a committee headed by Shri Ajeet Jogi, member of Rajya Sabha was constituted (1989) by the State Government. The Committee gave valuable suggestions, the State cabinet took various valuable policy decisions for rationalisation of schemes, including grass-root planning at ITDP level, raising the financial outlays for TSP areas and decentralising the financial allocations and powers at the field level. In this regard A 'pool' of funds from the state plan at least equal to the proportion of the Scheduled Tribe population percentage of the State had to be earmarked and out of which funds were to be allocated to different sectors looking to their priorities in the sphere of Tribal development. Greater emphasis had to be given to the distt. Sector schemes. Besides in the field of minor forest produce, the State cabinet also took radical decision to cooperatizating the

Tendu Patta trade. Similarly, to tight on the protective measure, the M.P. Land Revenue Code, 1959 was amended to ensure the restoration loan distributed to Scheduled Tribes.[63]

Tribal education was boosted by establishing a new directorate of tribal education, revising the rates of scholarship and stipend and encouraging the voluntary organisation, check the land alienation and special attention was paid to vulnerable groups and the primitive pockets. The programme planning for primitive tribes had been lined with essential infrastructure facilities. The Tribal Development Sub-Sector under the backward classes sector supplemented the tribal economy and took care of dispersed tribals.

The Tribe Advisory Council (TAC) under the Chairmanship of the Chief Minister, held several meetings during the plan period to review the tribal development in the State and gave several important recommendations in order to boost the tribal development activities in the State.

Despite, the massive efforts to boost the tribal development in the Seventh Plan, the package of programme approach could not be made feasible in desired manner under the individual/family benefit oriented network due to lack of sectoral coordination and channelisation of the programmes and lack of full utilisation of Special Central Assistance (SCA). The Government of India did not permit the development sectors to spend SCA on the development of some of the basic infrastructure programmes needed to facilitate the implementation of schemes of economic assistance. The field level monitoring system could not be suitably strengthened at all the levels. Spot concurrent evaluation of the programmes at the ITDP level were not done timely. These are the main reasons that development sectors failed to some extent to achieve physical targets fixed for tribal sub-plan area during the Seventh Five Year Plan. Besides, no proper attention could be paid towards the dispersed tribal population residing outside TSP area, except identifying a few clusters. No proper way out could be sorted out to percolate the economic benefits to the ST population living in these cluster.[64]

Fourth Tribal Sub-Plan—Eighth Five Year Plan (1992-97)

Seventh Five Year Plan was implemented in full swing, not only by expanding the coverage of tribal areas having preponderance of ST population, but managing more financial resource from all possible sources. In the Eighth Five Year Plan, while preparing fourth Tribal sub-plan, efforts were intensive to bridge the gap between the level of development of STs and the other sections of the society (non-tribals). It has been through because of two reasons: First during the annual plans (1990-91 and 1991-92 Plans holidays), consolidated and compressive steps could not be taken up to gear up the tribal development activities/programmes by all the development sectors due to untimely political intervention in the State by the Central Government; and secondly, launching of Three Tier Panchayati Raj System in the State due to enactment of M.P. Panchayati Raj Act, 1993. Therefore, after considering and conceptualising all the contemporary political factors likely to effect the administrative mechanism at the State and field levels, the following priorities were laid down by the planning and implementing wings of the State Government:

- To make programmes more result oriented and purposeful;
- Filling the gaps of last three plans;
- Raising the TSP quantification through 'Pool System;
- To allocate funds to beneficiary oriented schemes and the schemes which are beneficial to STs;
- Narrowing the gap between tribals and non-tribal communities;
- Emphasising on development of education, vulnerable groups and dispersed tribes;
- Decentralising of planning process and accordingly designing the administrative set up; and
- Stringent implementation of protective measures.

In case in the context of above laid down priorities, the sectoral performances made are evaluated, it is found that 21.25 per cent fund (2922.48 lakh) from the State Plan was earmarked during the Eighth Plan for Tribal development under TSP, but only 18.44 per cent could be utilised by the development sectors; it was lowest (18.21 per cent) for the annual plan 1992-93 a highest (19.49 per cent) for the last year (1996-97) of the plan period. Further, out of the total expenditure (2536.20 lakh) made, against it only 12.51 per cent and 15.82 per cent expenditure could be incurred on Agriculture and allied sectors and rural development programme and about 40.51 per cent funds could be utilised on Social services programmes. The indepth scrutiny has revealed that the major factors responsible for spending less amount (not proportionate to the population percentage of ST) have been as under:

1. Instead of 23.27 per cent, 21.25 per cent fund from the State plan could be earmarked under TSP in the Budget;
2. Due to financial constrains, the State Government made financial cut to the extent of 15 per cent to 20 per cent on TSP fund earmarked under different Demand Heads in the budget and due to such cut the budget fund was not allocated to the respective development departments and whatever funds allocated were not released in times due to administrative/financial reasons;
3. New items (schemes) were not sanctioned and cleared in time;
4. Rationalisation of scheme was not done under TSP as required;
5. Under three tier of Panchayat Raj system the decentralisation of scheme/programme and administrative powers were not transferred/done by the State Government as per the field requirement; and
6. There has been lack of coordination's and also over lapping between the working of Three Tier Panchayati Raj Units and the District Government, which adversely affected the TSP strategy in the State and with the result the ITDPS became dorments by all means.

The irony of situation is that as mentioned earlier, the State Government made some of the special efforts at the financial front. Separate 'Demands Numbers' were created to earmarks and to channelised the funds under 'Pool Fund' generated to provide extra allocation for the income generating programmes and also to provide grants under TSP to Panchayats for urban and rural tribal areas. Besides, rationalisation TSP schemes were done and Project

Advisory Boards (PAB) were strengthen at ITDP levels and separate Tribal Corporation (Adivasi Vitta and Vikas Nigam) was created to provide financial assistance to generate employment potentials for the unemployed tribal youths (self employment scheme) further. Special Primitive Tribal Agencies (Abhikarans) were established in 14 districts of their habitations, but, despite of all these initiatives, the pace of tribal development could not be accelerated the funds under TSP, were less utilised.

The Review

The review of the total situation has revealed that during Fifth, Sixth, Seventh and Eighth Five Year Plans, the pace of tribal development, both on the economic and non-economic fronts, could not be accelerated in the State, after deploying well remitted administrative structure and incurring financial investments.[65] The agreed level of investment from the State plan for the sub plan area of the State during the Fifth Sixth, Seventh and Eighth Five Year Plans have been shown in the Table—4.3.

Table—4.3 Agreed Financial Outlays Made During the Fifth, Sixth, Seventh and Eighth Five Years Plant From the State Plan Under Tribal Sub-Plan (TSP)

Plan Period	*Agreed Flow to TSP from State Plan*	*Percentage Flow of Fund from State Plan to TSP*	*Increase in Percentage Flow from the Previous Plan Outlay*
Fifth	210.00	15.03	
Sixth	629.03	16.55	218.70
Seventh	1298.70	18.55	106.47
Eighth	2922.48	21.35	154.10

It is clear from the above table that the level of flow to Tribal Sub-Plan areas from the State plan for the implementation of Tribal development programme rose sharply since Fifth Five Year Plan. It enhanced 218 from Fifth Plan to Sixth Plan; 106.47 per cent from Sixth Plan to Seventh Plan and 154.10 per cent from Seventh Plan to Eighth Plan. Besides, investments have also been made for the TSP area from the Special Central Assistance (SCA) received from GOI, Central Sector and the Institutional Finance. The analysis of the computation of the flow of funds to TSP reveals that in the beginning of the Sub-Plan, expenditure incurred in the TSP areas used to be taken as the flow. But as the strategy progressed, further refinements were introduced to enhance the real flow of funds.[66]

The national economy as well as economy of the State comprises the organised and the unorganised sectors. The former comprises the modern industrial sectors and the associated infrastructure, commercial organisation and economic institutions, modern, social and professional services and the variegated apparatus of the State. The unorganised sector includes agriculture and allied activities, Village and household industries, traditional professional services and such like. It is the revealing fact that the bulk of benefits of the organised sectors largely goes to those who have the benefit of being nearer to the emerging centre of power and urban/semi-urban areas, while majority of the activities in the un-organised sector face the backlash. With the result the differential between the two sectors is widen at the fast rate. The trend made under tribal sub-plan during the Fifth and Subsequent Sixth, Seventh and Eighth Five Year Plans shows that during the Fifth Five Year Plan, only 69.87 per cent and during the annual plan 1979-80 69.68 per cent funds could be spent on the tribal development out of the total outlay provided under TSP. Both organised and unorganised sector were not able to utilise the funds. Because during pre-Fifth Plan period these sectors used to implement a few specific programmes for the benefit of tribals in the State. After the new strategy of tribal development adopted in the Fifth Plan, their style of functioning remained more or less the same. However, in the absence of due appreciation of these sectors/developments, they overlapped their jurisdictions and blurred the responsibilities.[67]

During the Sixth Plan, efforts were made to control and regularise the financial outlays/system implementation of the sectoral programmes on the infrastructural development programmes and direct on family benefits programmes. But maximum amount were spent under the organised sector than un-organised sector. On the sectors like irrigation, flood control, power, transport and communication, industry and minerals more than hundred per cent of the allocations were utilised while the pattern of expenditure was poor in the un-organised sectors like agriculture and allied services (85.28 per cent), special rural programmes (74.19 per cent), and economic services (53.71 per cent). Thus, led to heavy backlash and did not help in promoting the uneconomic aspects of the life of the tribals, specially residing in the backward/primitive regions of the State. Similarly, in the Seventh and Eighth Five Year Plans about 90 per cent and 95 per cent amount of the total allocation was earmarked for the organised sector under the Tribal Sub-Plan. The unorganised sector were facing severe backlash of development of all the variations and with the result the social and economic status of the tribals could not improve and their participation in the whole process of development was lacking. This has been the main reason that the real benefit could not reach to the majority, of tribals and the interior primitive regions/pockets falling in the tribal areas. Only a small number of tribal people, say tribal elites or educated persons have been benefited. Such process of polarisation is gradually growing within the unorganised sectors in general and tribal economy in particular Commissioner, SC/ST Commission in his Twenty Eighth Report has also observed, "It is only in a comparatively smaller comparising services under Government and Public Sector in which the policy of positive discrimination has enabled the member of Scheduled Tribes to get a foothold. The big differential in the access to education and the initial start has thus created a setting of unequal competition for the opportunities in the organised sector, bulk of which have gone to the members of higher cates. Thus, the inter-sectoral and intra sectoral polarization has acquired a social base".

While concluding the discussions done in the fore going paras, it is clear that to overcome and eliminate the policy of isolation, the policy of integration has been adopted through *compensatory* discrimination using different provisions made in the Indian Constitution for overall development and protection of the Scheduled Tribes and their areas of inhabitation. The TSP strategy has stipulated the funds of the Centre and State Governments on the population proposition basis of STs with budgetary mechanism to ensure accountability, non-diverse ability and utilising for the welfare and development of STs in Madhya Pradesh. But even after fifty six years of independence, so many issues have been left unresolved and several problems are persisting with regard to the tribals. The unresolved issues comprises, displacements of Tribals, indebtedness, deprivation of tribal rights on forests, land alienation and bringing them in the mainstream of Indian society. The Planning Commission has also confessed in the mainstream of Indian society. The planning commission has also confessed in Tenth Plan document (chapter 4.2 page 457) that "Tribal Communities continue to be vulnerable even today, not because they are poor, but assetless and illiterate compared to general population; but often their distinct vulnerability arises from their inability to negotiate and cope with the mainstream economy, society, cultural and political systems, from all of which they were historically protected by their relative isolation (para 4.2.49).

The persisting problems are spread over viz. low literacy a high drop out rates in the school, inadequate and inaccessible health service, nutritional deficiencies and diseases and lack of adequate irrigation facilities, extreme/abject poverty, endangering of intellectual property rights, crimes/atrocities against STs, neglect of forest villages and settlements of tribals on the encroached forest land extinction of Primitive Tribal Groups (PTGs), ineffectives implementation of PESA, 1996 and routinised mechanism of TSP with regards to the implementation of TSP. The Planning Commission in its same chapter has also mentioned "...The strategy of TSP, as is implemented, has also become very much routinised. Thus its impact on improving the conditions of STs is not being felt." (Page 463). This observation of Planning Commission very much applies in the State of Madhya Pradesh, where TSP is being implemented in highly reutilised manner. It looks sound on this paper, but implementation is very poor, specially under the Three Tier Panchayati Raj System. So Pace of Tribal Development in the State is slow and in case it continues in this manner, it would be devastating to the tribals. The glimpse of such scenario is appearing in the shapes and action of mass reaction of tribals against their exploitation and conflicting situations, specially in the context of forests and other persisting problems/issues as mentioned above. Therefore, empowerment of tribals is must in the existing democratic system of Governance, so that they could be able to deal with their problems. The Planning Commission has also shown its anxiety and it is worth to quote the Commission's directive (P. 470 para 4.2.93 and 94), "As the empowerment of tribals goes beyond the existing framework of the welfare and development, the efforts of the Central and State Governments will be to adopt both effective and innovative strategies/action plans by involving the tribal people and their institutions at all levels and the executive governmental agencies in a synchronizing manner. Consultation with the tribal people before taking decisions about their welfare and development will, therefore, become a functional pre-requisite for ensuring both acceptance/involvement of the tribal people besides effective implementation of programmes towards empowering them. Finally, the absence of a laid-down national policy for empowerment of tribals has been the most obvious missing link and also a big gap in the planning process of empowering the tribals".

REFERENCES

1. Sharma, B.D. *Tribal Development Planning*, National Institute of Community Development, Hyderabad, p. 5.
2. Raizada, Ajit, *Tribal Development in Madhya Pradesh—A Planning Perspective*, p. 30.
3. Dhebar, U.N., *Report of Scheduled Areas and Scheduled Tribes Commission 1961*, p. 32.
4. Dube, S.C., *Tribal Development—Illusion and Reality*.
5. Sharma, K.N., *Development Planning for Madhya Pradesh Tribes*—A Review Article, Bulletin of Tribal Research Institute, p. 16.
6. Census of India, 1971 & 1981.
7. Singh, Bhupinder, *Training of Trainers in Tribal Development Administration*.
8. Ramkrishnan Mission: *The Tribals of Madhya Pradesh Vivekananda Ashram Raipur Development and Challenges*, Souvenir.
9. The Report of the Advisory Committee on the Revision of the List of Scheduled Castes and Scheduled Tribes G.O.I. Department of Social Security 1965, p. 6.
10. Naik T.B. *What is Tribe Conflicting Definition—Applied Anthropology In India*. Edited by L.P. Vidhyarthi, 1968, pp. 92-93.
11. Sharma, B.D., *Tribal Development in India-–Brief Revision, Occasional Papers on Tribal Development No. 28*, G.O.I.M.O.H. 1980 p. 15.
12. Naik T.B., *What is Tribe Conflicting Definition Applied Anthropology in India*, Edited by Dr. L.P. Vidyarthi 1968, p. 91.
13. Ibid Page No. 97.
14. Singh, Yogendhar, *Modernisation of Indian Tradition*, 1973, p. 1.

15. Lous Dumont, *Chage Interaction and Comparison, Contribution to Indian Sociology No. VII March, 1964*, p. 10.
16. Sharma B.D., *Tribal Development The Concept and the Frame, 1978*, p. 2.
17. Smelesor, Neil, J., *The Sociology of Economic Life*, 1965, p. 100.
18. *Ibid* p. 101.
19. Sharma, B.D., *Tribal Development—The Concept & Frame*.
20. Report of the Scheduled Areas and Scheduled Tribes Commission, G.O.I., 1961 p. 8.
21. Sharma B.D. ,*Tribal Development—The Concept & Frame 1978*, p. 1.
22. Singh K.S., *Colonial Transformation of the Tribal Society in Middle India Occasional Papers on Tribals Development No. 22 GOI not 1982*, p. 9.
23. *Ibid* p. 10.
24. Singh K.S. *Colonial Transformation of the Tribal Society in Middle India—Occasional Paper on Tribal Development, 1982*, p. 2.
25. *Report of Scheduled Areas and Scheduled Tribes Commission GOI, 1961, Page No. 21 26.* Singh K.S., Colonial Transformation of the Tribal Society in Middle India—Occasional Papers on Tribals Development 1982, p. 2.
26. *Ibid* p. 11.
27. *Ibid* p. 11.
28. *Ibid* p. 11.
29. *Ibid* p. 11.
30. *Ibid* p. 15.
31. *Ibid* p. 13.
32. *Ibid* pp. 13 and 14.
33. *Ibid* p. 14.
34. *Ibid* pp. 14, 15, 16.
35. *Ibid* pp. 16, 17.
36. *Ibid* p. 17.
37. The Report of Scheduled Areas and Scheduled Tribes Commission GOI 1961, p. 29.
38. Chandra, Vimal—*A Historical Review of the Progress of Education Amongst the Scheduled Caste Applied Anthropology in India*—Edited by Dr. L.P. Vidyarthi—1968 No. 299-300.
39. Report of Scheduled Areas and Scheduled Tribes Commission, GOI 1961.
40. Raizada, Ajit, T*ribal Development in Madhya Pradesh 1984*, p. 7.
41. Mathur K.S., *Some Problems of Tribal Rehabilitation in Madhya Pradesh Applied in India*, Edited by Dr. L.P. Vidyarthi 1968 p. 22.

42. *Ibid* p. 423.

43. Mathur K.S., *Some Problem of Tribal Rehabilitation in Madhya Pradesh Applied Anthoropology in India*, Edited by Dr. L.P. Vidyarthi, p. 422.

44. Report of Scheduled Areas and Sch. Tribes Commission 1961 p. 30.

45. *Ibid* p. 32.

46. *Ibid* p. 32.

47. Raizada, Ajit, *Tribal Development in Madhya Pradesh*, p. 6.

48. *Ibid* pp. 16 and 17.

49. *Ibid* pp. 16 and 17.

50. *Ibid* pp. 16 and 17.

51. *Ibid* pp. 16 and 17.

52. *Ibid* pp. 17 and 18.

53. Saxena R.N., *The Changing Tribes in India—Applied Authropology in India* 1968, pp. 264-66.

54. Leuva K.K., *Impact of Constitutional Safeguards on the Sch. Tribes. Applied Anthropology in India*, Edited by Dr. L.P. Vidyarthi, 1968.

55. *Ibid* p. 276.

56. Roy Burman, B.K., *Anthropology Concept on Problems and Planning & Research for Social Development—Applied Anthropology in India*, Edited by Dr. L.P. Vidyrathi, 1968 pp. 42, 43 and 45.

57. *Ibid*.

58. *Ibid*.

59. Tribal Development—*A New Strategy—Occasional Papers on Tribal Development No. 4*, GOI MOH, 1976, Self No. 11.

60. *Occasional Papers on Tribal Development No. 4*, GOI MOH, 1976, Self No. 11.

61. *Ibid* p. 12.

62. *Draft Tribal Sub Plan Document—Tribal Area Development and Planning*, Govt. of M.P. Th. Bcd, 1984 p. 9.

63. *Ibid* p. 67.

64. Tribal Sub Plan Draft (1990-95).

65. *Tribal Sub Plan Draft—Tribal Area Development and Planning*, Govt. of M.P. Th. and Bed, 1990 pp. 7, 8 and 9.

66. Report of Commissioner of Sch. Caste & Sch. Tribes Commission (Twenty Eighth Report).

5

Ails of Tribal Development

Dr. I. Satya Sundaram

Planning in India has bypassed some regions and some sections of the population. The tribal people constitute a marginalised section. They formed 8.2 per cent of the country's total population according to 2001 census.

Peculiar Environment

All the developmental activities undertaken by the government to uplift the poor sections of the tribal and non-tribal communities had benefited the better-off-sections—the peasants and landlords of the non-tribal community only. Also benefited were traders and middlemen.

Despite Adivasis self sustaining lifestyles, the governments fail to protect their right to use resources on their lands in a sustainable way. Forests officials assume the role of policing and not of conservation.

Women in tribal society are forced to undertake productive work for economic reasons. They collect minor forest products like honey, tamarind, medicinal roots, fruits and bamboo products. Most of the tribal women are working in the primary sector.

The tribal people sometimes depend on their traditional wisdom. Take the case of *Jhum* cultivation. Researchers found that this system is extremely efficient in maximising the use of scarce labour. The aim is to produce enough for self consumption.

Forest ground is soft and needs no tilling. Burning eliminates all weeds; so, no weeding is required. The system aims at minimising labour input, rather than maximising output. The fertility of patch diminishes in a couple of seasons, so the tribe moves to another forest patch, leaving the first one fallow to regain fertility.[1]

The Dhabar Commission (1961) recommended an integrated approach, giving due importance to the minimum needs.

The Task Force on the Development of the Tribal Area (1972) suggested that ecological, occupational and social parameters of development of the tribal population should be properly assessed for the formulation of a policy.

The Dube Committee (1972) tried to design a unique approach for the tribal development. It felt that the problems of tribal development should be defined at the national level. It favoured area development approach with due respect to sentiments and aspirations of the tribal people.

Policy Initiatives

The tribal development strategies in India aimed at improving the quality of life of tribal people by implementing minimum needs programme; infrastructure development in tribal regions; development of human resources through appropriate education and training, and finally expansion of credit and marketing facilities through cooperatives.

In the Second Five Year Plan period (1956-61), a special multi-purpose tribal project was implemented in select tribal areas.

The Third Five Year Plan (1961-66) witnessed the implementation of Tribal Development Block system.

It aimed at not only improving conditions of tribal areas but also involving tribal people in the development process.

The Fourth Five Year Plan aimed at integration of the tribal economy with the mainstream economy.

The Fifth Plan witnessed the formulation of tribal sub-plan (TSPs). It included all the scheduled areas and blocks where tribal population formed more than 50 per cent of the total population.

The Sixth Five Year Plan adopted 'Modified Area Development Approach' to enlarge coverage of tribal population.

The Seventh Five Year Plan laid stress on cluster approach and 47 clusters with tribal concentration were identified.

In the Eighth Year Plan, the emphasis was on a substantial increase in the flow of funds for tribal area development.

The Ninth Plan adopted a holistic approach, with stress on empowering the tribal people. The aim is to see that the development benefits reach the unreached.

The Tenth Five Year Plan wants to insulate the tribal economy from the adverse effects of globalisation.

As marketing continues to be a major problem for tribal people, most State Governments have established Girijan Cooperatives Corporations. The Corporation is an exclusive agency by minor forest and agricultural produce from the tribals at a fair price and to supply domestic requirements at reasonable prices.

An outlay of Rs. 1,146 crore was provided in the Annual Plan 2004-05 (Rs. 1087 crore in 2003-04) for undertaking various welfare and developmental works to empower tribal people.[2]

Special Central Assistance (SCA) to Tribal Sub-Plan (TSP) is a 100 per cent grant to undertake a number of developmental schemes with a focus on family oriented income generating schemes, creation of critical infrastructure and also to extend financial assistance to self-help groups, community based activities, primitive tribal groups and forest villages.

Grant-in-aid under Article 275 (1) is being provided to the states with a view to raising the level of administration in the States covered under Scheduled Areas to bring them on par with other states.

The Scheduled Tribes (Recognition of Forest Rights) Bill 2005 seeks to make Adivasi communities active protectors of the forest while strengthening their livelihood possibilities.

It secures 13 rights for the Adivasis that include access to and ownership of minor forest produce, grazing rights, habitat and habitation for primitive tribes, settlement of old habitation and unsurveyed villages and the community right to intellectual and traditional knowledge relating to forest and cultural diversity. The vested forest rights are heritable but not alienable or transferrable.

Clearly, the Bill is not just about rights. It is also about responsibilities. Hunting is not permitted. It is clearly stated that the rights may be exercised only for *bona fide* livelihood needs and not for commercial purposes.

Major Problems

Given the low level of literacy and general ignorance most tribal people are not aware of the various schemes launched for their benefit. The benefits had mostly accrued to the more advanced among the tribal population.[3]

Despite many good safeguards provided in the regulation Acts, the shrewd landlords and moneylenders manage to cultivate the lands belonging to the tribal people. The situation worsened because of the frequent filling of writ petitions in the court by the affected non-tribals.

In many cases, the tribal department has no resource inventory nor the exercises about their optimum utilisation. It has no idea about occupational and income pattern. Most planners have impressionistic ideas about the tribal economy. No independent surveys were undertaken about the tribal economy. Ad hoc programmes cannot raise the income of the tribal people permanently.[4]

The setting up of bit industries in tribal regions would not solve the tribal problems. For instance, the Rourkela Steel Plant was set up in a tribal region in Orissa, but the region made no progress. The tribal way of life has been completely destroyed. The steel plant conferred no benefits on the tribal people for the simple reason that neither its inputs nor products have any local significance.[5]

There has been adversarial relationship between Adivasi communities and the Forest Department. Very often the Adivasis are deprived of their traditional rights of access for even rudimentary needs of adivasis such as fodder, fuel and housing timber.

The Ministry had itself stated in its affidavit to the Supreme Court in July 2004 that its order of February 5, 2004 was "based on the recognition that the historical injustice done to the tribal forest dwellers through non-recognition of their traditional rights must be finally rectified. It should be understood clearly that the lands occupied by the tribals in forest areas do not have any forest vegetation."

The Ninth Five Year Plan (1997-2002) noticed that in the TSP, the infrastructure takes away the major share (up to 37 per cent) of the plan funds.

The TSPs are handicapped by low level of people's participation, very poor literacy rates and inadequate medicare.

In spite of government insistence on earmarking of funds for TSP, some states did not make the requisite provision. In some states, the heavy outlays earmarked resulted in implementation of schemes in a hurry.

The marketing system in the tribal economies is in very bad shape. The tribal economies have their own peculiar geographical, climatic and economic features.

The marketing habits and practices are so traditional that they are unable to realise a fair value for their produce as middle men continue to exploit them.

Measures Needed

Forest land is a primary source of income for most tribal people. Hence, the Adivasis who own lands need financial and technical support to develop their lands.

Laws are there to prohibit non-tribal occupation of tribal lands. The Supreme Court observed that transfer of land to State instrumentatives like the Andhra Pradesh Mineral Development Corporation or to a cooperative of tribals may be allowed. The Court also observed that 20 per cent of the net profit should be set apart as a permanent fund, and the same should be used for tribal welfare—setting up schools, hospitals, transport and sanitation facilities.

In the past, the A.P. Government expressed its desire to hand over som' tribal lands in the Srikakulam District to a Dubai based compan' vhich wanted to exploit bauxite resources. There was a hue and cry at the government move. Experts say that industrialisation should not be handicapped by tribal laws, and when tribal lands are taken over by the corporates, the tribal people should be duly compensated, in addition to providing employment.[6]

The tribal people depend heavily on forests. There is need for integration of tribals and forest economics. Forest based industries need to be encouraged for providing productive employment to tribal people. We have to ensure strong backward and forward linkages between forestry and other development sectors.[7]

There is need for strengthening the Grain Bank Schemes of the Ministry of Tribal Affairs by simplifying procedures and extending it to the entire country, covering all the endemic, drought and migration prone areas with concentration of tribal population, and also in other tribal areas.[8] It is better to store the grain in the village itself because this will act like a share capital provided by the government as a one-time grant.[9]

The best way to raise the socio-economic status of tribal women is formation of self-help groups (SHGs). The SHG-bank linkage (the mechanism of micro credit) has brought about a sea change in the earning capacity and status of tribal women.

The tribal people have to be taught to learn self-help. They should be free to be their own in their own surroundings. There is an erroneous impression that tribal development should be brought out without disturbing the existing socio-cultural practices. This is not possible. We should aim at change amongst the tribal people so that they themselves jettison irrelevant practices. Also, there should be social audit of the works undertaken.[10]

The tribal development strategies should be based on the cultural characteristics, environmental peculiarities and traditional skill etc. of the tribal population. This is necessary to prevent migration.[11]

No doubt, special programmes are being implemented for the development of tribal areas. But, these are not producing the desired results. One reason for this is they are not integrated with other development programmes. Also, the schemes are not based on the peculiar environment of the tribal people. Special care should be taken to meet the education, training and health needs of the tribal regions.

REFERENCES

1. Swaminathan S. Anklesaria Aiyar: '*Tribals and the Growth Puzzle*', The Economic Times, April 27, 2005.
2. *Economic Survey 2004-05*, Ministry of Finance, Government of India, p. 243.
3. Vinod Joseph: '*Tribal Development during the Five Year Plan*', Kurukshetra, June, 2003, p. 24.
4. O.S. Shrivastava: 'Interface of the Tribals in Madhya Pradesh: Sub-plan Strategy' in *Emerging Trends in Indian Economy* Edited by A.D.N., Bajpai et al. 1995. Atlantic Publishers & Distributors, New Delhi. p. 478.
5. Sachitanand (1970): '*Pitfalls of Rural Industrialisation*', The Hindu, July 9.
6. R.J. Rajendra Prasad: '*Eyeing Tribal Land*', The Hindu, July 11, 2000.
7. Roy Burman, B.K. 1982. *Report of the Committee on Forest and Tribals in India*. Tribal Development Division. Ministry of Home Affairs, New Delhi.
8. S.K. Naik: '*Towards a Hunger Free Tribal India*', Yojana, September 2002. p. 37.
9. *Ibid*, p. 38.
10. O.S. Shrivastava, *op.cit*, p. 479.
11. Dilip Shah: '*Tribal Development: Planning and Performance*', Kurukshetra, June 2003, p. 22.

6

Development of Indian Tribes

Anthropological Analysis

Dr. Bindu Ramachandran

According to 1991 Census 67,758,380 tribal people in India are found to settle in all most all States and Union Territories except the States of Punjab, Haryana J & K and Union Territories of Delhi, Chandigarh and Pondicherry. 1991 Census depicts that Mizoram is the State where highest number of tribes (94.8 per cent) and Uttar Pradesh is the State with lowest proportion (0.02 per cent) of Scheduled Tribes. The British rulers after establishing their colonial rule in pre-independent India adopted the policy of isolation towards the tribal people because they never liked to disturb the isolated condition of the tribal people. Besieds colonial interest, the British people had many other motives behind this sort of policy decision. This has resulted in a kind of emotional detachment of the tribals from the rest of the mainstream society and accelerated the growth of exploiters like moneylenders, non-tribal migrants, feudal lords and Christian missionaries.

The British rulers encouraged Christian missionaries to work among the tribal people with definite purposes. One was to do welfare works and development activities and the other was to convert tribal people to Christianity. But this policy of British Govt. took sudden all when India won independence. Anticipating all the existed and existing problems of tribal people, Union Govt. of independent India adopted entirely different strategies for the development of Indian tribes. Important among them are protection of the tribal interests through administrative and legal support and implementation of development programmes to enhance their standard of living. As part of administrative and legal support tribals were provided with safeguards and policies for development and various programmes were implemented covering all sectors of tribal life. This paper is an attempt to analyse the socio-cultural background of Kerala tribes which acts as hindrance in the way of their development and the disabilities from the part of authorities in selecting the beneficiaries and methodological strategies in its right context.

Scheduled Tribes of Kerala

There are 35 communities in the list of Scheduled Tribes in Kerala. According to 1991 Census their population was 320,967 persons which is 1.10 per cent of total population of the State (29098518). According to 2001 census the Scheduled Tribe population was 364,189 persons which is 1.1 per cent of total population of the state (31,841,374). The tribe-wise and gender wise population of Kerala State, according to 1991 census in given in Table—6.1.

Table—6.1 Tribewise and Genderwise Population of Kerala State (1991 Census)

S.No.	*Tribe*	*Male*	*Female*	*Total*	*% of total tribal population*
1	2	3	4	5	6
1.	Adiyan	4792	4898	9690	3.02
2.	Arandan	94	102	196	0.06
3.	Eravallan	1617	1522	3139	0.98
4.	Hill Pulaya	1463	1388	2851	0.89
5.	Irular/Irulan	10983	10853	21836	6.80
6.	Kadar	1022	999	2021	0.63
7.	Kammara	56	67	123	0.04
8.	Kanikkar/Kanikaran	7946	8518	16464	5.13
9.	Kattunayakan	6271	5884	12155	3.79
10.	Kochu Velan	18	18	36	0.01

(Table Contd...)

1	2	3	4	5	6
11.	Konda Kapus	1	4	5	0.001
12.	Kondareddis	227	215	442	0.14
13.	Koraga	826	825	1651	0.51
14.	Kota	17	19	36	0.01
15.	Kudiya, Melakudi	381	370	751	0.23
16.	Kurichchan	14386	13901	28287	8.81
17.	Kurumans	11855	11589	23444	7.30
18.	Kurumbas	955	865	1820	0.57
19.	Maha Malasar	14	22	36	0.01
20.	Malai Arayan	12504	12445	24949	7.77
21.	Malai Pandaram	1570	1369	2939	0.92
22.	Malai Vedan	3105	3226	6331	1.97
23.	Malakkuravan	292	255	547	0.17
24.	Malasar	577	484	1061	0.33
25.	Malayan	3822	3720	7542	2.35
26.	Malayarayar	2699	2796	5495	1.71
27.	Mannan	3565	3520	7085	2.21
28.	Marati	13170	12872	26042	8.11
29.	Muthubvan/Mudugar Muduvan	8762	8616	17378	5.41
30.	Palleyan	118	118	236	0.07
31.	Palliyan	773	745	1518	0.47
32.	Palliyar	79	76	155	0.05
33.	Paniyan	33273	34675	67948	21.17
34.	Ulladan	7424	7422	14846	4.63
35.	Uraly	5316	5019	10335	3.22
36.	Unclassified	839	738	1577	0.49
	Total	**160812**	**160155**	**320967**	**100.00**

Out of the 35 communities listed in the 1991 census records, recently some of the communities are omitted and in that place new ones are added. According to the list published by Ministry of Tribal Affairs (Annual report 2002-03), seven communities are omitted from the census list and eight ones are newly added to the list.

Scheduled Tribes of Kerala

The latest amended list of Scheduled Tribes is detailed below.

Annual report 2002-03. Ministry of Tribal Affairs.

1. Adiyan
2. Arandan, Aranadan
3. Eravallan
4. Hill Pulaya, Mala Pulayan Kurumba Pulayan, Pamba Pulayan
5. Irular, Irulan
6. Kadar, Wayanad Kadar
7. Omitted
8. Kanikaran, Kanikkar
9. Kattunayakan
10. Kochuvelan
11. Omitted
12. Omitted
13. Korga
14. Omitted
15. Kudiya, Melakudi
16. Kurrichchan, Kurichiyan
17. Kurumans, Mullukuruman, Mullakuruman, Malakuruman
18. Kurumbas, Kurumbar, Kurumban
19. Maha Malasar
20. Malai Arayan, Mala Arayan
21. Malai Pandaram
22. Malai Vedan, Malavedan
23. Malakkuravan
24. Malasar

25. Malayan, Nattu, Malayan, Konga Malayan (excluding the areas comprising the Kasargode, Cannanore, Wayanad, and Kozhikode Districts)
26. Malayarayar
27. Mannan
28. Omitted
29. Muthuvan, Mudugar, Muduvan
30. Palleyan, Pallyyan, Palliyar, Paliyan
31. Omitted
32. Omitted
33. Paniyan
34. Ulladan
35. Uraly
36. Mala Vettuvan (in Kasargode and Kannur districts)
37. Ten Kuruman, Jenu Kurumban
38. Thachonodan, Thachanadan Moopan
39. Cholanaicken
40. Mavilan
41. Karimpalan
42. Vetta Kuruman
43. Mala Panicker

The Scheduled Tribes of Kerala are numerically predominant in Wayanad, Idukki, Palakkad and Kasargod districts. They are distributed in other districts also but the number is less when compared to the above mentioned districts. 35.82 per cent of the total tribal population of the State lives in Wayanad which forms 17.11 per cent of the total population of that district. The districtwise S.T. population according to 1991 census in given in Table 6.2.

Table—6.2 Schedule Tribe Population of Kerala State (1991 Census)

District	*Total population*	*Tribal population*	*% of total population of the district*	*% of total tribal population of the state*
Thiruvananthapuram	2946650	16181	0.55	5.04
Kollam	2407566	3884	0.16	1.21
Pathanamthitta	1188332	6922	0.58	2.16
Alapuzha	2001217	2801	0.14	0.57
Kottayam	1828271	17996	0.98	5.61
Idukki	1078066	50269	4.67	15.66
Ernakulam	2817236	4941	0.18	1.54
Thrissur	2737311	4051	0.15	1.26
Palakkad	2382235	35465	1.50	11.05
Malappuram	3096330	10555	0.34	3.29
Kozhikode	2619941	5407	0.21	1.69
Wayanad	672128	114969	17.11	35.82
Kannur	2251727	18243	0.81	5.68
Kasaragod	1071508	29283	2.70	9.12
Total	29098518	320967	1.10	100

Though 35 communities have been notified in the Scheduled Tribe list of the state, communities like, Kammara, Kondakapus, and Kondareddis are not found in Kerala. However, they have been enumerated in various censuses. The reason for this is that during census enumeration, the enumerators record the community names as revealed by the individuals, and they do not verify validity of which. Certain communities though a single entity, have been classified under different titles and serial numbers in the list. For instance, Palleyan, Palliyan and Palliyar form a single community, but classified under different serial numbers (item numbers 30, 31 and 32). Similarly Malai Araya (item number 20) and Malayarayas (item number 26) form a single entity. Likewise, Kochuvelan (item No. 10) is a synonym of Ulladan, classified as item number 34. Though Maha Malassar and Malasar form a single community, they are enlisted as two distinct communities as item number 19 and number 24 (KIRTADS...) Among the 35 tribal groups of Kerala, five communities i.e. Kattunaicken, Koraga, Kurumbar, Kadar and Cholanaicken are classified as primitive tribal groups considering their relative isolation and subsistence economy from the rest of the tribal population. In Wayanad district, there are two tribal communities; Mullukuruman and Uralikuruman classified under single title 'Kurumans' (item number 17). But their subsistence pattern and culture are entirely different. Among the Scheduled Tribe population of Kerala, Paniyan form the numerically predominant community. At present the tribal population of Kerala are generally classified under different economic categories such as food gatherers, agricultural labourers and settled cultivators. Landless people are working as wage labourers under tribal and non-tribal landlords and also in forest department.

Anthropological Analysis

Tribal development has been accepted as the main issue of debate and public policy by the nation. Anthropologists advocated the method of sharing and development effort by the beneficiaries of a community and this is so particular in the case of tribes. If development is a structured and orderly transition of one social system or values from lower to higher order, the transition can be measured by verifying the capacity of a community to respond to the complex situations of biological and social environment. Chamber says, 'I take the term development to mean deliberate attempts to alter human interaction with the natural and built environment through innovations in agriculture, new energy exploitation and conversion of the construction of modern transportation systems, improvement in housing and so on. (1985: 81).

When reaches application level the confusions regarding development gives to so many problems. In most cases any failure in the proper implementation of development strategies is often blamed on the strict and tradition bound cultural beliefs and practices of the actual beneficiaries. In Kerala, Govt. has implemented a number of programmes for the welfare of tribal communities especially in the fields of education, health, housing etc. As far as tribal education is concerned, providing educational facilities on large scale is one thing while the utilisation aspect is another thing. According to the data collected from four districts of

Kerala regarding tribal education, the progress of education among food gatherers and agricultural labourers does not commensurate with the all round facilities available in the area. They have late enrolment in schools. Detailed investigation on the school going children and their academic performances revealed that their standard is staggeringly poor and the dropout rate is very high. It is also understood that economically well of families are interested in imparting education to their children by admitting them in hostels. There are many reasons for the irregular attendance of tribal children. When we probe into the situation, it is clear that irregular attendance is directly proportional to their attitude towards education on one end and their social and economic background on the other. Most of the tribal children are from families where both father and mother are working for wage labour. In such houses it is his duty to look after the young ones in the house. If there is more than one school going child, they take alternative days duty to look after the young. In such circumstances regular attendance of that boy or girl is interrupted. In some of the families if mother or father take one day off from their daily work due to any physical unfitness, that time the school going boy has to earn the livelihood for the family by doing some minor jobs. The drop-out details are given below:

District-Wise Dropout

No.	District	Total ST students		Drop-out			
		Male	Female	Male	%	Female	%
1.	Idukki	1371	1381	45	3.28	45	3.25
2.	Palakkad	1900	1725	70	3.68	45	2.60
3.	Wayanad	4511	3705	300	6.65	280	6.20
4.	Kasaragod	1080	1025	47	4.35	58	5.65

Data relating to dropout depicts that Wayanad district has very large percentage of dropout as compared to other districts. The male and female ST students dropout is higher in Wayanad (6.65 for males and 6.20 per cent for females). It is clear that drop-out rate is higher in tribal areas where the social and economic condition of the inhabitants is very low and backward, and most of them belong to primitive category like Kattunaicken and Paniyan.

Many of the tribal families of Kerala are not having adequate land for cultivation except a few percentages of settled agricultural families like Mullukurumba, Kurichiyan ... etc. Land is one of the stumbling blocks in the path of development Since the tribal families do not have any documents of ownership the land is generally alienated due to their unawareness. Govt. has given lands to landless food gatherers and agricultural labourers. But some families of the food-gatherers are not interested in agricultural activities because of their gathering nature of economy. If they are diverted to land based economic development programmes, they can very well utilise the land for obtaining subsistence. Distribution of adequate land and creation of awareness regarding the utility of land ensures employment and there by an upliftment in the present economic condition. If the principal Act (Kerala Scheduled Tribes Act 1975) is implemented and the alienated land is distributed among the tribal families irrespective of the period or nature of alienation, that can help the landless to improve their economic condition to a certain extend.

As part of tribal development, Govt. has built houses for the rehabilitation of tribes. Not only the construction of these houses very poor, but also the basic norms of good housing have not been fulfilled. Proper ventilation is absent and the houses are found leaking in rainy seasons. The disadvantages in Govt. housing forced them to vacate the allotted houses and they themselves constrained to the traditional method of housing. But there also they have to face another restriction. The traditional hut of most of the Kerala tribes is made with bamboo and logs collected from the forest. The introduction of forest laws do not allow to enter the forest areas without an entry pass from the department officials and tribal people are not allowed to take a single stick from the forest. These kinds of legal restrictions and other measures prevent the targets of tribal development in utilising and maintaining the resources. If Govt. adopts the methodology of taking the opinion of beneficiaries before implementing any programme, they will be benefited more than more within their cultural traditions.

Drinking water is another important area requires urgent attention. Even though Kerala is blessed with number of rivers and streams pure drinking water remains a problem in tribal areas.

Most of the tribal colonies are provided with drinking water facilities by installing pipes. But in major areas it is of no use. The pipes are dry in all the seasons and women have to go in search of water from other sources or they have to depend on their traditional method of fetching water. Govt. has also provided wells in most of the colonies but the inhabitants have not maintained it neatly especially in the colonies of primitive tribes. Actually they are not aware of the role of pure drinking water and proper sanitation. They used to put all the unwanted materials in the well and use it as 'waste tank'. In rainy seasons this types of waste tanks accelerates the growth of mosquitoes and other insects. If the concerned officials give a detailed picture of all the aspects of pure drinking water, sanitation and hygiene, before implementing the programme, the beneficiaries can utilise the advantages of each programme.

Occupational status of the tribal population of Kerala shows that 60 per cent of them are engaged in agricultural labour and other wage labours. It is true that Govt. has given land to cultivate, tried to teach them new method of cultivation and has even supplied with agricultural tools and implements. However, a large percentage of the food-gatherers are not interested in agriculture. After the initial expenditure involved in agriculture and the difficulties in learning a new mission, when wild animals destroy their crops or if they do not get sufficient outputs they naturally feel that their efforts are wasted. More over the non-tribal neighbours used to take the agricultural implements supplied by Govt. for cheap prices and the tribal gradually lost their interest in agriculture. If the concerned authorities systematically inspect the output, this sort of exploitations can be checked to a certain extent. The Govt. can also explore other economic opportunities if the beneficiaries are not interested in agriculture. Their skill in bamboo work which could be developed for basketry and if they can be taught modern methods of extracting honey and encouraged to do bee keeping at home.

Road network and transportation facilities are poor in the tribal areas of Kerala. In the districts of Idukki and Palakkad, of the tribal settlements are situated in hilly areas and it is too difficult to reach there especially in rainy seasons. Poor transport facilities also stand as a hindering block to the education of the tribals as they have to walk long distance to reach educational institutions.

The most important thing is the tribes of Kerala, to a certain extent lost their ecological balance as a result of the inequalities in rehabilitation programme on the one hand and the disappearing forest resources on the other land. It is a fact that they cannot continue their traditional style of especially the subsistence patterns with these depleting forest resources. So it is high time to think about the alternative strategies for better survival. Before implementing any development programme the Govt. should consider the cultural background of the community and their suggestions. Therefore, development efforts may be designed specifically to suit the tribal group to ensure their success.

REFERENCES

Bindu, B., 1997. Ethnographic Study on the Kattunaickens—A Food Gathering Tribe of Wayanad, Kerala. *Journal of Human Ecology*, Vol. 8, July 1997.

Luiz A.A.D., 1962. *The Tribes of Kerala*, New Delhi: Bharathiya Adimjathi Sevak Sang.

Menon, T Madhava, 1986. *Encyclopedia of Dravidian Tribes*. Trivandrum: ISDL.

Mathur, P.R.G., 1997. *Tribal Situation in Kerala; Trivandrum*: Kerala Historical Society.

Misra, Rajalakshmi, 1971. *Mullukurumbas of Kappala*; Calcutta: ASI.

Parthasarathy, J., 1996. Kattunaicken; in Sachidananda & B.R. Prasad (ed), *Encyclopaedia Profile of Indian Tribes*; New Delhi: Discovery Publishing House.

Panur, K., 1963. Keralathilae Africa; Kottayam: National Book Stall.

Thurston, E., 1909. *Castes and Tribes of Southern India*; Madras: Govt. Press.

Vidyarthi, L.P., 1976. *The Tribal Culture of India*; New Delhi: Concept Publishing Co.

7

Indian Tribes and Gender Disability in Female Education

Dr. Nabakumar Duary

The members of feminine gender in India and many other parts of the world are taken considered as low status in the traditional male dominated societies. They face a lot of problems since childhood till old age. Female is caught in a 'no win' situation. It is generally found that the girl child is often neglected in feeding, health care and education. She feels that the male child is preferred to her in the family. Ultimately she adjusts herself and makes the mental make up in this situation. Durkheim has stated that, "the two sexes do not share in social life. Man is actively involved in it, while women does little more than look on from a distance. Consequently man is much more highly socialised than women. His taster, aspirations and humour have in large part a collective organ, while his companion is more directly influenced by her organism" (1897: 385).

Gender disability is a barrier in any developmental process for a society. The Indian tribes are socially and economically disadvantageous group. Naturally they are educationally backward also. The year 1975, celebrated as the 'International year for women'. So, the year was devoted for over all development of women. There are 461 Scheduled Tribes of which about 172 are segments (Singh, 1994: 2). According to the 1991 census total tribal population in the country stands 67, 758,380 (i.e. about 8.08 per cent). These tribal people differ from one group to another in their ethnic identity, language/dialect, culture, habitat and also in basic economy. They live mostly in remote places where the advanced groups of Indian population do not reach and do not put impression there (Basu, et. al, 1972: 71).

Before independence no attention had been paid to the education of the tribals. The earliest efforts in tribal education were made by the foreign missionaries, then Indian institutions were set up in 1940's. Though credit for spreading education among the tribals in pre-independence period goes to the Christian missionaries and other voluntary agencies (Roy Burman, 1965: 121). The Government of India has made many constitutional provisions for various development programmes from time to time for the upliftment of the tribals, but result is not satisfactory, particularly in education. The Article 45 of constitution of India has provided free and compulsory education for children until they complete the age of fourteen years, another Article 46, made for promoting educational and economic interests of Scheduled Castes, Scheduled Tribes and other Weaker Sections to protect them for social injustice and all forms of exploitation. Morever, National Policy on Education, 1986 provided many provisions for educational development of the tribals. The Acharya Ramamurti Committee reviewed the education policy and strongly recommended that education should be made socially relevant and meaningful (Arulandram, 1993:1). Because this policy is more socially relevant along with core curriculum, establishing of school, opening of hostels in every district, identifying teachers from educated tribals, expanding Ashram schools, providing pre-primary education. It is also stated decentralised and micro level of planning should be improved in order to cater local educational needs. Therefore, this education policy is known as 'people's policy

In spite of this policy the picture we get clearly indicate that the tribal literacy rate is increasing very slowly and female literacy as recorded in the census reports also is very low. Nevertheless it is also acceptable fact that the female literacy rate is higher among few Christian tribal societies in North-East India (i.e. the Mizos of Mizoram) and other parts of the country including Andaman Islands (Christianity 149 tribal communities and i.e. 23.4 per cent of the total tribal population in India), where it is observed that tribal female literacy rate is higher than the total and / male tribal literacy rate in India. The main reason is that the tribal societies in these are socially more advanced than the non Christian tribal people of the country. In this context Sundaram has also made similar observations as early as in 1960's that there are certain places in these regions where the average level of literacy and education exceeds the prevailing rate of literacy even in the advanced areas of India (1965: 6). It has been observed that Rajasthan is one of the educationally backward state of the country. The Bhil is the large populated tribe in this state. The male and female literacy rates among the Bhils are 13.83 and 0.83 per cent respectively. Nevertheless there are living one P.T.G. Seharias and this female literacy will be poorest or negligible. Therefore, it is clear that tribal total literacy rate of the nation or state constitute by some progressive tribal groups and or male tribal folks.

In the field of tribal education studies have been made by many scholars like Ambasht (1970), Bapat (1964), Bhagat (1989), Bose (1970). Bhowmik (1980), Bhowmik (1985), Biswas (1966), Basu (1971), Bose (1970), Das Gupta (1963), Das Gupta and Danda (1984), Duary (1995, 1996, 1998), Elwin (1963), Karve (1957), Khurana (1978), Lakshmaiah (1991), Mahapatra (1967), Malhotra (1986), Naik (1986), Patel (1984), Rathnaiath (1977), Roy (1989), Roy Burman (1967, 1985), Roy Chowdhury (1964) Sachchidananda (1964, 1965, 1968), Singh (1991), Srivastava, (1966, 1967), Sujatha (1987), Sundaram (1966), Toppo (1979), Vidyarthi (1955) and other. They have identified many societal problems viz. poverty, socio-cultural dogma, medium of instruction, environmental conditions, structural constraints, stagnation, wastage, absenteeism, enrolment, dropout of the student, educational policy, administration etc. and suggested for educational development among them. Moreover, they also observed many aspects of the tribal life and education, which have traditional role i.e. youth dormitory and its changing form, growth of tribal literacy, formal education and development role of Government and non government agencies in the development, problems in educational planning etc.

It is also a notable fact that tribal education has remained problematic for the planner since their intensive efforts from the last four decades have not yielded the desired result. In this regard Biswas has aptly remarked that 'the cultural diversity of the Indian tribals makes any educational programme directed towards them a very difficult and some what risky enterprise. He suggested that the educational schemes should be formulated in such a manner that the adult tribals as well as their children can be benefited from the implementation of the tribal educational programme in the most desired way (1963: 3). In general female tribals have been suffering from the number of problems due to gender issue as social disadvantage and as a result it affects their life and i.e. prime barrier in developmental work among them. So, it is the appropriate time to discuss the issues of female gender which are great hindrances in the education, economy, health and so on. Education should be an important element that contribute to social, justice and development of the society. It enriches world of view, develops the logical reasoning and provide knowledge skill to a level that would lead a gainful, creative life. The fact is that tribal people treat boys and girls equally. But because of some socio-cultural and psychological factors the tribal appears to be less interested in female education (Duary, 1995: 107).

This article is based on secondary data as well as primary data. Therefore, data published as per the census of India. For the analytical treatment of the gender discrimination in tribal educational development, a field work was conducted in tribal concentrated district i.e. Medinipur, Bankura and Puruliya in western border Bengal during the year 1991-1995. The areas are inhabited by nine tribal communities of four different types of traditional economic activities i.e. hunter gatherer—Birhor, Kheria and Lodha (Primitive Tribal Groups), Bamboo artisans-Mahali, Earth workers—Kora and Agriculturists—Santal, Munda, Oraon and Bhumij (Hinduised tribe). During the field work observation were made on the situation of educational infrastructure in primary level i.e. schools, hostels, teachers, environmental situation of the schools, etc. standards anthropological tools were adopted for this study.

Objectives

The present study has following objectives:

(i) to findout the growth of the tribal literacy rate (1961-1991) in India, state wise tribal literacy rates (1961-1991), literacy rates of Scheduled Tribe female (1961-1991), gender wise literacy rate of the tribes (1991), highest level of education attainment of the tribal females (1988-1989) as surveyed by the education department and gender wise drop out rates of the scheduled tribes (1988-1989);

(ii) to findout the gender disability in the education of tribal women in India.

Result and Discussion

This discussion reveals that the tribal literacy rate in India is still lagging behind in comparison to the Indian population in general. The growth of literacy in India is given in Appendix—I, it reveals that literacy rate among the tribals has been increasing gradually since 1931 census (that was only 0.75 per cent). Though it also shows that female literacy rate among the tribals are less than their male counterpart. The highest literacy rate observed during 1981-1991 and it is noted that during the years of 1981-1991 tribal female literacy rate was increased more than two times than 1971-1981 (i.e. from 8.04 to 18.19 per cent).

The state-wise literacy rate of the Scheduled Tribe from 1961-1991 is given in Appendix-II. The differential rate of literacy is found in different states and region of the country. The highest percentage of literates were found in Mizoram in 1981 and 1991 census i.e. 59.63 and 82.73 per cent respectively. In 1961 and 1971 the highest literacy rates was found in Manipur. The tribal literacy rates of Andhra Pradesh shows very poor condition in every census and has been increased very slowly (only one per cent in every decade). It also shows that the literacy rate has been double during the 1981-1991 census, except the Manipur, Meghalaya, Nagaland, Tamil Nadu, Goa, Daman and Diu. The inter tribal difference in this literacy rate of the Mizoram has achieved high i.e. 78.70 per cent, they are educationally advance group in this country. But the neighbouring states like Arunachal Pradesh in North-East region possess only 8.86 per cent. This picture is prevalent all over the country and which is primarily related with their socio-economic conditions and educational infrastructural facilities.

It reveals State-wise female literacy rate is given in Appendix-III, the literacy rates of the tribal female varies from states to states and from territory to territory. During the 1961-1971 the highest percentage of tribal female literates are found in Manipur i.e. 17.67 per cent, Lakshadweep i.e. 28.94, 42.62 per cent and Mizoram i.e. 78.70 per cent respectively and lowest percentage is only found in Rajasthan i.e. 0.28, 0.49, 1.20 and 4.42 per cent in all census (i.e. 1961-1991). In a few states and in one Union Territory female literacy rate achieved very poor state which is below of the national average literacy rates in every decades. These States are Andhra Pradesh, Bihar, Madhya Pradesh, Orissa, Rajasthan, West Bengal and Dadra and Nagar Haveli. It is quite interesting to note that the female literacy rate of all States and Union Territories has been increased more than two times to three times except, Kerala, Manipur, Meghalaya, Mizoram, Tamil Nadu, Andaman and Nicobar Islands and Lakshaweep. The range of variation among the tribals by gender is about 10-18 per cent in the above mentioned States.

The literacy rates in total population and of Scheduled Tribe population by gender (in 1991 census) is discussed in Appendix-IV. It mentions the achievement of literacy secured by the individual states and the Union Territories. The highest percentage of general and tribal literacy rate by sex is achieved by Mizoram i.e. 82.77, 82.73 and 78.70 per cent respectively. The lowest percentage of it is observed in Andhra Pradesh i.e. tribal male 21.25 and tribal female 8.68 per cent only. In Union Territories the highest and lowest percentage of literacy rates are presented in Lakshadweep and Dadra and Nagar Haveli respectively. But it is also worth mentioning here that most of the cases of tribal female literacy rate achieved from the states like Andhra Pradesh, Assam, Medhya Pradesh, Orissa, Rajasthan, West Bengal and of the Union Territory i.e. Dadra and Nagar Haveli remained below of the average tribal female literacy rate. Highest female literacy rate has been reported from Lakshadweep i.e. 71.72 per cent. This is remarkable that in 1991 census the tribal literacy rates of seven States i.e. Kerala, Manipur, Nagaland, Sikkim, Mizoram, Andaman Nicobar and Lakshadweep and higher than the general literacy rate of India i.e. 52.11 per cent.

Appendix-V reveals that the level of education among the tribal females, which is based on State wise/Union Territories sample survey (i.e. state wise sample size was 1000 tribal females) conducted by Department of Education, New Delhi, during 1988-89. From this table it is observed that in India 876 tribal females are illiterate out of 1000 sample population, the highest number i.e. 57 literate female are found in below primary level of education and after the higher secondary or in senior secondary level there is no tribal female literates in India. This is notable fact that after primary level of education the number of educated females have decreased. In case of all individual States the highest number of female illiterates i.e. 965 population is found in Rajasthan and lowest in Lakshadweep i.e. 326 females only. The highest number of tribal female literates without formal education is present in Mizoram i.e. 50 population and lowest this number is represented in Dadra and Nagar Haveli. In the primary level of education the tribal females of Andaman and Nicobar Islands achieved the numerically highest i.e. 189 and its lowest in Rajasthan i.e. 16 females only. The female literate in primary and middle levels of education are found in Mizoram i.e. 251 and 151 respectively and its lower number found in Andhra Pradesh i.e. 16 females and only one female in Rajasthan. In secondary and higher secondary levels of education highest female literates were found in Lakshadweep i.e. 42 and 4 respectively. In few states the female are graduate and above level of education and very few poor number of females hold the diploma of technical education. From this table it is clear that the maximum number of tribal females are educated upto primary level and so, their level of education attainment is very limited. But in this compare in the level of education attainment of non-tribal female is higher than the tribal female in India.

The state-wise/Union Territories dropout is given in Appendix-VI. From this Appendix it is observed that in India the highest percentage of dropout is found is secondary level (I-X) and there girls dropout rate is quite higher i.e. 89.91 per cent than the boys. Among the States the highest dropout rate in primary (I-V) and middle (I-VIII) levels of education is found in Goa and in primary level the lowest dropout is present in Andaman and Nicobar Islands. In the secondary level (I-X) of education the highest girls dropout is found in Rajasthan i.e. 94.33 per cent and then Bihar i.e. 93.64 per cent. From this appendix it is stated that in all the educational levels and in all individual States or Union Territories the girls dropout rates are higher than the boys. But in case of Mizoram this difference is very less in percentage.

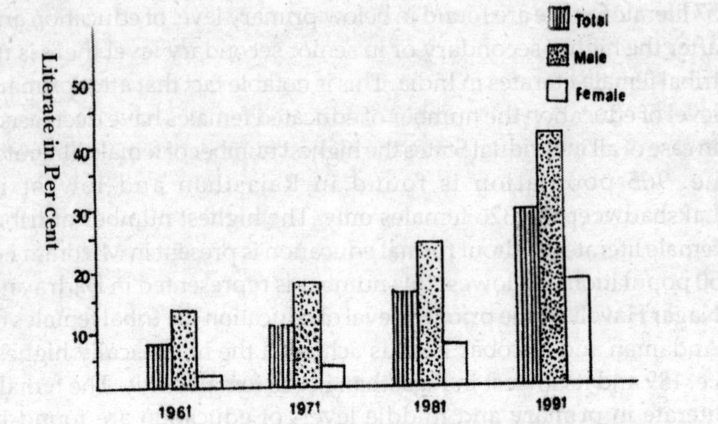

Fig. I: Growth of Tribal Literacy Rate in India, 1961-1991.

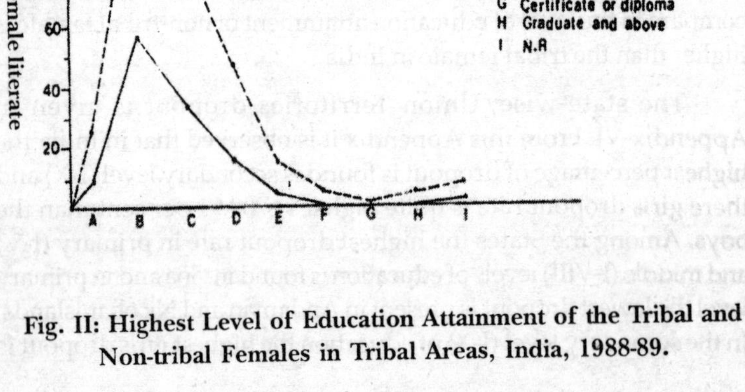

Fig. II: Highest Level of Education Attainment of the Tribal and Non-tribal Females in Tribal Areas, India, 1988-89.

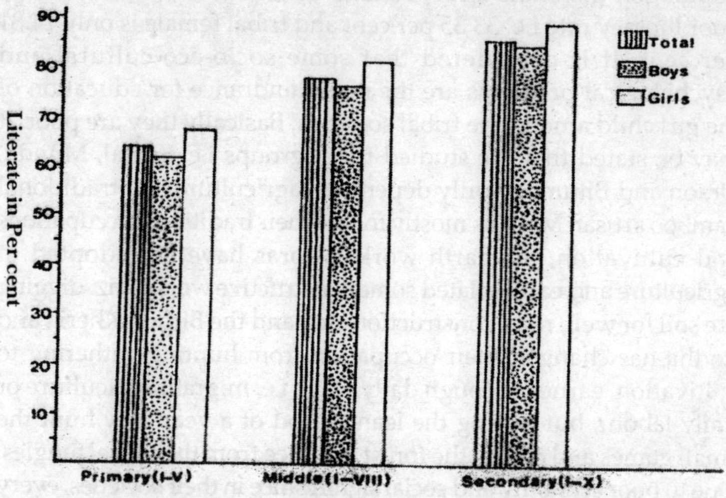

Fig. III: Drop-out Rates Among Tribal Students in India, 1988-89.

Field Situation and Findings

The problems of education among the tribal people are of varying nature. In the field of tribal education a number of problems were identified in different studies. It is observed that still the tribal of the study area (western border Bengal) are suffering from the same type of problems with the variation of degree. These are the basic problems of their society like poverty, socio-cultural, psychological conditions. But other problems are of languages, curriculum, text books, non availability of schools at approachable distance, lack of physical facilities, educational equipments, hostel boarding facilities and in few cases existing hostels are in unhygienic condition due to inadequate management. There were also absence of adequate number of trained teachers, tribal teachers, night schools. Morever, lack of proper financial aids from the State Government such as annual aids for school, adequate stipend, scholarship etc. Even single teacher schools remain closed if teachers take leave where. Teacher students ratio is 1: 44. Some schools are running without building. There is no governmental special initiative in girl child or female education. The causes of illiteracy or dropout are many related to above mentioned educational problems. As the result achieved from the studies sampled tribal population (i.e. Male 2,126, Female 1,973 and total 4,099) shows poor literacy rate i.e. 33.35 per cent and tribal female is only 14.81 per cent. It is considered that some socio-eco-cultural and psychological problems are the main hindrance for education of the girl child among the tribal societies. Basically they are poor. It may be stated that the studied tribal groups i.e. Santal, Munda, Oraon and Bhumij mainly depend on agriculture, the traditional bamboo artisan Mahalis mostly follow their traditional occupations and cultivation, the earth worker Koras have not adopted in agriculture and earth related some constructive works (viz. digging the soil for well, road construction etc.) and the Birhor, Kheria and Lodha has changed their occupation from hunting-gathering to cultivation, earned through daily wage i.e. migrant agriculture or daily labour, but during the lean period of a year they hunt the small games and collect the forest produce from their local jungles. Due to poor economy and social significance in their societies, every girl child in a family assists the parents more than the male child in economic activities and as well as in domestic works. Most of them try to perform routined duty since dawn to dusk, from courtyard to working field, house to market/jungle/cattle grazing area and from kitchen to school. Morever, the girls look after youngsters and in some cases she carries the infant (brother or sister) to working mother's place or field for breast feeding. It is observed that all tribal students assist their parents in economic activities, domestic works and in parallel they continue their study. But after at primary level of education they face more problems in school education due to above mentioned reasons and other like lack of parental guidance and awareness in education. Most of the families have not suitable physical and social environment for study. They are habituated for early taking of food and early going to bed. So, naturally their result is not satisfactory in class promotion examinations. Thus it indirectly influences the dropout at primary level. The dropout rate of the girls is higher than the boys. There is found only 33.8 per cent girl student out of 530. It is reported by the teachers that the poor parents of the hunting-gathering societies send their children to schools, for being looked after by the teachers. Because parents get busy for whole day in search of livelihood. Even when the children attain 8-10 years of age they leave the schools for assisting their parents. Most of the parents like to have their daughters educated up to primary level but only few of them allow it up to middle-secondary level of education. Because, till she will join 14-16 years age of marriage. Where as the parents show interest in case of male child education. Because a male child is expected to look after the family. According to their knowledge it is difficult to findout a suitable educated groom for an educated girl in future. As for example in this study the highest female literates i.e. about 57 per cent is found in primary level and only 7 per cent literate females are in secondary level of education. Among the tribal societies early marriage is one of the hindrance in education. So, parents are more interested to trained their girl child in all sorts of domestic works since her childhood than to encourage for education. The scarcity of Governmental service and educated unemployed problem is also discouraging towards their children education. The another factor is laxity of sex which hinders the development of female among the tribals. Free mixing or love affairs is permissible and it is started from early childhood. As the result from the different case studies that some of brilliant students (in middle or secondary level) has shown sudden deterioration in school examination, which end up in marriage. It is observed that primary schools are situated in or around the studied villages and in most of the cases the secondary schools are located far way from villages. As a result large number of girl students discontinue or end up their education after primary schooling.

A number of social scientists have carried our several studies on tribal education in India, to findout the loopholes sytematically and they identified the many problems. Therefore, the Government have launched several special plan-programmes for the development of education among the tribals. But fact is that still they are backward in education particularly the tribal females. As observed in a scientific review of the Census data (from 1961-1991) on literacy rate, educational attainment and dropout of the tribal female in India, it closely shows that their educational development is very low in national average. This is acceptable that some improvement has been observed during the thirty years, in the literacy rates, educational attainment of the younger generation. In spite of all efforts, young tribal girls still lag behind. They are far away from the national educational goal. From the foregoing paragraphs, numerical figures in tables and graphical representations a clear picture is made concerning one of the prime barrier in educational development among the tribal female is apathy towards the feminine gender. But communities in India, it varies from tribe to tribe. As for example the Mizos of Mizoram, literacy rate is highest in India and their gender difference in literacy rate is marginal due to impact of Christianity and advance culture. Therefore, they are in progress in all sphere i.e. education, economy, health and soon. It is the crucial time to think about importance of female education among the tribals. If they will progress in education, they can solve many problems and automatic increase in their awareness in economy, health, mass participation in family welfare etc. As it will reduce the maternal mortality rate, child or infant mortality rate, vanish the superstition and will make aware them to keep the ecological balance, environment and so on. It should be kept in mind that no welfare programmes will succeed without spreading of education among the tribals as well as the tribal women, because only an educated mother, will be able to make her child educated.

REFERENCES

Adhikary, Asim Kumar, 1984, *Society and World View of the Birhor*, Anthropological Survey of India, Calcutta.

Ambasht, N.K., 1970, *A Critical Study of Tribal Education (with Special Reference to Ranchi District)* S. Chand & Co., New Delhi.

Arulandram, H.B.S., 1993, Summester Development Education Programme, *University News*, Vol. XXI, No. 25, New Delhi.

Bapat, N.V., 1964, A Few Thoughts on Tribal Education, *Vanyajati*, Bharatiya Adimjati Sevak Sangh Vol. XII, No. 4, New Delhi.

Bhowmik, P.K., 1963, *Lodhas of West Bengal*, Punthi Pustak, Calcutta.

1980, *Some Aspects of Indian Anthropology*, Subarnarekha, Calcutta.

Bhowmik, K.L., 1985, *Some Observation on Literacy Situation in India*, State Resource Centre for Adult Education, Calcutta.

Basu, M.N., 1958, The Role of Anthropology in Education of Aborigines in India, *Tribal Research Bureau*, Vol. III, Bhubaneshwar.

Basu, M.N., B.B. Ghosh and M.K. Chowdhuri, 1972, Level of Tribal Literacy in India, *Society and Culture* Vol. 1, Calcutta (Reprint).

Bose, A.B., 1970, Problems of Educational Development of Scheduled Tribes, *Man in India*, Vol. 50 No. 1, Ranchi.

Chottopadhya, K.P., 1953, Tribal Education, *Man in India*, Vol. 33, No. 1, Ranchi.

Dasgupta, N.K., 1963, *Problem of Tribal Education and the Santals*, Bharatiya Adimjati Sevak Sangh, New Delhi.

Duary, Nabakumar, 1996, Language Problem in Educational Development of Santals: An Observation in Frontier Bengal, *Vanyajati*, Adimjati Sevak, Sangh, Vol. XLIV, No. 2, New Delhi.

1995, *Tribal Education in Western Border Bengal: Retrospects Prospect*, Anthropological Survey of India, Calcutta, (Unpublished Project Report).

1998, Education Among The Primitive Tribal Groups: Example from West Bengal, *Man and Life*, Vol. 2-4, No. 122.

Elwin, Verrier, 1960, *Report of the Committee on Special Multipurpose Tribal Block*, Ministry of Home Affairs, New Delhi.

Govt. of India, 1986, *National Policy on Education*, New Delhi.

1991, *Provisional Population Total Rural Urban Distribution*, Series-1, Paper-2.

Karve, Irawati, 1957, Social Education of the Scheduled Tribes, *Vanyajati*, Bharatiya Adimjat Sevak Sangh Vol. V, No. 4, New Delhi.

Lakshmaiah, T., 1991, Education and Social Change: A Study of Tribal Students, *Man in India*, Vol. 71, No. 4, Ranchi.

Malhotra, O.P., 1986, *Tribal Education in Andaman and Nicobar Islands*, S. Chand & Co. Ltd., New Delhi.

Naik, J.P., 1972, Education of Scheduled Tribes (1965-66) *ICSSR, (Occasional Monograph)*, New Delhi.

Patel Tara, 1984, *Development of Education Among Tribal Women*, Mittal Publications, Delhi.

Rathanaiah, E.V., 1977, *Structural Constraint in Tribal Education: A Regional Study*, Sterling Publishers Pvt. Ltd., New Delhi.

Reddy, G.P., 1970, Causes of Wastage in Tribal Education of Andhra Pradesh, *Vanyajati*, Bharatiya Adimjati Sevak Sangh, Vol. XVIII, No. 3, New Delhi.

Roy, Chowdhury, B.K., 1964, Tribal Education in West Bengal. *Bulletin Cultural Research Institute*, Vol. 3, No. 2, Calcutta.

Report of the Symposium, 1966, *Problems of Education of the Tribal People of India* (Held of February 11, 1965, New Delhi).

Report of the National Seminar, 1967, *Tribal Education in India*, (Held at Udaipur, September 13-18) NCERT, New Delhi.

Roy, Kanchan (Ed.), 1989, *Education and Health Problems in Tribal Development: A Study of National Integration*, Concept Publishing Co., New Delhi.

Sachchidananda. 1968, Education and Changes in Social Values, *Man in India*, Vol. 48, No. 1, Ranchi.

1985, Economic Development, Education and Social Change in Arunachal *Man in India*. Vol. 65 No. 1, Ranchi.

Saxena, Sateshwari, 1979, *Educational Planning in India: A Study in Approach and Methodology*, Sterling Publishers Pvt. Ltd., New Delhi.

Sharma, K.P., 1991, *Educational Life Style of Tribal Students*, Classical Publishing Co., New Delhi.

Singh, K.S., 1994, *The Scheduled Tribes, People of India*, Vol. III, Anthropological Survey of India, Calcutta.

Singh, Shyama Nanda, 1991, *Tribal Education in India*, Uppal Publishing House, New Delhi.

Sinha, Diskhit, 1984, *The Hill Kheria of Purulia: Impact of Poverty on a Hunting and Gathering Tribe*, Anthropological Survey in India, Calcutta.

Srivastava, A.R.N., 1957, *An Annotated Bibliography on Tribal Education in India*, National Council of Educational Research and Training (NCERT), New Delhi.

Sujatha, K., 1987, *Education of the Forgotten Children of the Forests: A Case Study of Yenadi Tribe*, Konark Publishers Pvt. Ltd., New Delhi.

Toppo, Sita, 1979, *Dynamics of Educational Development in Tribal India*, Classical Publication, New Delhi.

Vidyarthi, L.P., 1955, Education in Tribal Bihar, *Man in India*, Vol. 35, No. 1. Ranchi.

APPENDIX—I

Growth of Literacy Rate in India, 1961-1991 Census

Year	*All population*			*Scheduled Tribe*		
	Total	*Male*	*Female*	*Total*	*Male*	*Female*
1961	24.00	27.86	16.69	8.53	13.89	3.16
1971	29.45	33.80	17.11	11.30	17.63	4.85
1981	36.20	46.89	24.82	16.35	24.52	8.04
1991	52.11	64.13	39.29	29.60	40.65	18.19

APPENDIX—II

Literacy Rate Among Scheduled Tribes During 1961, 1971, 1981, 1991 Census

Sl. No.	*Name of state/U.T.*	*Year*			
		1961	*1971*	*1981*	*1991*
1.	Arunachal Pradesh	4.41	5.34	7.82	17.16
2.	Assam	23.58	26.03	–	49.16
3.	Bihar	9.16	11.64	16.99	26.78
4.	Gujarat	11.69	14.12	21.14	36.45
5.	Haryana	–	–	–	–
6.	Himachal Pradesh	–	15.89	25.93	47.09
7.	Jammu & Kashmir	–	–	–	–
8.	Karnataka (Mysore)	8.15	14.85	20.14	36.01
9.	Kerala	17.26	25.72	31.79	57.22
10.	M.P.	5.10	7.62	10.68	21.54
11.	Maharashtra	7.21	11.74	22.29	36.79
12.	Manipur	27.25	28.71	39.74	53.63
13.	Meghalaya	–	26.45	31.55	46.71
14.	Nagaland	14.76	24.01	40.32	60.59
15.	Orissa	7.36	9.46	13.96	22.31
16.	Punjab	16.46	–	–	–
17.	Rajasthan	3.97	6.47	10.27	19.44
18.	Sikkim	–	–	33.13	59.01
19.	Tamil Nadu (Madras)	5.91	9.02	20.46	27.89
20.	Tripura	10.01	15.03	23.07	40.37
21.	U.P.	–	14.59	20.45	35.70
22.	West Bengal	6.55	8.92	13.21	27.78
23.	Arunachal Pradesh	0	5.20	14.04	34.45
24.	Goa	–	12.73	26.43	42.91
25.	Mizoram	–	–	59.63	82.73
	Union Territories				
26.	Andaman Nicobar	11.10	17.85	31.11	56.62
27.	Dadra & Nagar Haveli	4.40	8.90	16.86	28.21
28.	Chandigarh	–	–	–	–
29.	Delhi	–	–	–	–
30.	Lakasadweep	22.27	41.37	53.13	80.53
31.	Pondicherry	–	–	–	–
	All India	8.53	11.30	16.35	29.60

Source: Census of India, 1961, 1971, 1981 and 1991.

APPENDIX—III

Statewise Female Literacy Rates of Schedule Tribe (1961 to 1991)

S. No.	States/U.T.	1961	1971	1981	1991
	India	3.16	4.85	8.04	18.19
1.	Andhra Pradesh	1.48	2.13	3.46	8.68
2.	Assam	15.72	17.16	–	38.98
3.	Bihar	3.18	4.83	7.75	14.75
4.	Gujarat	4.09	6.15	11.64	24.20
5.	Himachal Pradesh	1.74	5.53	12.82	31.18
6.	Karnataka	2.81	7.67	10.03	23.57
7.	Kerala	11.92	19.40	26.02	51.07
8.	Madhya Pradesh	0.97	2.18	3.60	10.73
9.	Maharashtra	1.75	4.21	11.94	24.03
10.	Manipur	17.67	18.87	30.35	44.48
11.	Meghalaya	–	22.79	28.91	43.63
12.	Nagaland	10.57	17.68	32.99	54.51
13.	Orissa	1.77	2.58	4.76	10.24
14.	Rajasthan	0.28	0.49	1.20	4.42
15.	Sikkim	–	–	22.37	50.37
16.	Tamil Nadu	2.73	4.48	14.00	20.23
17.	Tripura	2.31	5.76	12.27	27.34
18.	Uttar Pradesh	–	15.58	8.69	19.86
19.	West Bengal	1.76	3.09	5.01	14.98
20.	A. & N. Islands	6.45	11.10	23.24	48.74
21.	Arunachal Pradesh	–	1.70	7.31	24.94
22.	Dadra & Nagar Haveli	0.41	2.59	8.42	15.94
23.	Goa, Daman & Diu	–	5.08	18.89	41.49
24.	Laksadweep	10.61	28.94	42.62	71.72
25.	Mizoram	–	–	–	78.70

Source: Census of India, 1961, 1971, 1981 & 1991.

APPENDIX—IV

Literacy Rates for Total Population, Scheduled Tribe Population by Sex-1991

Sl. No.	State/ Union Territory	Total Population	Persons	Males	Females
			Scheduled Tribe Population	Scheduled Tribe Population	Scheduled Tribe Population
1	2	3	4	5	6
	India*	52.21	29.60	40.65	18.19
	States				
1.	Andhra Pradesh	44.09	17.16	25.25	8.68
2.	Arunachal Pradesh	41.59	34.45	44.00	24.94
3.	Assam	52.89	49.16	58.93	38:98
4.	Bihar	38.48	26.78	38.40	14.75
5.	Goa	75.51	42.91	54.43	29.01
6.	Gujarat	61.29	36.45	48.25	24.20
7.	Haryana	55.85	00.00	0.00	0.00
8.	Himachal Pradesh	63.86	47.09	62.74	31.18
9.	Karnataka	56.04	36.01	47.95	23.57
10.	Kerala	89.81	57.22	63.38	51.07
11.	Madhya Pradesh	44.20	21.54	32.16	10.73
12.	Maharashtra	64.87	36.79	49.09	24.03
13.	Manipur	59.89	53.63	62.39	44.48
14.	Meghalaya	49.10	46.71	49.78	43.63
15.	Mizoram	82.77	82.73	86.67	78.70
16.	Nagaland	49.09	22.31	34.44	10.21
17.	Orissa	49.09	22.31	34.44	10.21
18.	Punjab	58.51	0.00	00.00	0.00
19.	Rajasthan	38.55	19.44	33.29	4.42
20.	Sikkim	56.94	59.01	66.80	50.37
21.	Tamil Nadu	62.66	27.89	35.25	20.23
22.	Tripura	60.44	40.37	52.88	27.34
23.	Uttar Pradesh	41.60	35.70	49.95	19.86
24.	West Bengal	57.70	27.78	40.07	14.98
	Union Territories				
1.	Andaman & Nicobar Islands	73.02	56.62	64.16	48.74
2.	Chandigarh	77.81	0.00	0.00	0.00
3.	Dadra & Nagar Heveli	40.71	28.21	40.75	15.94
4.	Daman & Diu	71.20	52.91	63.58	41.49
5.	Delhi	75.29	0.00	0.00	0.00
6.	Pondicherry	74.74	0.00	0.00	0.00
7.	Laksadweep	81.78	80.58	89.50	71.72

* Excludes figures of Jammu & Kashmir where 1991 census was not taken.

APPENDIX—V

Per Thousand Distribution of Females by Highest Level of Education Attained Separately for Tribals and Non-Tribals of Tribal Areas

Rural

S. No.	States/ U.T.	Highest level of education attained											No. of females			
		House hold	Net literate	Literate without formal education	Literate below primary	Primary	Middle	Secondary	Higher Secondary	Certificate or Diploma	Graduate & above	N.R.	All	Estd. (00)	Sample
(1)	(2)	(3)	(4)	(5)	(6)	(7)	(8)	(9)	(10)	(11)	(12)	(13)	(14)	(15)	(16)
1.	Andhra Pradesh	T	943	4	33	6	4	2	–	–	–	3	1000	11520	1649
		NT	789	16	90	49	33	15	7	–	1	1	1000	63574	1912
2.	Assam	T	686	33	133	94	43	8	3	–	0	–	1000	9477	994
		NT	507	83	165	117	80	40	6	–	1	1	1000	14928	872
3.	Bihar	T	893	12	36	21	32	4	1	0	0	–	1000	23769	2643
		NT	806	35	56	25	33	7	–	–	1	36	1000	33640	2180
4.	Gujarat	T	896	8	71	55	17	8	1	0	2	3	1000	28244	2009
		NT	511	7	270	110	65	28	3	4	2	–	1000	20704	1048
5.	Himachal Pradesh	T	755	16	161	47	12	7	–	–	1	–	1000	942	502
		NT	636	14	133	134	56	15	10	–	–	3	1000	5626	497
6.	Karnataka	T	704	4	121	115	33	11	1	–	–	12	1000	1231	372
		NT	714	38	91	58	42	17	9	3	3	26	1000	57151	1813

(Contd...)

(1)	(2)	(3)	(4)	(5)	(6)	(7)	(8)	(9)	(10)	(11)	(12)	(13)	(14)	(15)	(16)
7.	Kerala	T	555	4	175	123	125	12	–	–	–	5	1000	863	434
		NT	322	21	180	207	166	70	22	10	2	–	1000	16586	858
8.	Madhya Pradesh	T	922	3	53	15	3	1	1	–	0	2	1000	52101	5299
		NT	759	12	123	71	20	7	4	0	1	2	1000	54361	3558
9.	Maharashtra	T	81	12	66	37	10	2	0	–	0	1	1000	20866	2739
		NT	615	21	132	132	75	19	3	1	4	1	1000	57906	2311
10.	Meghalaya	T	656	35	112	108	60	25	3	–	1		1000	5467	1338
		NT	706	55	35	114	65	25	–	–	–	–	1000	283	116
11.	Orissa	T	918	11	40	12	16	2	0	–	0	–	1000	24154	2409
		NT	677	33	139	82	52	8	6	–	3	–	1000	36140	1970
12.	Rajasthan	T	965	5	16	10	1	1	0	–	–	2	1000	18811	2111
		NT	842	14	60	27	14	2	2	0	38	–	1000	39329	1635
13.	Sikkim	T	680	35	156	69	39	7	1	1	–	12	1000	323	736
		NT	613	64	141	102	51	12	12	3	3	–	1000	850	662
14.	Tamil Nadu	T	888	–	64	28	15	1	–	–	–	4	1000	1601	321
		NT	627	16	162	110	45	18	5	2	4	11	1000	38434	1139
15.	Tripura	T	792	48	93	49	14	1	–	0	0	2	1000	1773	706
		NT	414	98	199	188	56	5	6	2	9	23	1000	1638	421
16.	Uttar Pradesh	T	903	11	52	27	7	0	–	–	–	–	1000	1010	530
		NT	914	4	26	18	10	2	0	1	0	25	1000	9562	451
17.	West Bengal	T	905	5	48	29	8	1	1	1	–	3	1000	14506	1863
		NT	637	46	123	108	55	11	5	3	9	2	1000	48556	1326

(Contd...)

(1)	(2)	(3)	(4)	(5)	(6)	(7)	(8)	(9)	(10)	(11)	(12)	(13)	(14)	(15)	(16)
18.	Andaman &	T	550	25	189	145	83	10	–	–	–	–	1000	89	488
	Nicobar Islands	NT	547	1	151	219	58	23	1	–	–	–	1000	35	89
19.	Arunachal Pradesh	T	774	14	60	82	25	5	–	1	0	38	1000	1990	997
		NT	501	90	173	93	75	28	17	–	24	–	1000	217	154
20.	Dadra &	T	852	1	56	77	12	2	–	–	–	–	1000	407	359
	Nagar Haveli	NT	514	2	220	129	36	95	–	–	4	–	1000	61	136
21.	Laksadweep	T	326	56	244	179	145	42	4	3	–	–	1000	103	297
		NT	165	37	11	71	304	268	47	37	6	–	1000	4	52
22.	Mizoram	T	336	50	176	251	151	24	4	1	–	6	1000	1524	1254
		NT	304	–	147	519	30	–	–	–	–	–	1000	7	57
23.	All India	T	876	10	57	33	16	4	1	0	0	2	1000	222457	30762
		NT	690	26	119	82	47	15	5	1	5	7	1000	499644	23719

Source: Education of Scheduled Cast and Tribes 1988-89 Department of Education.

APPENDIX—VI

Statewise Drop-out Rates Scheduled Tribes 1988-89

State/UT		Primary I-V			Middle I-VIII			Secondary I-X		
		Boys	Girls	Total	Boys	Girls	Total	Boys	Girls	Total
1	2	3	4	5	6	7	8	9	10	11
1.	Andhra Pradesh	63.70	68.97	65.66	84.21	90.14	86.42	88.83	92.77	90.34
2.	Arunachal Pradesh	64.77	59.92	63.01	75.60	79.35	76.95	80.49	89.30	83.37
3.	Assam	71.90	70.71	71.40	66.06	68.17	66.95	56.15	77.21	68.18
4.	Bihar	69.51	77.14	72.19	84.53	88.65	85.94	90.30	93.64	91.42
5.	Goa*	83.79	95.36	89.91	96.63	97.21	96.89	–	–	–
6.	Gujarat	55.61	68.50	61.21	77.70	84.03	80.34	85.68	90.10	87.50
7.	Haryana	–	–	–	–	–	–	–	–	–
8.	Himachal Pradesh	24.39	28.16	25.89	33.97	46.97	38.65	55.88	65.33	59.27
9.	Jammu & Kashmir	–	–	–	–	–	–	–	–	–
10.	Karnataka	35.80	45.77	40.18	59.61	70.07	64.03	69.06	80.52	73.97
11.	Kerala	21.19	16.37	18.94	45.30	37.94	41.82	72.94	67.39	70.43
12.	Madhya Pradesh	47.12	59.69	51.80	70.75	80.85	73.79	83.26	93.18	86.20
13.	Maharashtra	57.89	68.83	62.60	73.00	83.04	77.10	83.34	90.94	86.18

(Contd...)

1	2	3	4	5	6	7	8	9	10	11
14.	Manipur	77.20	78.09	77.61	84.87	85.82	85.30	85.12	86.79	85.88
15.	Meghalaya	73.21	81.76	77.40	72.85	73.09	72.96	91.63	93.37	92.47
16.	Mizoram	61.88	62.70	62.28	31.17	24.66	28.08	75.91	78.49	77.17
17.	Nagaland	34.94	35.70	35.29	64.41	58.67	61.99	79.64	83.86	81.53
18.	Orissa	75.41	77.74	76.19	83.99	85.72	84.59	87.34	92.69	89.23
19.	Punjab	–	–	–	–	–	–	–	–	–
20.	Rajasthan	66.77	79.07	69.63	72.34	86.07	74.44	83.09	94.33	84.72
21.	Sikkim	66.99	57.19	62.87	70.89	62.25	67.19	86.78	88.83	87.64
22.	Tamil Nadu	42.61	44.31	47.95	51.45	59.72	54.90	75.47	77.13	76.15
23.	Tripura	73.96	78.41	75.86	84.75	88.17	86.17	90.83	93.44	91.81
24.	Uttar Pradesh	41.73	51.60	45.14	55.83	63.69	58.10	79.30	83.88	80.68
25.	West Bengal	63.76	67.55	65.03	83.27	87.03	84.39	92.35	92.74	92.47
26.	A. & N. Islands	8.95	13.33	11.00	35.20	38.13	36.50	42.76	64.31	52.97
27.	Chandigarh	–	–	–	–	–	–	–	–	–
28.	D & N Haveli	41.26	57.58	47.60	69.67	79.94	74.04	87.62	93.01	89.94
29.	Daman & diu	–	–	–	–	–	–	–	–	–
30.	Delhi	–	–	–	–	–	–	–	–	–
31.	Pondicherry	–	–	–	–	–	–	–	–	–
32.	Lakshadweep	–	10.94	–	29.72	50.41	39.61	71.11	73.78	72.34
	Total	**61.94**	**68.73**	**64.53**	**76.21**	**81.45**	**78.08**	**84.87**	**89.91**	**86.72**

* Includes Daman & Diu.

Source: Education of Schedule Tribes 1988-89 Department of Education.

8

Development of Primitive Tribes

A Critical Appraisal

Dr. Pratibha Kumari

Primitive tribes are distinguished from other Scheduled Tribes as they constitute the lowest layer among the Scheduled Tribes, having preagricultural stage of economy and very low literacy level. The tribes of newly formed Jharkhand State are mostly confined in the plateau of Chhotanagpur and Santhal Paragana constituting about 28.05 per cent of the total population of the State in 1991 census. Out of thirty Scheduled Tribes of the State eight tribes have been identified as primitive tribes namely Asur, Birhor, Korwa, Sauria, Paharia, Mal Paharia, Birjia, Parahiya and Savar constituting about 1.06 per cent of the total population and 3.81 per cent of the Scheduled Tribe population of the State.

These primitive tribes belong to different economic categories like hunters and food gatherers, shifting cultivators, marginal farmers, artisans etc. They have distinct culture and social organisations different from the tribal peasant neighbours like Munda, Oraon, Santhal etc.

Since independence till the present time a variety of programme and schemes have been formulated and implemented for the welfare and development of the tribes.

During the Sixth Five Year Plan Primitive tribal groups got a pointed impetus for the first time when separate funds were earmarked for the development of primitive tribes under Special Central Assistance. Also top most priority to their welfare was to be accorded from the grants received under Article 275 (1) of the constitution.

Till 1st June 1989 seventy four Scheduled Tribes have been identified as primitive tribes and separate micro-projects have been identified for each of them. Microprojects have undoubtedly benefited the primitive tribal groups in varying degrees. But all the families among the larger primitive tribal groups have not been brought within the purview of microprojects. Central Government funded for centrally sponsored schemes like construction of hostels, establishment of residential schools, construction of houses through Indira Awas Yojana through State government on 50 per cent matching basis. Besides central plans are also available for many other schemes. Allocation of funds for the development of tribal communities during different plan periods shows a gradual increase of the funds from the Fifth Plan onwards.

The Seventh Plan laid emphasis on income generating family oriented schemes, but it is found out that in spite of all the strategies and efforts of all these years 85 per cent of the tribal families remain below the poverty line compared to the national average of about 38 per cent.

The Government of India have liberally agreed to support the state efforts to boost up the economic development schemes for these people. Emphasis has also been laid on the programmes of social service sectors like education, health, housing etc. which could emancipate the tribals from the clutches of exploitative agencies have also been supported.

The present paper highlights the success and failure of different developmental schemes implemented for the welfare of two primitive tribes namely Birhor and Sauria Pahria of Hazaribagh and Santhalpargana districts respectively of Jharkhand State.

The Primitives and Area

Birhor of six colonies (*tandas*) of the different blocks of Hazaribagh district and Sauria Paharia of four villages of Taljhari block of Sahebganj district were selected for the research work in late nineties.

So far as the Birhor tribe is concerned, they represent hunting and gathering type of economy. They are found in Ranchi, Gumla and Hazaribagh district of Chhotanagpur plateau of Jharkhand. They number about 5017 as 1991 census reveals. Ethnically they belong to Proto-Australoid group and linguistically to Austro-Asiatic Mundari group. During early eighties Birhor have been settled in different colonies through the Government. So they are no more nomads, through they have continued their traditional occupation of collection of forest produce, rope making and trapping small games. After their settlement in permanent houses, they have taken up wage labour work to take out their livelihood alongwith their traditional economic activities.

Sauria Paharia are one of the three sections of Paharia inhabiting Santhal Pargana plateau. The other two sections are known as Malpaharia and Kumarbhag. The Saurias are also known as Maler. E.T. Dalton in his "Descriptive Ethnology of Bengal" (1872) has recorded "The Maler call themselves the Asal Paharia because they have not subjected themselves to any restriction in regards to what they eat. The other two sections of Paharias refrain from beef eating and they regard Sauria as unclean." The difference is quite distinct and Maler have no matrimonial relation with other Paharias leaving few exceptions. Sauria Paharia live on the hilli slopes and hill tops of Sahebganj and Godda district of Santhal Pargana plateau. They also belong to Proto-Australoid racial group and speak 'Malto' which comes under Dravidian linguistic group. They also speak Hindi which is their language of communication with other tribal and nontribal communities.

They still practice shifting or slash and burn cultivation known as 'Kurwa' in their dialect on hilli slopes. They grow millets, cereals, vegetables in Kurwa cultivation. They have also taken up wage labour work in stone quarries and crusher nearby the Block.

Village-wise household, population and gender ratio of Birhor and Sauria Paharia is given in Appendix-I. Among Birhor of the studied 'Tandas' females outnumber the male member. Male female ratio and women children ratio are 42.12 and 62.74 per cent respectively. Among Sauria Paharia studied sample male female population is nearby equal having gender ratio 50.22 per cent and women children ratio 53.88 per cent.

So far as literacy is concerned male and female literacy rate among the Birhor of studied colonies are 26.28 and 12.12 per cent respectively whereas among the Sauria Paharia of the sample villages male literacy is 23.2 per cent and that of female is 13.24 per cent.

Though residential schools both for girls and boys have been opened since decades in the blocks where these communities reside, the literacy rate among them does not present satisfactory picture, the reason may be attributed to their poor economy which forces the children to perform economic activities during school hours.

Schemes

For the welfare of the primitive tribal groups several schemes were implemented and have been proposed by the Central as well as State Government during different financial years. Some of the schemes have shown good results where as few of them did not serve the propose.

The schemes were implemented and purpose mainly for the economic development of the concerned tribes.

Scheme such as basketry, goatary, poultry, rope making deep boring, house building, trench digging, land levelling were implemented in the Birhor colonies during the period 1992 to 1996 though the State Government. Training for making craft items with lamp fibres was imparted to few Birhors of the colonies namely Sijhua and Tilra of Ichak Block in the year 1985 by the state Tribal Development Corporation Ltd. Trainee Birhor of these colonies have been prepared beautiful items with lemp fibre which serve both decorative and utility purposes and are sold in town markets and emporia.

The raw material of the craft items are provided to the Birhor craftmen through the agent of BSTDCL who visit the Birhor colonies monthly. Sixty per cent of the total cost of the craft item is given to the craftperson as their labour cost. Agent of BSTDCL visit Birhor tandas for the collection of finished product as well as to give them remuneration.

Appendix-II shows the different types of implemented schemes, number of families benefited, amount sanctioned and welfare of Birhor of different 'tandas'. Birhor folk work on wages for success of schemes such as land levelling, trench digging, deep boring, house construction etc. Grants for house construction under Indira Awas Yojana were given to the Birhor families who were living in dilapidated houses. The construction work was done by member of the family.

The scheme of basketary was totally for females, but it did not bear good result.

The grant for making bamboo baskets was given to family each of the two colonies. But the sum was not utilised for the purpose it was given. The beneficiaries deposited the sum in bank to get the interest. It was found out that distribution of agriculture apparatus to the Birhor of Tilra colony did not prove fruitful due to the lack of irrigational facilities. Birhor of this colony grew vegetables in their kitchen garden for their home consumption only. Besides, all the families living in a colony do not get benefit of the scheme. The sourceful and influential persons of the community get the benefit of the implemented schemes. Other schemes like deep boring, trench digging, land levelling etc. benefited the entire households of Birhor colonies as the adult members of each family of the colonies or 'tandas' work as labourer and got the wages for making the schemes a success.

So far as the Sauria Paharia are concerned several schemes were implemented as well as a number of them have been proposed for being implemented. Under TRYSEM (Tribal and Rural Youth Self Employment) rope making machines were distributed to selected Saurias for preparing ropes with Sabai grass (Pollinidium angustifolium) which grow up abundantly in the local area. After a little span of time those rope making machines were turned useless and the fabrication of rope with local raw material did not bring positive result. Cattle such as oxen, goats, pigs, chicken were distributed to Sauria for rearing up in the year 1997, but most of the cattle died of diseases and due to the lack of proper care. In the financial year 1995-96, bee boxes were given to the selected Sauria families, but they were not trained properly for bee keeping and the programme also failed. In the same financial year grants were given to the selected and needy Sauria families of few villages under Indira Awas Yojana. Tiles were also distributed alongwith the sum. Other raw materials required in house building such as bamboo, clay, straw, wood were procured from the surrounding forests by Saurias themselves. House construction work was done by the sharing of labour by the other Saurias living in the same village. Cooperation of community level can be observed as far as the contribution of physical labours is concerned.

Hand pumps were also sunk for each Sauria village at the foot hill for getting potable water as there is dearth of clean drinking water on their hilli habitat. Perennial small springsletsor 'chua' are their only sources of getting water on hills which also dry up are sometimes during the summer. After the installation of hand pumps Saurias at least get drinking water coming 200 to 300 ft. down from their dwellings.

Grants were also given to them for mixed crop cultivation as well as for bean cultivation. Bean locally called *'Barbatti'* is abundantly grown at *'Kurwa'* field on hilli slopes. Seeds of bean locally called *Ghaghra* (*Vigna catjang*) are stored and sold usually to the middlemen or *'Sawkar'* who frequently visit the Sauria villages for purchasing their agricultural produce. Schemes of rearing goats was also succeeded as the goats were shared and sold to the plain dwellers by the beneficiaries.

Appendix-III shows the types of schemes implemented in the Taljhari block of Sahebganj district which consists of the studied four Sauria village amount sanctioned and spent and number of beneficiaries.

It is clear from the Appendix that most of the implemented schemes are concerned with agriculture followed by cattle rearing. The majority of the schemes have shown positive result.

A number of schemes have been proposed and are yet to be implemented. Those schemes include vegetable cultivation, land levelling, piggery, pisciculture, basketary, making of leaf plates, construction of cheekdam, bridge, pond, road, village panchayat building, sweater knitting etc. Sauria folk labour will be hired for the putting these schemes in action.

Sauria have been always reluctant to settle in planes even after several attempts done by the Government since pre independence time. Their adaptation in the surrounding environment of their 'hilli' habitat is century old and they have sacred centres and cultural values which can be maintained on hills only, as their name '*Paharia*' (living on hills) indicates. They consider themselves as King of hills.

If the foregoing proposed schemes will be carried out properly the Sauria will be benefited immensely.

The purpose of the implementation of different schemes was mainly the economic development of the tribal groups but it was found out that primitive tribals development strategy lacked in any micro level comprehensive planning. The achievement has not been commensurate with the inputs provided. The development needs of PTG vary from tribe to tribe, sometimes even village to village, so the generalised nature of schemes at times did not cater to the specific village need. The development programmes initiated by the State Government has not brought marked improvement in the life of these primitive tribal groups.

In implementing the development schemes the local political leaders had played their role beginning from the selection of beneficiaries to the execution at the last stage and in this regard of officers had little or no control over it. Uneven development among the tribes have been found out.

It is suggested that the welfare programmes should be based on the felt needs of the people. Planners should be acquainted with these needs and should find out the way to meet them taking into consideration the natural resources, existing human resources, available inputs of technical know how and infrastructure arrangements.

REFERENCES

Behura, N.K. (1993), Tribes of India: Planned Development, *Social Change* 18 (2 & 3).

Dalton, E.T. (1872), *Descriptive Ethnology of Bengal*, Govt. Printing, Calcutta.

George, Ose & S.S. Sreekumar (1993), Conceptual Framework for Tribal Development, *Social Change*, 18, (2 & 3), New Delhi.

Kapthuama, B.B. (1995), Bihar Tribal Sub Plan, Bulletin of Bihar Tribal Welfare Research Institute, XXXIV (2) Ranchi.

Risley, H.H., (1891), *Tribes and Castes of Bengal*, Vol. II, Calcutta.

Roy, S.C. (1925), *The Birhor: A Little Known Jungle Tribe of Chhotanagpur*, Man in India, Ranchi.

Roy, S.N. (1974), The Sauria Paharia—A Socio-economic Study, *Bulletin of Bihar Tribal Welfare Research Institute, XVI* (1 & 2), Ranchi.

Roy Burman, B.K. (1997), Critical Issues Relating to Tribal Development during the Eight Plan in George Pfeffer et. al. (eds.) *Contemporary Society: Tribal Studies*. Vol. 2, Concept Publishing Company, New Delhi.

Sarkar, R.M., (1986), Sedentarization of the Nomadic Birhor: A Case Study *Vanyajati*, 34 (1), New Delhi.

APPENDIX—I

Village-wise Population and Gender Ratio of Birhor and Sauria Paharia

S. No.	*Primitive Tribe*	*Name of Tanda/Village*	*No. of Household*	*Population (in No.)*			*Ratio*	
				Male	*Female*	*Total*	*Gender*	*Child women*
1.	Birhor	Sijhua	9	197	210	407	42.12	62.74
		Tilya	20					
		Baladohar	5					
		Durukasmaur	55					
		Govindpur	2					
		Demotanr	22					
		Total	**113**	**197**	**210**	**407**	**42.12**	**62.74**
2.	Sauria Paharia	Chhotabanapara	7					
		Hanriakol	25	224	222	446	50.22	53.88
		Sitapahar	9					
		Dhamdhamia	54					
		Total	**97**	**224**	**222**	**446**	**50.22**	**53.88**

APPENDIX—II

Village-wise Schemes, Amount Sanctioned and Spent, in Birhor

S. No.	Name of Tanda/Villeges	Scheme		Amount (Rupees)		Beneficiaries (No.)
				Sanctioned	Spent	
1.	Sijhua	(1)	House construction	14,125	14,120	5
		(2)	Deepboring	25,000	25,000	8
2.	Tilra	(1)	Agriculture	15,000	15,000	15
		(2)	Appavatus			
3.	Tilra Jarga		Deep boring	25,000	25,000	34
4.	Demotanr	(1)	Giotary	6,450		
		(2)	Basketary	5,000	5,000	1
		(3)	Rope making	1,90,000		
5.	Durukas -maur	(1)	Trench digging	94,854	94,551	41
		(2)	Basketary	5,000	5,000	1
		(3)	Land levelling	50,000	22,500	42
6.	Govindpur Land levelling			30,238	28,758	15
7.	Baladohar Land levelling			14,000	11,500	7

APPENDIX—III

Village-wise Schemes, Amount Sanctioned and Spent and Beneficiaries in Sauria Paharia

S. No.	Name of Village	Scheme	Amount (Rs.)		
			Sanctioned	Spent	Beneficiaries (No.)
1.	Taljhari Block	(1) Grant for cultivation	38,000	38,000	38
		(2) Mixed cultivation	44,160	44,160	69
		(3) Barbatti cultivation	1,25,856	1,25,856	138
		(4) Mustard cultivation	1,25,000	–	–
		(5) G. tary	22,500	22,000	10

9

Development of Naikas

Dr. Md. Azeez Mohidden

Developmental Programmes

The Government of India introduced numerous programmes for the development of tribals. In 1951, Five Year Plans were formulated which included special schemes for tribal development. In 1952, Community Development Projects were initiated in rural and tribal areas. But in 1954, Multipurpose Tribal Development Blocks were started in tribal areas including the Naika territory to meet the special needs of the tribals. The three tier Panchayat Raj Institution came into operation in 1963 in Naika land. This system idealised better participation of the people in planning process and effective implementation of developmental programmes. However, the results of this system were not encouraging. Neither the Community Development Blocks in general not the Tribal Development Blocks in particular were touching the target groups and greater effort was needed to meet basic problems of the tribals. In the Fifth Five Year Plans (1973-1978), the tribal development policy was drastically revised and changed. The concept of Integrated Tribal Development of the Scheduled Tribes and Scheduled Areas was evolved. As a result of this eight Tribal Area Sub-plans have been formulated for accelerating overall socio-economic development of most of the tribal areas, including the Naika habitat. Besides some voluntary organisations have also formed and tried for reform and development among the Naikas.[1]

In the past fifty years, the axis of Valsad-Pardi-Vapi region embracing much of the Naika territory is fast growing as an industrial belt[2] and quite a number of Naikas have taken to industrial labour and other jobs and important means of livelihood.[3]

At present there are several governmental programmes like the Tribal Sub-plan, the integrated Child Development Scheme and the Small Farmers Development Agency functioning for the development of tribes all over Gujarat including the Naikas.

In addition to these governmental programmes, there are two trusts the Atul Rural Development Fund set up in the year 1978 and the Atic Rural Development Fund set up in the year 1979 specially meant for the development of the Naikas found distributed in about 40 villages located in Chikli, Valsad, Dharampur and Pardi Taluks of Valsad District. These two trusts are co-ordinating the efforts of the Government and Non-Government agencies in order to make the Naikas reap maximum benefits by utilising at the governmental schemes to the maximum possible extent.

Voluntary Organisations

Apart from the developmental programmes and the trusts meant for bettering the socio-economic conditions of the Naikas, there is a voluntary organisation which tried to reform the Naikas. Some of the educated Naikas of the erstwhile Dharampur and Gaikwad States in Surat District had formed an association called Naika Mitra Mandal as far back as on 29-3-1921. The aim of the association was to bring social reformation and unity amongst all the Naikas. In this context, the association was successful in weaning the Naikas from drinking during marriage functions and rituals like death and other social gatherings, in removing backwardness among the Naikas and in eliminating the inferiority complex from the minds of the Naikas. Especially, the educated Naikas in Pardi, Dharampur, Bilimora and Valsad towns and the city Surat were its trusted agents for carrying out the work of the association all over the Naikas of erstwhile Dharampur and Gaikwad States.

During the First World War, the association ceased to exist. So, another association known as Naika Samaj Sudharn was formed in October, 1969 at Vasiyar village located in Valsad Taluk.

Its aim was similar to that of the Naika Mitra Mandal. For sometime it was active. In April 1976, at its Chikli Taluk general meeting it unanimously decided to stop serving liquor during marriage functions and rituals of death and other socio-religious occasions. But it has become inactive since the beginning of the period of national emergency is from 1975 to 1977.

Impact of the Developmental Programmes

The different developmental programmes influenced the Naikas and changed their attitudes and behaviours toward family, education, language, achievement, secularism, democracy, social image and group identity. The rigorous campaign undertaken by the Family Welfare Programme has influenced the Naikas to realise the importance of small family and to adopt small family norm. Some Naikas in Bamti, quite a few in Chanwai and almost all in Atul have adopted family planning, mostly vasectomy and rarely tubectomy.

Introduction of school education in numerous tribal villages has raised their literacy levels. In this context, establishment of primary and secondary schools in a number of Naika settlements, appointments of teachers from tribals, introduction of mid-day meal scheme for school children, free supply of books, slates and other materials for children, and grant of scholarships to all tribal children have helped the Naikas acquire more literacy and encourage education among their female children also. Further, the adult literacy programmes particularly in Atul have also helped the Naika men and women to attend night schools and acquire literacy in terms of reading and writing to a considerable extent.

Under the Housing Improvement Scheme sponsored by the Government, a vast majority of the Naikas were able to construct brick-walled houses with tiled-roofs. The Naikas submit an application to the Taluk Development Officer, after it is being endorsed by the Taluk Panchayat President locally known as Pramukh, and get 750 Mangalore tiles free of cost, provided they are able to bear the transport charges. On account of this facility, more than 70 per cent of the Naikas were able to construct brick-walled houses with tiled roofs and nearly 20 per cent of them were able to replace the thatched houses with tiled-roofing.

It is significant to observe that under the influence of Tribal Sub-Plan programmes, the Naikas in Bamti and Chanwai are able to use improved varieties of seeds, and improved methods of farming. In Chanwai, most of the Naikas have realised the importance of regular earning from public and private organisations in cash terms as opposed to dependence on agriculture which is not only unkind but also is uncertain and fluctuating with droughts, pests and other unexpected conditions. In Atul, the Naikas have completely done away with their traditional agricultural life. They are earning their livelihood by non-agricultural occupations. Many young people feel that they can achieve higher status and better prestige within their own society, and also outside it, by being employed in some government or private organisations other than the Atul Industrial Complex.

With the introduction of Statutory Gram Panchayats and Statutory Nagar Panchayats, the Naika Panch System has lost some of its importance. Even though panch is socially recognised as a traditional body of all-purpose leaders of the community, it has no formal recognition from the government, hence it has been relegated to the background. The Panch was an exclusive political body to look into the social irregularities and incidents of breach of social norms among the Naikas. Traditionally Panch was considered to be essential to maintain social integrity and keep the continuity of social traditions through generations. In the preserve setting these irregularities are sometimes attempted to be settled by the Statutory Gram or Nagar Panchayat. Sometime, if the accused or aggrieved party is not satisfied with the judgement, it simply sues in a Court of Law.

In the field of health, the developmental programmes have influenced the people to a small extent. Primary Health Centres in the Naika habitat are few and far between. Looking to the vastness of the area, these Primary Health Centres provide only meagre medical facilities to the Naikas. The contact of the Naikas in Bamti with the Primary Health Centres is slight but those in Chanwai is somewhat more and those in Atul is better. In Atul, the Naikas make use the private dispensaries also. Sometimes they go to Valsad in order to have appropriate medical treatment. Even then, the Naikas in Atul have not yet totally changed their ideas regarding the causes and cure of diseases. Divination, protective and ameliorating magic, chants and spells are still employed to ward off evils, cure of modern medical and surgical aids. Age-old prescriptions of indigenous herbs are generally still used for fevers and other common aliments in the initial stage. But as it takes serious turn the doctor is consulted for modern medical attention. In complicated and chronic cases, they often continue both the traditional and modern treatments side by side. Thus, it appears that respect for tradition on the one hand, and fascination towards the better effectiveness of the modern medicines on the other are playing their relative roles both hand in hand in affecting the mind of the Naikas culminating in some changes in the sphere of their religious life also. It is interesting to note the general tendency is still they have more faith in native medicines to tablets or tonics for instant relief.

Impact of Naika Samaj Sudharn

The Naika Samaj Sudharn formerly known as Naika Mitra Mandal, though inactive today, was active for about fifty years before it become inactive since 1976. In its fifty years of long active life, it had several achievements to its credit, especially with reference to reformation and unity among the Naikas.

The Naikas had been addicted to fermented palm juice (toddy) that was available in abundance in nature. They also drink local liquors distilled by themselves or by their caste neighbours. Ban on home distillation took them to the liquor shops where they had to spend considerable money as they required large quantities of liquor for some of their socio-religious rites and ceremonies. The traders had entered the field to make their economic collapse complete. Most of the families spent money in intoxicants at the cost of their basic needs. Economically of many families has been badly affected because of this pattern of expenditure. Many families had been found to be over-burdened with indebtedness, and seemed to sink into a dull and hopeless apathy. This situation had stimulated the minds of some of the educated among the Naikas to form a voluntary organisation to check up the situation. Therefore, they took reform and unity of the Naikas as their foci of attention for the betterment of the Naikas.

First, it is only an account of the rigorous campaign of the voluntary organisation, the Naikas have stopped spending money on liquor even at the cost of basic needs to a considerable extent. Secondly, the organisation was able to wean the Naikas from the traders and money-lenders and rescue them from indebtedness to a great extent. Thirdly, the organisation was able to make the Naikas conscious of their rights for benefits guaranteed by the Indian Constitution. Fourthly, it has impressed the Naikas how the Dhodias who are economically, educationally and politically strong are able to get out much of the benefits intended for the Scheduled Tribes and it has propagated the idea that unless the Naikas too acquire economic prosperity, educational benefits, political awareness, and appropriate representation in political bodies, the Naikas cannot dream of their socio-economic betterment. Finally, the organisation has encouraged the unity of the Naikas and the adoption of the language, food-habits, ritualism and social customs of the agricultural castes, especially the Patels. Consequent upon this, the Naikas have tried to imitate the way of life of the caste of Patels. Some of them recently have started adding the caste title Patel after their names. The Naikas now feel that they are agriculturists like Patels, that they like Patels, should have their names ending with the title Patel, and that they, like Patels should adopt non-agricultural occupations befitting the dynamics of Hindu Society. All this had helped the Naikas to build a better social image than their earlier stance vis-a-vis other tribes.

REFERENCES

1. Lal, R.B., 1982, Modern Industry and the Tribals: A Study of the Effects of Industrialisation on the Tribals in South Gujarat Ahmedabad: Tribal Research and Training Institute, Gujarat Vidyapeeth, 1993, pp. 20, 30-33.

2. Padmanabham, P.B.S.V and Md. Azeez Mohidden, (1984), *"Tribes in Contemporary India-Naikas of Gujarat* (Unpublished Report), 1984.

3. Trivedi, Harshad R., 1993, *Tribal Land System, Land Reform Measures and Development of Tribals, (1982)*, New Delhi: Concept Publishing Company, pp. 64-67.

INDEX